. . . And Justice For All?

"And Justice For All?"

A Dissenting Opinion of the American Legal System

JOHN C. SULLIVAN

ISBN: 0-88290-330-6
Horizon Publishers' Catalog and Order Number: 2020

Printing: 1 2 3 4 5 6 7 8 9 10

Printed and distributed
in the United States of America by

Horizon Publishers
& Distributors, Incorporated
P.O. Box 490 Bountiful, Utah 84010-0490

John C. Sullivan

Dedication

This book is dedicated to

—my beloved parents,
—my wife, Edith,
—my daughter, Martha Anne, and
—my son, Paul.

All have shared in my struggles and successes.

Acknowledgments

This book was developed from over 20 years of trial experience, personal interviews and extensive research. The latter was long and expensive. I found no book that covered the whole spectrum of the American legal system.

To present a full analysis, it was necessary also to rely on many authors and authorities. It is impossible to thank all the people and institutions who contributed to the book's completion. The major contributors are listed in the endnotes and to them I am especially grateful. Dozens of others remain unnamed, whose insights and contributions are also appreciated.

Many pre-law and law students begin studies with little or no information as to what lie ahead in the practice of law. I have written this book in the hope that it will, in some degree, inform and awaken the minds of some of these students and novice lawyers, and also many laymen. It is my desire that it will increase their understanding and that it will contribute to a lessening of injustice.

Table of Contents

Preface

Why This Book Was Written

This book is a critique of the American legal system. It is limited in scope to the state courts and principally the lower courts of general jurisdiction because these are the courts most Americans face and the courts they can do the most about.

This book has three purposes. First, it is written to inform and enlighten the public about:

- the inadequacies of legal education;
- how the American bar associations and their satellites, the state bar associations, strangle the practitioner with a viselike hold;
- what happens in the trial courts relative to judges and juries;
- the futility of appeal, in many instances;
- the injustice of the criminal law system;
- suggestions for reform.
- how the practitioner operates and how to find a good lawyer;
- and what can be done to ensure competent legal representation.

The second purpose of the book is to warn the law student and young lawyer about some of the pitfalls of practice. The chapters in Part II of the book were written particularly for the successful bar examinee preparing to enter practice. For those who choose to go it alone, these road maps with markers and guideposts for the route of travel should save him from many errors and much grief.

Part III is a plea for sweeping reforms, with detailed suggestions of specific remedies which would correct many of the tremendous deficiencies in America's present legal system.

Lawyering is mostly always about money, influence, power and status. The few exceptions are those brave and courageous lawyers willing to risk reputation, status and income by defending unpopular clients and causes. The average lawyer hesitates to participate in heavy controversial issues for fear of what other clients might think. Instead, he listens to the enemy within. Timidity is one of the most disqualifying defects a lawyer can have, yet, an enormous number of frightened people practice law.

The Need for Changes in America's Legal System

Today, more than ever, scholars, lawyers and judges are calling for the improvement of the trial bar. Until his retirement, Chief Justice of the United States Supreme Court Warren Burger was the most outspoken. He has gone on record at annual meetings of the American Bar Association with charges that the system is in a state of disrepair; that we have too many lawyers and that one-third to one-half of them are incompetent in the courtroom. In his remarks, or "Burgerisms," he has noted: "We may be well on our way to a society overrun with hordes of lawyers and brigades of judges in numbers never before contemplated." He has admonished judges for the many delays in court that take years for cases to be resolved. He has recommended that certain disputes, such as personal injury cases, be taken out of court and submitted for negotiation and arbitration; and he has requested that we examine the English system with its solicitors and barristers and limit the right to practice in our courts only to those of proven skills.

Law Schools Fail to Prepare Students Adequately for the Practice of Law

Our law schools are institutions of legal training but they fail to fully prepare the student for the practice of law. The law school faculties, only three generations removed from their patron saint, Christopher Columbus Langdell, still hold to conventional orthodoxy. Many law professors have never passed a bar examination and are detached from the legal profession. Aloof from public life, they sit in their plush ivory tower offices unaware of what is going on at the ground level of controversy and law practice. All thought, context and questions are supplied by the instructor who channels the students' thinking along the outmoded path of legal precedent. Students need to be taught the skills required in and out of the courtroom, about the legal problems of the poor and about a jury system that requires overhauling.

The American Bar Association—the "Gentlemen's Club"

The first chapter scrutinizes the origin of the American Bar Association (ABA) and its state affiliates, the state bar associations, and their dictatorship over all phases of lawyering. Organized in 1878, in the luxurious surroundings of Saratoga Springs, New York, the ABA has always been a "gentlemen's club" for the protection of the corporate giants and the well-to do . In its original bylaws is a provision for the promotion of justice, yet for years, it denied admission to blacks, women, Jews and other ethnics. Today, membership is open to almost all, in return for dues needed to support ABA's large budget and for hiring lobbyists in the state legislatures and the U.S. Congress.

The Cult of the Robe

Legends and myths have grown up about the judiciary that serve to obscure realities. There's the cult of the robe, its sanctity and sacredness. Judges are human and make mistakes, as do all of us. But for their blunders, which can bring death to the criminal defendant and financial loss to the civil plaintiff, they are rarely disciplined. A small few are alcoholics, womanizers, tyrants, and crooks. They come in all sizes, races, and quality.

However, all are not bad, and I have seen many stand for justice. But many are elevated to the bench who don't belong there. Backgrounds and political ties pattern a consistency in the way each categorizes, approaches, and resolves social and political conflicts. It is in the trial court that their awesome power resides.

During election campaigns many judges sell themselves as fund-raisers to persons and organizations and contribute sizeably to campaign budgets. We can well wonder when such judges might begin to solicit money for themselves.

The press, in many instances, refuses to get involved, telling nothing about court delays, unfair treatment of the poor, or inept and unethical judges.

The Jury System and Low-quality Justice

There is a growing minority who would do away with our jury system in civil cases, as has England. Juries promote a low quality of justice; they are almost never a true cross-section of the community or of one's peers. Where knowledge is sorely needed, ignorance has been permitted to sit in places of judicial decision. There is no guarantee that juries will deliberate wisely or decide well, as is commonly assumed. Differences in background, personality and attitudes influence each juror's decision.

America is the most litigious society in the world, having three times as many lawyers as England and twenty times as many as settlement-oriented Japan. We need a justice system that stands the test of common sense.

Flaws in the Criminal System

The chapters on *"The Criminal Law Jungle"* and *"Justice Denied"* deal with the many flaws in the criminal system. In state courts, the sixth amendment joined with the fourteenth amendment guarantees "That in all criminal prosecution, the accused shall enjoy the right to a speedy and public trial by an impartial jury. . . ." But there is no assurance that the trial will be fair or meet the constitutionally-mandated due process; nor is there any any guarantee that the defendant's lawyer will be competent. A well-known myth, one never taken to heart by judges and juries, is that the accused is presumed innocent unless proven guilty beyond reasonable doubt. When the press gets underway in reporting a crime and all the circumstances, this information is absorbed in the minds of the judge and jury and is never removed. The imprint is indelible.

The real aim of prosecutors is to win and they rarely seek justice under the Rules of Professional Responsibility and legal ethics, and are seldom disciplined for breach of the rules. They labor as hard for a conviction as a personal injury lawyer strives for a large monetary verdict. The grand jury is a pawn of the prosecutor; it should be done away with as in England many years ago.

Mistaken identity is a leading cause of miscarriage of justice. It is understandable that many witnesses to crimes of violence are excited or catch only a glimpse of the culprit. Bank tellers, liquor store employees and storekeepers generally, all potential victims, head the list of unreliable sources of identification.

Public defenders are among the legal bureaucrats most entrenched in the trial courts. Seldom do they attack the system of injustice they recognize as present, and they are far more likely to plead their clients guilty. Judges and prosecutors prefer them and their company because, working together, they can sweep mistakes under the rug.

Plea bargaining has crept into the system with increasing intensity. There is no trial, no jury of one's peers, no exhaustive search for truth and no exacting legal rules. Furthermore, it is sanctioned by the U.S. Supreme Court and the ABA. Lazy judges and lawyers are those who promote it, and the appellate courts affirm it. A lawyer barters away a client's rights along with the so-called presumption of innocence on which the American system rests. Everyone pays lip service to justice.

White collar crime such as fraud, bribery, and embezzlement costs American business $40 billion a year. Defense lawyers routinely plead their clients guilty, then plead for mercy because of the defendant's "good" character, family and community standing. The defendant is customarily let off with a slap on the wrist and possibly sentenced to some form of community service as opposed to the street crime defendant who is jailed for petty misdemeanors. In the more serious crime of murder, we do not hear of a millionaire being sentenced to execution or a long prison term. It is a double standard of justice that America practices.

In capital offenses the public clamors for revenge under the Old Testament edict of "an eye for an eye and a tooth for a tooth," despite the earnest protests of churchmen, lawmen who care, and scholars who understand that capital punishment is not a deterrent to others. Crime prevention is more important than revenge because revenge does nothing for the victims or their families. England acknowledged the futility of capital punishment and abolished it in 1965.

Radicals and reformers are not the darlings of their times. Future generations may regard them with respect, but their contemporaries consider them cranks and pests. Chapter Ten discusses reforms that would bring about a more just and fair system.

The English refuse to be controlled by precedent or *Stare Decisis* and have overridden much of the common law established by Sir William Blackstone, the legal saint and jurisprudence giant. The system in England is revised from time to time or as the occasion demands, by the House of Lords, or by judicial fiat or by statute in the House of Commons. The test of any progressive system is the willingness to reform.

Basis of the Author's Personal Perspective

What prompted me to study law at the cessation of World War II were the many avenues of service the law profession offered. I quit my factory job in 1939 to study for the theological profession. During World War II, as an officer of the court of the military justice system, I witnessed many inequities and wondered whether civilian law practice was similar. I attended the International Military Tribunal in Nuremberg, Germany, in February 1946. From the visitors' gallery I watched as Nazi leaders were tried, one by one. Later I questioned the validity of War Crimes Indictment Count Two, "Crimes Against Peace," which was read to each prisoner: "All the defendants, with diverse other persons, during a period of years preceding 8th May 1945, participated in the planning, preparation, initiation, and waging of wars of aggression which were also wars in violation of international treaties, agreements and assurances. . . ." Here was law operating retroactively—*ex post facto* law. Commentaries and books abounded on the matter of *ex post facto* laws being applied, and I wondered if the same laws applied in the American justice system.

My night school law training was confined solely to the Langdellian case method of study. I was to learn how totally unprepared for law practice it left me. Although my pre-law and law studies were done in leading institutions in the nation's capital with its many courts and agencies, no part of the curricula included court visits to observe the practical side of law practice. Clinical training had not arrived.

I was a few months shy of 45 when I opened my law office in January 1960 in the county of my birth. A solo practitioner, I had no mentor or family member to emulate. Advanced education had no part in my family's way of life. My brother and I quit school in our early teens to perform unskilled factory work.

Once in law practice, I quickly learned it is every attorney for himself. Disillusionment struck fast and set in permanently. My continuing education was to take many forms and was not limited to periodic seminars which I religiously attended. Our county was no different from many others in which I have studied and practiced, and there was the so-called establishment at the helm; join the clique or suffer. I chose the latter. I had two young infants to feed with my wife and myself, but I chose the independent route. It took a little longer, but it brought clients and respect. I wasn't interested solely in money. For eighteen years I challenged and fought the established system. My son, Paul, joined me in 1977 as the only partner with whom I would associate. On December 31, 1979, I retired from the pressures and demands of the office with its eighty-hour weeks. I had received a few honors and a few scars incident to the profession. In 1985 I joined him for two years to assist in his overload of cases. Now I have entered my second retirement.

Early in my practice I knew that someday I would write about the profession I had diligently and perseveringly sought. I retained most of my files and prior to retirement I examined all the court files and cases in which I had been involved. I then traveled thousands of miles visiting libraries, courtrooms, law schools and medical schools, and also conducted interviews in preparation for this book. During a personally-guided tour of the English legal system in London in the spring of 1984, I visited the sixteen courtrooms of Old Bailey Criminal Court. I observed court proceedings in many of the 48 trial and appellate courtrooms of the High Court on the Strand. I spent time in the magistrate courts on well-known Bow Street and watched hundreds of cases tried—traffic and misdemeanors—that affect society so much. I saw the manner in which the robed and wigged clerks, barristers, judges and other court functionaries perform their work. I visited the Four Inns of Court, the educational institutions, and I interviewed solicitors and barristers. I entered the beautiful and ancient Law Society library with its volumes dating back to the Norman invasion. I frequented the pubs at lunch, downing healthy tumblers of ale and stout with lawmen. I interviewed members of the judiciary, including Lord Justice Michael Kerr, appellate judge.

At his Lincoln Inn office I spent an hour with the beloved and controversial Right Honorable Lord Denning, former member of the House of Lords, who, before his retirement in 1982, held the highly prestigious office of Master of the Rolls. On a Sunday visit to the Speaker's Corner in Hyde Park I heard individuals speak from platforms and boxes, unmolested and under police protection. It was a great example of freedom of speech and expression, and a lesson in constitutional law, such as is purportedly guaranteed in the first amendment to the U.S Constitution.

This book is not an autobiography, but observations based on the times and events during my practice in the trial and appellate courts, and drawn from personal experience, interviews and extensive research. It is a book of views and opinions shared by myself and renowned authorities—not necessarily connected with the law profession—and tested in the laboratory of experience. This is a story of what I have felt and the conclusions to which these feelings have led me.

JOHN C. SULLIVAN

Part I

A CRITIQUE OF AMERICA'S LEGAL SYSTEM

I

The ABA: Overlords of Lawyering

I find no pleasure in saying that the majority of lawyers who appear in court are so poorly trained that they are not properly performing their job and that their manners and their professional performance and their professional ethics offend a great many people.

Former Chief Justice Warren Burger

Formation of the American Bar Association

On August 21, 1878, seventy-five lawyers gathered at Saratoga Springs, New York. Their purpose, besides having a good time, was to establish a national association of lawyers.

Saratoga Springs, 180 miles from New York City, was a thriving retreat for the wealthy, a city of opulent charm, dispensing culture, learning, healing waters and money, with an abundance of fun. Opportunity for amusement brightened each day. There were orchestras and thoroughbred racing. An early watering hole for politicians, Saratoga had served as the informal headquarters of the Albany Regency, an astute group described by historians as our first political machine. The attraction of "The Springs," as it was known, was neither the waters nor the climate, but the carefree and ever-changing company, especially of the wealthy class. The cascading springs of the region attracted the high and the mighty, including U.S. presidents from Millard Fillmore to Benjamin Harrison, with the exception of Abraham Lincoln. George M. Pullman of railway fame, William Waldorf Astor,

William Vanderbilt, John Wanamaker, Diamond "Jim" Brady—these were but a few of the notables.

It was here too that the American Bankers Association had its beginnings that year. The bankers brought along "Coal Oil" Johnny Steele loaded with Pennsylvania oil money and James C. "Jubilee Jim" Fisk, looter of the Erie Railroad, together with Jay Gould.

The legal profession was changing rapidly with the railroad lawyer and business lawyer emerging as the dominant figures.

The first annual banquet of the ABA was held at the lavish, super hotel, the Grand Union, claimed as one of the two largest hotels in the world and occupying seven acres in the center of town. It was in this atmosphere that this coterie of well-heeled lawyers—a club of intimates—met to transact organizational business.

A constitution was adopted under the leadership of Simeon E. Baldwin of New Haven, Connecticut, acknowledged to be the moving spirit and driving force and veritable founder of the ABA.

The original constitution, which still substantially defines the organic character of the ABA, fixed the name and defined the objectives as:

> To advance the science of jurisprudence, promote the administration of justice and uniformity of legislation throughout the Union, uphold the honor of the profession of the law and encourage cordial intercourse among the members of the American Bar.

For the next ten years the membership chose this pretty upstate village with cool pine-scented air descending from the foothills of the Adirondacks and its medicinal springs for its annual meeting.[1]

Restrictive Membership Practices

Over the years the annual meetings moved on to Chicago and other leading cities and the organization became an exclusive set or group. Jethro K. Lieberman has given us a description of the early membership:

> You could become an invitee to membership if you were white, Protestant and native born, preferably with a British surname, and attended the elite law schools such as Harvard, Yale and Columbia; only then did you have a chance of prospering. Catholics, Jews, women and blacks were automatically excluded from membership. This exclusion was necessary to the elite bar's sense of identity.

> Any fraternity is defined not only by whom it accepts but also by whom it excludes. The Association also pinned the stigma of immorality on the lower class of lawyers as shysters who talked, dressed and acted differently.[2]

The "accidental" admission of the first black members has been described by Allan Gerson:

> In 1912 The Association made a costly mistake or accidental election to membership when it admitted three black lawyers which was unknown to the membership committee. The executive committee immediately passed a resolution rescinding the admission under the settled practice of the Association. . .to elect only white men as members. The membership chairman saw the issue of keeping pure the Anglo-Saxon race. A compromise was struck whereby the three were permitted to retain their membership provided that all future applicants were required to identify themselves by race. Twenty-seven years later the Association questioned the wisdom of pressing for membership the distinguished judge, William Hastie, a black Harvard Law School graduate.[3]

Biased Control Through The Canons of Ethics

Subsequently, the association became an instrument of considerable power, controlling the entire profession with its Canons of Ethics. The canons freed the elite bar from any restraints whatsoever since the canons had no bearing on the way the elite practiced; and the canons also gave the association power to regulate those who it claimed were giving the profession a black eye. Thus, the rules helped crush competition and enhance the position of big firm clients, as well as ensure that the lower strata of the bar could not dictate to those in charge. It was a masterly strategy and it worked. The bar became a monopoly.

The failure of the ABA to make legal assistance available to the poor over the years has been appalling. The northern lawyers who joined with the small band of southern lawyers to undertake cases for the poor, the black and the disregarded, were thwarted by the community and by fellow lawyers. In Mississippi, Virginia and North Carolina, lawyers faced disbarment charges as a result of involvement in racial issues. The ABA stood by and did nothing. Many a lawyer from another state, making a *pro-hac-vice* appearance was stopped in his tracks.

According to Philip M. Stern in *Lawyers on Trial*,

> When Lennox Hinds, president of the National Conference of Black Lawyers, made a comment on a criminal trial he thought unfair, the Organized bar initiated a formal complaint against him. When Hoyt Augustus Moore of the Wall Street firm of Cravath, Swaine and Moore publicly admitted having paid a bribe of $250,000 to a federal judge, not one disciplinary finger was raised against him. Bribing a federal judge is a felony as well as an effort to corrupt the administration of justice. Mr. Moore continued his highly prosperous practice until his death at 88.[4]

Or, take the case of Richard Kleindienst, once the U.S. Attorney General. He pleaded guilty to a peculiar charge: failing to disclose information to Congress. This obscure violation was cooked up so that Kleindienst might sidestep the more serious charge of perjury. As Deputy Attorney General, he lied to a member of Congress during hearings on his nomination as chief law officer of the U.S. in the District of Columbia. He was suspended from practice for twenty days in the District of Columbia. His home state of Arizona tapped him on the wrist with a censure. He now has a practice in Washington.

In Stern's book he has cited other cases:

> The lawyer: Daniel T. Taylor III of Kentucky, frequent defender of blacks and civil rights activists. Alleged offense: accusing the judge in a highly charged murder trial of calling him a "dirty son-of-a-bitch." Bar-recommended punishment: suspension from practice (that is, denial of Taylor's means of livelihood) for five years.
>
> The lawyer: Philip Hirschkop of Virginia, co-founder of the Virginia Civil Liberties Union, instrumental in striking down Virginia's law against interracial marriages and bringing about widespread prison reform. Alleged offense: telling newsmen that his clients (a liberal prison administrator and others) were "the good guys." Bar-recommended punishment: disbarment. He was exonerated.
>
> Compare the five-year suspension recommended for Daniel Taylor and the disbarment effort against Philip

Hirschkop with the Bar's kindlier treatment of other attorneys.

The lawyer: George E. Spater, board chairman of American Airlines. The offense: admitted knowingly violating federal law by arranging an illegal $55,000 corporate contribution to the Nixon campaign. Bar disciplinary action: a public "admonition." Ordinarily, Mr. Spater's felonious behavior would have called for automatic disbarment.

The lawyer: Orin E. Atkins of Kentucky, board chairman of Ashland Oil Company. The offense: pleaded guilty to arranging illegal corporate contributions to the Nixon campaign. Bar disciplinary action: none.

The lawyer: Harry S. Dent of South Carolina, White House counsel under President Nixon and manager of the "Townhouse" operation that received most of the illegal corporate campaign contributions for the 1972 Nixon re-election campaign. The offense: pleaded guilty to various Federal campaign law violations. Bar disciplinary action: none.[5]

Elite Control Over Rank-and-File Lawyers

THE DOUBLE STANDARD: One for the bar elite and their prosperous clients, another for the rank and file of lawyering with more modest clients.

Wrote Stern:

> The same duality prevails in the enforcement of those rules, in at least three distinct areas:
>
> a. Aggressive bar initiatives against lawyers who threaten the status quo in the legal profession as opposed to bar passivity toward Establishment lawyers.
>
> b. Harsh treatment of political mavericks and "boat-rockers" contrasted with mild treatment of mainstream attorneys.
>
> c. The allocation of scarce bar disciplinary personnel to pursue and punish comparitively mild rule violations by rank-and-file attorneys while permitting the bar elite to go unpunished.[6]

Gerson, writing on this, said:

> An organization that promotes the administration of justice and encourages cordial intercourse among the members of the bar should not demonstrate bias and discrimination. Such was not the case in the following: Leaders of the bar, Chief Justice of the U.S. Supreme Court Harlan Stone and William Taft made no bones about their dislike of Jewish lawyers who, in Stone's words, "exhibit racial tendencies toward study by memorization and a mind almost in its fidelity to the *minute* of the subject without any controlling rule or reason." Other complaints of the Eastern European immigrant, "with little inherited sense of fairness, justice and honor as we understand them."
>
> When President Wilson nominated the great Jewish lawyer, Louis Brandeis (there is a University in his name now) to the Supreme Court, the leaders of the ABA lined up solidly against him. The bar president, Elihu Root, declared "that Brandeis was not a fit person to sit on the court."
>
> The position taken by the elite lawyers was to impose their own conception of legal ethics and increase their power over the profession. Character committees sprang up over the country with the function of screening prospective lawyers. As a result of the standards of the Association, a high percentage of Russian Jew boys, Catholics and blacks and other ethnics were left out as undesirable.[7]

It is the associations, both American and state, that maintain a stranglehold on the sole practitioner and small law firms. In more than half the states there is the integrated bar. To be a regularly admitted member of the bar in these states, a lawyer must be a member of an official state organization, i.e., the state bar. The U.S. Supreme Court has upheld the compulsory nature of such organizations against a challenge. The most unusual grounds is the common law point that practicing lawyers are public officials, officers of the courts, and consequently subject to regulation by the courts, including compulsory associations if the court so desires.

The first state to integrate the bar was North Dakota in 1921 and the action was upheld in the State Supreme Court. Not until 1960 was it litigated in the U.S. Supreme Court. David McKean Dayton in *The Integrated Bar* has supplied the details:

> Trayton L. Lathrop, a young Madison, Wisconsin, attorney, paid under protest annual dues of $15 to the treasurer of the association. In his letter of protest he said he did not want to be coerced to support an organization "which is authorized and directed to engage in political and propaganda activities. I believe that when such coercion is by the judiciary, it is extremely distasteful and alarming" and that a payment of dues was in violation of his state and federal constitutional rights. He felt that a very grave wrong was being forced upon him which affects the very foundation of society. The case went to the U.S. Supreme Court on a *Writ of Certiorari* from the state supreme court. The Supreme Court upheld the lower court but was not without its dissenters, Justices [Hugo] Black and [William] Douglas. Part of Justice Black's opinion was that the lawyer's money is taken out of his pocket against his will and put into a collective fund, part of which is used for the propagation of ideas he is against. Justice Douglas held: "This regimentation appears in humble form today. Once we approve this measure we sanction a device where men and women to almost any profession or calling can be at least partially regimented behind causes which they oppose. . . .[8]

So runs the power of the state bar associations over the practitioner. It is the lawyers who pay their way through school, sacrifice and suffer defeat many times in the process, and then, reaching the ultimate of practice, must give obeisance to an overlord: the bar association. Maryland, my home state, is not an integrated bar as a requirement for practice.

Millions Spent in Lobbying

The ABA and many of the respective state bar associations spend millions lobbying in legislatures and in congress with the primary goal to maximize the profits of its members and their clients. The association influence stems from the fact that many of its members are committee heads in the legislatures and congress. The ABA has its second largest office of over 200 employees in the palacial surroundings of elite Connecticut Avenue in Washington, D.C., where it houses the Governmental Affairs Group. The group serves as the eyes, ears and voice of the organized bar in the nation's capital. It communicates the status of important bills and regulations weekly to state and local bar associations and provides in-depth analyses of major governmental activities affecting the legal profession. It also provides numerous governmental entities with its views on a broad range of issues.

The bar associations have great impact on the selection of both state and federal judges. Association membership is a prerequisite for consideration for a judgeship. Each state governor looks to the input and recommendations of the bar associations. The ABA's Standing Committee on Federal Judiciary has been consulted by every U.S. president on almost every federal judicial appointment since 1952. Moreover, the U.S. Senate, through its Judiciary Committee, has requested the opinion of the committee on every federal judicial nomination since 1948.

"Ambulance Chasing" vs. "Corporation Chasing"

"Lawyers giving unsolicited advice to a layman shall not accept employment resulting from that advice," the bar canons direct, but as Stern has pointed out, "While the bar winks at in-person solicitation in the locker room or over a martini, the rule is likely to be more strictly enforced against in-person advice to the indigent and powerless."

To substantiate this claim, Stern cites an example:

> Thus, in the summer of 1973, attorney Edna Primus told a group of welfare mothers that their legal rights may have been violated when they were sterilized as a condition of receiving continued Medicaid treatment. Later, when advised that one of the women, Mary Etta Williams, wished to bring a lawsuit against the doctor, attorney Primus wrote her to say that the American Civil Liberties Union would pay for the suit, and to suggest a conference with Ms. Williams to explain what is involved.
>
> Attorney Primus never, in fact, represented Ms. Williams, because while she was waiting one day to have the doctor see her critically ill child, the doctor's attorney persuaded Ms. Williams to sign a legal release, without explaining to her that this foreclosed a lawsuit. One might have thought the parties would have been content to end the matter there. Not the South Carolina Bar Association. After the passage of more than a year, Ms. Primus suddenly found herself charged, and then convicted, by the State Disciplinary Board, of "soliciting" employment by Ms. Williams. While the United States Supreme Court later overturned the action, it was no thanks to the South

> Carolina Bar Association, which, in this most benign example of "solicitation"—an attorney for a nonprofit organization advising a group of poorly informed women about their legal rights—filed a still legal brief against Ms. Primus.[9]

Ambulance chasing, though frowned on by the fat cats of the profession, is big business in large cities. It is a scramble between insurance claims agents and the lawyers to see which can reach the injured claimant first. Ambulance chasing is considered reprehensible, but "corporation chasing" carries the ABA seal of approval. Chasing is the natural reflex or defensive response to the unfair methods of claims adjusters.

In *Verdict on Lawyers*, edited by Ralph Nader and Mark Green, we read:

> Large firms do not use runners to attract business but do spend large sums of money for membership to country clubs and other similar amenities of social activity. The primary purpose is to attract business and all amenities are tax deductible. It is a dignified method of solicitation and has the United States government paying a substantial portion of the cost.
>
> There is the approved device for soliciting clients in the impressive volumes of Martindale-Hubbell. This purely and simply self-laudatory advertisement is called a "card" and directed to potential clients. Not every attorney is permitted to advertise his or her professional autobiography in Martindale-Hubbell. It is not available to the ordinary lawyer. One must await an invitation from the publisher to apply for an "A" rating which can be achieved only upon submission of favorable references from judges and attorneys who have themselves already received an "A" rating. For all other members of the profession, Martindale-Hubbell is a closed book. Other means include attorneys' registers and directories distributed free to banks and trust companies, banks and financial institutions who are believed to be prolific forwarders of substantial legal matters. That is the way solicitation is done by lawyers seeking to represent those of wealth and privilege. The problem of impropriety arises only, of course, for those who seek to represent the other socio-economic group on the lower rung of the ladder, or the lower strata.[10]

A Self-perpetuating Clique

The ABA whose creed is "the promotion of the administration of justice," was designed as a self-perpetuating clique, with little on its record to justify a claim to leadership. It typified to the full, the blindness of a ruling class and was the most reactionary of a reactionary profession. It has never participated actively in the social issues of the day—such as the integration of schools and colleges. It opposed the 1890 Sherman Anti-trust Act, and fought Roosevelt's New Deal. Earl Warren resigned from the ABA because of its intolerance of Supreme Court decisions in free speech. It remained silent and took no position when the poor immigrants, Sacco and Venzetti, were sent to the execution chamber after a trial that was hailed as a mockery of justice. In 1969 it came out against no-fault insurance. It fostered a loyalty oath that was akin to McCarthyism; it has opposed consumer class actions as being "unwise, unnecessary and inefficient" and deemed them a burden to the courts and a bonanza to plaintiffs' lawyers. It has been characterized variously as "the Brahmins of the Bar," "the toll collectors," "the blue noses," "the snubs and the holier-than-thou clique," and "the stiff necks."

Opposition to Advertising and Price Competition

The idea of operating a legal clinic in the same manner as a medical clinic was unheard of until 1972 when two young men decided to test the waters and open a clinic. For an account of this happening we turn to Lieberman:

> Leonard Jacoby and Stephen Meyers were brave young men. Their purpose was to make legal aid available to more people, especially the middle class who were left out in the cold in many instances. The two faced disbarment for unethical conduct under the code of ethics. It was a common-sense approach toward high quality, low cost services. This was too much for the local bar to contend with. In March 1973 not long after opening for business, they were charged with ethical violations by the state bar association and charged with having conducted themselves dishonestly and engaging in corrupt law practice. The bar association did not realize they had two plucky barristers out to challenge the powers-to-be and the antique system in effect. The disciplinary committee shouldered its arms ready to fire and first recommended suspension of 45 days coupled with an order to remove the clinical signs. The pair simply came out for reform ahead of conventional

> wisdom and were now paying for their foresight. The case went to the California supreme court who held that it was unconstitutional to discipline lawyers for reaching out to the public with reduced fees or rates in the form of a clinic.[11]

Lieberman has described an Arizona case dealing with the same question.

> "...Two young law grads, John R. Bates and Van O'Steen modeled their claims after Jacoby and Meyers and used the media to advertise their wares. The case went all the way to the U.S. Supreme Court with the state bar association of Arizona as party plaintiff. Justice Blackmun, in speaking for the court, ruled that the first amendment protected advertising of routine legal services and the price of those services.[12]

Thereafter, the ABA redrafted its model code and left it to each state to adopt its own rules.

Warren Burger, a strong opponent of legal advertising whose criticism has often stung his colleagues, said, "Legal advertising has become much like the hawking of automobiles, dog food, cosmetics and heart tonic."

The lawyer's duty, according to the legal code, is to make legal services available to the public. But Jethro Lieberman has cited at least two instances in which the bar associations have opposed such assistance.

> In 1963 . . . a miners' union in Illinois hired an attorney and put him on an annual retainer to serve all union members. From 1963 to 1966 he collected more than three million dollars for his clients, charging the union only $12,000 per year. In 1966 the Illinois Bar Association filed an injunction enjoining the attorney from conducting the legal assistance program. The Illinois Supreme Court ruled that the attorney must sever his relationship. On an appeal to the U.S. Supreme Court, Justice Hugo Black in an eight man majority ruled that the bar association interference with the union's legal program was a violation of the First Amendment right of all persons to form associations to protect their legal rights. It showed that the Illinois Bar had committed a major tactical blunder on behalf of the entire American legal monopoly. The decision shook the

> organized bar and revealed its insensitivity to the legal needs of people.[13]

Again turning to Lieberman:

> In 1971 the U.S. Supreme had occasion to consider another group legal services case. The Michigan State Bar brought action to enjoin members of the Brotherhood of Railroad Trainmen from engaging in activities undertaken for the stated purpose of assisting their fellow workers, their widows and families to protect themselves from excessive fees at the hands of incompetent lawyers in suits for damages under the Federal Employees Liability Act or workman's compensation claims, while injured on the job. The union recommended to its members a certain number of lawyers who agreed to take cases on a 25 percent fee of recovery. The Michigan Supreme Court issued the injunction; however, in an appeal to the U.S. Supreme Court the court reversed in sweeping language that collective activities undertaken to obtain meaningful access to the courts is a fundamental right within the protection of the First Amendment.[14]

Habitual charging of fees less than the minimum fee schedule established by the local bar was always evidence of unethical conduct, and subject to disciplinary action. The ABA emphasized minimum bar fees and each state bar association established fees and passed the order down to the locals.

Eventually this was challenged and Lieberman has given us an account of the circumstances:

> A Fairfax, Virginia couple, the Goldfarbs, decided to purchase a home accompanied with a mortgage. The latter meant title insurance and the services of a lawyer. The buyers looked around the legal fraternity to bargain for fees and found that a set price was set by the Virginia Bar Association being 1 percent of the purchase price. No attorney would take less including the young budding novice. He was stuck with the minimum fee. The couple then brought charges against the Virginia Bar Association under the theory of price fixing under the anti trust act and that lawyering was a business and controlled by the

act. The case was tried in the U.S. District Court of Virginia with a victory for the Goldfarbs. On appeal to the fourth Circuit Court of Appeals in Richmond, the case was reversed and held for the Association. On appeal to the U.S. Supreme Court, the court held that fee schedules and ethical opinions coalesced to create a pricing system that consumers could not realistically escape. The bar's activities constituted a classic example of price fixing; the matter of fee scheduling became a thing of the past.[15]

Resistance to Legal Self-help Materials

Bar associations, including the ABA, have strenuously fought self-help books and kits containing the necessary forms for the lawyerless handling of matters such as estates. Barbara R. Strock in her book, *It's Easy to Avoid Probate*, sets forth the steps to take to save much money and time by doing it yourself. She says that each week in America approximately $180 million dollars are taken from the pockets of unsuspecting bereaved families for the expenses of probate. She alleges that "Probate has been called a system designed by attorneys for the benefit of attorneys."[16]

When I went to Florida to open an estate for a Maryland client, I had to join with a Florida lawyer. This was a rule established by the Florida Bar Association. Many states, including my own, permit probate administration to be handled by the administrator noted in the will without a lawyer.

In every legal jurisdiction of America there exist Probate Courts, also called Orphans Courts or Surrogate Courts, for the handling of estates—property left by a deceased. The probate procedure is time-consuming and expensive, but for an attorney versed in estate planning and court work it can be a gold mine. Millions of dollars have been exacted in certain estates.

In the mid-sixties Norman F. Dacey published a self-help book, *How to Avoid Probate*. The book scorched the legal profession because it taught in easy lessons how to improvise and handle estate affairs without going through the costly Probate Court procedure. Not long after the book came out Dacey's native state bar association arranged for one of its members, Judge Marks, to issue an injunction without a hearing requiring Dacey to stop telling people how to avoid probate. The legal establishment was hell-bent on keeping it out of the book stores. Despite the association's efforts, over a million copies were sold and in thirteen weeks it became a best seller. Cries of outrage rattled the windows in the ABA headquarters in Chicago. The New York County Lawyers Association filed a complaint in the New York Supreme Court charging Dacey with criminal contempt of court for having written the book. The book was regarded as a threat to the lawyers' pocketbook. The New York section of the American Civil Liberties Union intervened and contended that any injunction would be a gross violation of one's constitutional rights and of the public's right to know. Dacey eventually won out after hard court battles in which the ABA and state bar associations used every stratagem to oust the book from the book stalls.[17]

In America it is estimated that one of every two marriages ends in divorce, yet the cost can be out of reach for many. In Florida where 70,000 divorces are granted each year, a former legal secretary, Rosemary Furman was jailed for thirty days for violating a 1977 court order prohibiting her from selling divorce forms. She was accused of practicing law without a license. Mrs. Furman was a self-styled champion of the poor in providing forms for filing for divorce. Her case was appealed to the U.S. Supreme Court where the lower court judgment was affirmed. Though fighting it to the end, the state bar association succumbed to a new state law of "do it yourself" prompted by crusader Furman.

Control of America's Legal Education System

Since the ABA's adoption of the first law school accreditation standards in 1921, state supreme courts and other bar-admitting authorities have encouraged the ABA's accreditation efforts, and the vast majority of states rely upon ABA to determine whether an applicant meets the educational requirements for admission to the bar. Thus, the ABA and its state satellites control the American legal education system.

The Axe Falls on Men of Authority

Only strong protests by reputable law school administrators, judges and trial lawyers have brought about changes in law school training. The association has been slow to implement or innovate. Clinical programs were adopted in the 1960s which the ABA was reluctant to introduce, believing that the Langdellian system of case studies should prevail.

In passing, we cannot forget to mention the law and order bar men of the Nixon administration and Watergate—the Palace Guards, the Liddys, the Deans, Colsons, Kroughs, Erlichmans, Kalmbachs, Mardians, Reineckes and Segrettis—all bar association members and all set down with either suspensions or disbarments. President Nixon resigned from the California Bar under threats of disbarment; he unsuccessfully attempted to resign from the New York State Bar. And finally the ax fell on the top law and order man of the century, John Mitchell, former U.S. attorney general and a devoted member of the ABA. The mighty fell from their high perch.

And there was Spiro Agnew, one step away from the highest office of the country until he resigned from the vice presidency in disgrace. On October 10, 1973, as a member of the Maryland Bar Association, he entered a plea of *nolo-contendre* (I am at your mercy, oh judge) in the U.S. District Court of Maryland in Baltimore. The charge was willfully and knowingly attempting to evade and defeat a large part of the income tax due and owing by him and his wife to the U.S. for the calendar year of 1967 by filing a fraudulent tax return. The presiding judge, Walter E. Hoffman, directed the entry of a final judgment, suspending sentencing for three years, conditioned on his good behavior and payment of a $10,000 fine. On November 12, 1973, Agnew was disbarred from the practice of law by the Maryland Court of Appeals.

And last but not least, another member of the Maryland Bar Association, Governor Marvin Mandell, met a similar fate—a prison sentence and eventual disbarment. Maryland was becoming a state known for crooked lawyers.

Chief Justice Burger, a leading spokesman for the ABA and a Nixon appointee, blamed much of the bar trouble on the law schools and the lack of trial lawyer skills for helping bring it all about. "The low state of American Trial Advocacy is a consequent diminution in the quality of our own entire system of justice," he said. He called for a special license system for trial lawyers to purge incompetent advocates and generally raise ethical standards.

The ABA had fits. What has happened to our system, it asked. Never in the history of lawyering had such a fate befallen such good men! The ax fell on the men of authority. The eagle's wings were clipped. The association responsible for promoting ethical standards and professional responsibility took it all to heart and insisted that all accredited law schools have at least one course in professional responsibility. Was it too late?

II

The Judiciary—High Priests of the Legal System

Certainly courts are not, and cannot be, immune from criticism, and lawyers, of course, may indulge in criticism. Indeed, they are under a special responsibility to exercise fearlessness in doing so.[1]

Former U.S. Supreme Court Justice Felix Frankfurter

No honest and sensible man who reads the newspapers and converses with his fellows can deny that a large class of people throughout the United States entertains growing distrust of our judges and judical systems.[2]

John A. Wright

The Awesome Powers Held by Trial Judges

They belong to one of the three departments of our government: the judiciary. They appear in black priestly robes in that sanctuary called the courtroom. They are entrusted with awesome power and authority. They exercise the power to take a life, to separate a loved one from his family, ruin his good name and reputation, to destroy his career and deprive him of his livelihood, or cause him to leave the courtroom penniless and naked. Too often, they favor the wealthy and despise the voiceless poor.

Their office workings are little known to the public except to that clan called lawyers, who must maintain a conspiracy of silence because of the weapon held over them. They can be arrogant and temperamental and unleash their venom on the private citizens who appear before them. They rule over witnesses and juries and cause them to tremble at times. They can take cases away from the jury in favor of corporate giants, including the insurance industry. They can deny you your day in court by summarily dismissing an action that has all the incidents of legitimacy. They decide what witnesses and attorneys can say or do in the courtroom. They can ride herd over attorneys—especially the weak and the beginners. They can force compromise settlements between parties. They set their own time schedule, but rebuke an attorney for being a few minutes late. Case files are clogged but those in the robe generally work a four-and-a-half-day week from nine to four. Laziness is an occupational disease. They grant delays in cases because insurance company attorneys are not prepared. Special training and continuing education are available to them, but they seldom avail themselves of it.

Many of them are indebted or in hock to the politicians for their position. Their selection is catch as catch can, the rewarding of the party faithful and the big givers. They must pass the bar, that is, be members of a bar association to qualify for appointment.

They are the most important officers of government and their individual personalities are the single factor in our law's administration. And of most importance, they set the tone of the proceedings, rushed or deliberate, serious or ridiculous.

And all these things they do in the name of Justice. They are our trial judges, in charge of courts of general jurisdiction.

It has been written:

> Judges are human beings, with mortal frailties and limitations subject to the influence of their environment, education and association. Political affiliations, economic views, social ideas and philosophy of life, play as great a part in the decision of the judge as in the acts of other public officials. It is foolish to imagine that by the assumption of the ermine a judge is transformed from an ordinary human being of flesh, blood, passions and leanings, to a cold, calculating and disinterested applier of the law.
>
> Judicial temperament is almost entirely a myth. The judges are not better or worse than other governmental servants. The stigma of graft and corruption is as frequently applied to judges as to others, and proportionately there

> are probably as many honest and sincere public servants in other branches of government as in the judiciary.[3]

Potential for "Twisting" the Law

The investment of the courts with discretionary power makes possible the abrogation of the Constitution and statutes by judicial fiat. In the words of Thomas Jefferson, this power makes the Constitution "a mere thing of wax in the hands of the judiciary, which they may twist and shape into any form they please."[4]

A form of lawlessness lies in the strained and illogical construction of statutes and constitutions for the purpose of reading into them the social, economic or political views of the judges.[5]

In some states in a criminal case, the jury is allowed a say in the sentencing of a guilty party in a first degree murder case. In the vast majority of cases, the jurors decide that the circumstances do not warrant the death penalty. Not so in Florida, which has more people on death row than any state in America. As of the fall of 1983, a fourth of the 320 men sentenced under Florida's 1972 capital punishment law were on death row against the wishes of the jurors who had heard their trials. The only woman ever sent to death row in Florida was sentenced against the wishes of her jurors. In three-fourths of the cases in which juries recommended life and the trial judge imposed the death sentence, the Florida Supreme Court has overturned the judge.[6]

As Herman Schwartz, a law professor and civil rights lawyer, wrote:

> Every trial lawyer knows from personal and often bitter experience that there are few more tyrannical figures than an autocratic trial judge, of which, sadly, there are more than a few. Glaring down from their elevated perches, insulting, abrupt, rude, sarcastic, patronizing, intimidating, vindictive, insisting on not merely respect but almost abject servility—particularly in the lowest criminal and juvenile courts, which account for most of our criminal business.

Judge Lois F. Forer, in her book, *Money and Justice,* wrote:

> Trial judges decide guilt or innocence of more than 90 percent of all persons accused of crime. Some of the important issues: the right to life, the right to die, the right to marry and divorce, custody of children, property rights, conditions of employment and access to jobs, safety of food

and air, qualifications of school teachers, doctors, lawyers, rights of school children, the mentally ill, the legality of strikes, the financial obligations of church and state are among the responsibilities of trial judges.

Blatant irregularities, indifference and politics as usual prevail in state judicial systems. Not all are honest, able and sensitive. Some courts have judges that are more liberal, moderate and conservative. Backgrounds are a major cause of division or of variance among judges. Many jurisdictions have judges of less than ten years experience and some have less than five years. The screening agent, the state bar associations, have not succeeded in eliminating all mediocre, biased and temperamentally unfit judges. Regardless of the legal scheme, political considerations play a large part in the selection of judges. Judiciary aspirants under all systems of selection must have political backing. It involves contributing to a political party. Judges are sold over to TV and campaigns which require money from lawyers and special interest groups which put them under obligation to donors. There is no foolproof method of selection. No one can tell whether he'll be arbitrary or autocratic.[7]

What Makes A Good Judge?

The question arises what qualities make the best judge. A couple of thousand years ago Socrates set forth the qualifications of a good judge: 'To hear courteously, to answer wisely, to consider soberly and to decide impartially.' The good trial judge is a referee, traffic cop and an umpire."

The trial judge must have patience, moral courage, a reputation for fairness and uprightness, good mental and physical health, and trial experience. He must be decisive, have a sense of humor, communicative skills, sensitivity and consideration for others, knowledge of the rules of evidence and procedure, and above all, integrity.

It is integrity that embraces honesty and impartiality. It is integrity that lies at the core of the ideal judicial character. Judges should be chosen with great care because they exercise great power over our lives and fortunes, our liberties and property. In some, their power goes to their head; they turn into mean spirited, vengeful, vicious tyrants. And some become lazy, drunks, and misfits.

Columbia law professor Harry Jones, in a brilliant essay on the subject, delineated what he considers the essential qualities of a trial judge:

> The demands and strains of his courtroom task require unusual emotional stability, exceptional firmness and serenity of temperament, and . . . great intellectual and psychic endurance. He must have unusual talents of communication. He needs to be empathetic and endlessly patient with jurors and witnesses, compassionate without being mushy headed in sentencing, at once sensitive and austere.[8]

"He must be able to take a lot of pressure," says F. Lee Bailey. "He should be strong and compassionate, he should have a quick mind and be right a fair amount of the time. If he's right all the time, he's slowing the trial so much that he's killing it, because he's looking everything up. Common sense helps, and so does knowledge of the community."

A striking feature of these highest-ranking attributes is that they tend to focus upon the personality or person—what he is rather than what he has done, his innate or intrinsic qualities, rather than his external attainments. They are more concerned with temperament, disposition, character and attitude than with background, training or formal achievement.

The Challenge of Maintaining Neutrality

Practicing lawyers attempt to learn the peculiarities of particular trial judges. If Judge Brown is a former law firm member who represented insurance companies and corporations, it is likely he will still represent them. If Judge Green is a former district attorney, that prosecution complex is hard to change. If Judge Blue was knee-deep in politics with a host of old buddies—including some lawyers—he cannot change now. Armed with this information, lawyers try to avoid having cases heard before certain judges.

In one instance during my trial practice, I filed a motion for a judge to remove himself from the case for prior knowledge of the evidence. In his intimidating manner he replied, "Do you want me to hold you in contempt of court?"

"When businessmen have a salesman," wrote former judge Bernard Botein, "they try to choose one who enjoys the good will of his trade. When they hire a lawyer, they sometimes try to choose one who enjoys the good will of the judge. They will then try to retain a good friend, a former colleague on the bench, or a politician to whom they think the judge is beholden for past favors or to whom he will be gracious in anticipation of future favors.[9]

It is not always easy for a judge to exercise neutral judgment when a friend appears before him; a weak judge may lean over backwards. One, of course, has several circles of friends of varying degrees of intimacy. Politicians expect judges to be grateful to the party which lifted them into the bench. Once on the bench, they state, "I must sever my ties with politicians"—but it is never done.

I call them Brass Gods. One of the most difficult facets for me in trial practice was to address the court as "Your Honor," or, "May it please Your Honor," particularly when I was aware of the cloudy character and mold of the judge. My firsthand experience with court operation tended to breed, if not contempt, at least disillusionment. The high priest judge you learn of in law school is not sacred, but sanctimonious. I placed him at first on a pedestal, but after my first year, my belief in the righteous and just judge had dissipated.

Judge Jerome Frank, in his book, *Courts on Trial,* adds:

> When it comes to finding the facts in lawsuits where the oral testimony is in conflict, obscure idiosyncracies in the trial judge are bafflingly at work. The judge's sympathies and antipathies are likely to be active with respect to the witnesses. His own past may have created plus or minus reactions to women, or blonde women, or men with beards, or Southerners, or Italians, or Englishmen, or plumbers, or ministers, or college graduates, or democrats. A certain facial twitch or cough or gesture may affect the judge's initial hearing or subsequent recollection, of what the witness said, or the weight or credibility which the judge will attach to the witness's testimony.
>
> Now the trial judge is a man with susceptibility to such unconscious prejudiced identifications originating in his infant experiences. Sitting at the trial, long before he has come to the point where he must decide what is right and wrong, just or unjust, with reference to the facts of the case as a whole, he has been engaged in making numerous judgments and inferences, as the testimony dribbles in. His impressions colored by his unconscious biases with respect to the witnesses, as to what they said, and with what truthfulness and accuracy they said it, will determine what he believes to be the facts of the case. His innumerable hidden traits and predispositions often get in their work in shaping his decision in the very process by which he

> becomes convinced what those facts are. The judge's belief about the facts results from the impact of numerous stimuli—including the words, gestures, postures, and grimaces of the witnesses—on his distinctive personality. That personality, in turn, is a product of numerous factors, including his parents, his schooling, his teachers and companions, the persons he has met, the women he married (or did not marry), his children, the books and articles he read.[10]

In the preface to his book, *Judges,* Donald Dale Jackson writes:

> Judges are no more or less human, struggling with their own imperfections and those of others, and their human reactions have as profound an influence on their decisions as the law they are sworn to serve. "Men's judgments are a parcel of their fortunes," Shakespeare wrote, "And things outward do draw the inward quality after them, to suffer all alike." The quality of our justice is a direct reflection of the quality—and qualities of our judges.[11]

"No man can be the sort of judge we expect an American judge to be," wrote Justice John Parker several generations ago, "unless he is absolutely honest, absolutely courageous, and blessed by God with an understanding heart. . . . And a judge should be a kindly man. The power he exercises is so great—he can easily make or break an ordinary man—that no one but a kindly man should be entrusted with it."[12]

> "The trial-court judge is The Man," wrote Jackson:
>
> Bigoted and tyrannical judges are the most widespread menace to our dream of equal justice. The manner and attitude of a trial judge are crucial to everyone concerned. The idea that the sins of a lower-court judge come out in the wash at the appellate-court level is fantasy; a top-heavy majority of all cases are not appealed, and equally imposing number of appealed cases are upheld by the higher court.[13]

William Kunstler, the chief counsel of the Chicago Seven, said, "All I expect a judge to do is to always opt for the Bill of Rights. Some do more than others, but I don't know any who will always do so. I think a good judge is one who understands the realities of American life and is consciously doing something to change them, to bring us closer to our professed aims of free speech, due process, and equality. There aren't any like that."[14]

"There is no character on earth more elevated and pure than that of a learned and upright judge," said Daniel Webster, flicking away a tear. "He exerts an influence like the dews of heaven falling without observation." Chief Justice John Marshall, glancing in the same direction, thundered the corollary: "The greatest scourge an angry heaven ever inflicted upon an ungrateful and sinning people was an ignorant, a corrupt, or a dependent judiciary."

"Such feverish rhetoric obscures a calm assessment of the American judiciary. The subject is unrelentingly emotional; great clouds of bias are forever overhead; a good judge inspires veneration, a bad one provokes contempt. Mediocrity is plainly unbearable.

"American judges are not all they ought to be. They are too often greedy, too often weak, too often tyrannical; they are far too often callously insensitive to human weakness; far too many are pedestrian, "gray mice," devoid of distinction. All this and more. Their means of ascension almost guarantees a sodden mediocrity. Judicial insensitivity may be the least offensive consequence of a selection system that puts a premium on cronyism and self-promotion. The nature of their work, especially in the lower courts, is not calculated to attract the best—"It's chopping wood, you're just another bureaucrat," a law professor said. And finally they are insulated, caressed, and protected by the brotherhood of the robe, the dusty deference that walls them off and chokes their humanness. Measured against what we expect of them, they fall pathetically short.

"In rebuttal, judges ask why they must be measured by such a standard. They are, after all, flesh of our flesh, no more touched by divinity than you or I. Short of an assemblage of saints, who could meet the demands we make of them? "It isn't fair," a judge complained after he heard a lawyer's speech cataloging complaints against judges. "Why can't we be judged like everyone else?" The lawyer's reply was swift: "Because you're not like everyone else. You have more power."[15]

Jack Newfield in his commentary, "The Ten Worst Judges," in Ralph Nader and Mark Green's book, *Verdict on Lawyers,* has this to say concerning the New York judiciary:

> Just spend a month inside the chaotic courtrooms and you will see judges with unstable temperaments, judges with unmistakable biases, judges who are insulting and sarcastic, judges who open court at 11:00 a.m., take long

> lunches and quit at 3:00 p.m., judges who are not intelligent enough to understand complex or subtle legal arguments, judges who are incoherent from too many martinis at lunch, judges who bend the law to favor clients of lawyers who are clubhouse cronies. You will see judges rule time after time against tenants, and then go out and have lunch with the landlord's lawyer. You will see defendants awaiting trial who have been locked in jail for six months on $250 bail because their files have been lost. . . . You will see judges coerce guilty pleas, improperly force settlements, malinger, manipulate the calendar, do anything to escape the mental labor of conducting a jury trial.[16]

The Process of Judging

"In the adversary system of litigation" one judge states, the state has been relegated largely to the function of furnishing the stadium and the referees; of booking, staging and deciding these civilized fights. . . . The court's decision anoints not the truth, but the winner of the brawl."[17]

"The process of judging," so the psychologists tell us, "seldom begins with a premise from which a conclusion is subsequently worked out. Judging begins the other way around—with a conclusion more or less vaguely formed. A man ordinarily starts with a conclusion and then tries to find premises which will substantiate it. If he cannot, to his satisfaction, find proper arguments to link up his conclusion with premises he finds acceptable, he will, unless he is arbitrary or mad, reject the conclusion and see another."[18]

A century ago, a great American judge, Chancellor Kent, explained in a personal letter his method of arriving at a decision. He first made himself "master of the facts," he wrote. "I saw where justice lay, and the moral sense decided the court half the time; I then sat down to search the authorities. . . I might once in a while be embarrassed by a technical rule, but I almost always found principles suited to my view of the case. . . ."[19]

Howard James' book, *Crisis in the Courts*, was developed from a series of articles that appeared weekly in *The Christian Science Monitor* and is based on his findings concerning the judicial process while on a nationwide tour investigating the state court systems, municipal and minor court systems, police procedures, bail and the right to counsel, juries, and the role of the citizen—all probed in his in-depth, comprehensive study. His travels and experiences revealed that incompetent judges can be classified into one or more of the following categories:

The Hacks: Rewarded for long and faithful service to a political party.

The Failures: Could not hack it at practice.

The Retirees: In last days they take judgeships. They are the long vacationers, long lunches and arrive late at work.

The Inattentive: Sleep on job, doodle or look out window.

The Misfits: Cannot cope with judicial ethics, are abrasive and short tempered.

The Informal: Most business done in chambers.

The Incapacitated: Old age, ill health and still draw full pay.

The Inexperienced: Never in court.

The Lazy: Speaks for itself.

The Weak: Favors friends, wants cases settled and plea bargainer.

The Prejudicial: Brings into the bench old views as to religion, ethnic background.[20]

Should Judges Be Selected or Elected?

Stanley Rosenblatt has written a scathing denunciation on the role of selection of judges:

> . . .Judges either run for office or are appointed by political figures. The judiciary has always been the shadowy branch of our government, and the people know a good deal less about their judges than they do about their legislators or executive officials. Usually they are protected and insulated from criticism. They are constantly defended by members of the bar. Lawyers know who the lousy judges are, but they are in an awkward position, for if they criticize the judge, and he is vindictive, he can hurt their clients. Besides, if the judge is a good politician, he is going to get elected anyway and the attorney still has to practice before him. This is why the attorneys seldom knock the judges in public.
>
> . . .Lawyers will laugh and become hysterical over the dumbest thing that a judge says, and they are often so polite and respectful that it becomes sickening. Many judges believe and many lawyers encourage them to believe, that their seat on the bench is a throne, and that everyone that comes before them are their subjects.[21]

Judges are elected in most of the state and local courts but bar associations are out to change that, particularly in jurisdictions where minorities make up a substantial percentage of the population. Maryland is one of the states that compels a circuit judge to stand for election following an interim appointment. In the city of Baltimore, which is predominantly black, white judges, after holding office for years, have been voted out in numbers and replaced by blacks. The state bar association would like to change that. Robert C. Murphy, chief judge of the Maryland Court of Appeals and former president of the state bar association, speaking at the 88th annual meeting of the state bar association, and in editorials, had this to say: "We must purge from the Constitution of Maryland, once and for all, that now destructive provision that requires circuit judges after initial appointment by the Governor of Maryland to stand for election in an expensive and 'crap shoot' political type contest against any and all comers. The judges of Maryland, acting through the Maryland Judicial Conference, have, for more years than I care to think about, undertaken wholly without success, to persuade the legislature to take circuit court judges out of the competitive election process."

As to the elective process, black Judge William H. Murphy, who retired to run for mayor of Baltimore, feels differently:

> "Many big corporate law firms complain that their lawyers won't apply for circuit court judgeships because they don't want to demean themselves by publicly going to community meetings, political gatherings, churches, mosques and synagogues to tell literally thousands of people who they are, what they've done and why they should be elected to judge them. They don't want to have their weaknesses, limitations or inadequacies publicly exposed by another lawyer who is running for the same seat, or, worse still, by some newspaper. They don't want to publicly raise money from lawyers and others who have to appear in their courts. They suspect that ordinary people really aren't capable of appreciating who they are. They don't believe that to be judges, they should have participated in broad-based community activities to know, understand and be a part of the people they will be judging.
>
> Many of these well-connected corporate law firms would rather play a more private politics where they can seek the support of the financial backers and close political associates of whoever the governor may be. Instead of

> attending hundreds of public meetings, they would rather campaign at a few well-chosen private ones. Instead of having their political and financial supporters known to the public as is required in open elections, they would rather vigorously campaign in the shadows. To them, the closed and often secret politics of private offices is more advantageous and more comfortable than the more open politics of contested elections."[22]

The result of judges' keeping a low profile has been summed up by Rosenblatt: "A judge may be on the bench for 20 years in a given community and still be a stranger to the public. He does not speak out on domestic or international questions, and the people have no idea as to whether he is liberal or conservative or where he stands on the great issues of the day."[23]

The principal methods of selecting judges are: (1) the democratic means by popular election. (Some say this is too political and controlled by political bosses.) There is the merit system which takes two forms. One is commonly called (2) the Missouri system (officially declared in Missouri in 1940), which provides for citizens to vote for or against judges appointed by the governor from nominations by a judicial selection committee consisting of lawyers and laymen. And (3) there is the process in which the governor appoints judges from select committee nominees, but the appointee must run for election after one or more years on the bench, at which time he may face opposition.

Judicial nominating commissions are silk-stocking bodies not reflective of the many groups in society, but many are representative of large law firms.

Where political machines exist, as they do in many larger cities, the "only way you get to be a judge," a distinguished New York lawyer with daily experience in the courts said, "is by running errands and kissing asses."

According to a report of the Illinois Committee on Courts and Justice:

> . . . [T]he path to judicial office in Cook County (Chicago) is not the high-road of education, scholarship, intelligence, character, independence, proven legal ability or standing or reputation in the legal community. . . . What really counts. . .are credits won as precinct captains or in other partisan political service, and political connections, political friendships and relationships with successful political families. . . . [T]he notion that judges are elected by the people is a cruel charade. They are in fact

> appointed—perhaps the word is anointed—by the ward committeemen and other party slatemakers as a reward for service to the party apparatus and the recognition that they are or will become "good old boys." The real vice of the present system is that it effectively limits opportunity for judicial office to the small segment of the Bar that has gained the price of admission by demonstrating qualities that have nothing at all to do with essential judicial qualifications.
>
> To put it in a nutshell, judgeships are bought.

In their monumental treatise on the government of New York, Wallace S. Sayre and Herbert Kaufman stated that "district leaders can extract (from a judge whom they "anoint") as much as a year's salary plus an additional 'campaign fund' of several thousand dollars." Murray Kempton has written, "The black robe is indeed the prime article of commerce remaining to the party organizations." In *To the Victor: Political Patronage from the Clubhouse to the White House,* Martin and Susan Tolchin point out that wives of judges indulge in wry jokes about how long it will take the family to pay for its seat on the bench.[24]

In the words of Strick, "Their Honors may be nonpareils of probity or remain in hock for all their professional lives to the governor who appointed them, the machine that pushed them, the mob that brought them."[25]

Elections have been won by duds and second raters, but on the whole, the voters' judgment has been at least as sound as that of the appointing authority. Anyone even slightly familiar with the way judges are selected for the non-elective courts is aware that political considerations are ever more present there as well. It is no more possible to take politics out of the selection of judges than it is for a hopeless cripple to climb Mt. Everest.

The Ethics of Judicial Conduct

Honorable judges need to guard against involvement in improper conduct situations, according to one author:

> An honorable judge may fairly ask why his attention should even be called to the records of the dishonorable ones. The reason is that, if he stays on the bench long enough, he will inevitably observe, or at least suspect, improper conduct somewhere in the judicial system. The honorable judge needs to guard himself against involvement in the dishonor, and he needs to think what he should do about it. He has obligations not only to his own integrity

> but to the honest administration of the law which he has sworn to uphold.

The new Code of Judicial Conduct adopted by the American Bar Association establishes minimum standards of judicial conduct and judges are asked to live up to higher standards than that prescribed, but it is binding only on the judges of any particular jurisdiction which officially adopts the code.[26]

The former chief justice of California, Roger J. Traynor, chairman of the committee that drafted the new Judicial Code, had this view:

> The easy answer is that a judge's personal morality is none of the public's business, but that's not the true answer. It doesn't do the judiciary any good if judges do things contrary to the mores of their community. It undermines public confidence. I'm not bothered if a Judge shoots crap at a casino, but if it's his constant habit to go to the races and bet heavily, it would harm the judiciary. It's a weasel worded answer, I know, but it's a question of balance. I don't like the idea of a judge going to a house of prostitution even if it's legal. It's a matter of moral behavior by commonsense standards of propriety.[27]

A judge should participate in establishing, maintaining and enforcing, and should himself observe, high standards of conduct so that the integrity and independence of the judiciary may be preserved, says Code I of the Judicial Ethics.[28]

Examples of Improper Judicial Behavior

Every student of legal ethics in law school should be familiar with the case of former Justice Martin Manton, Chief Judge of the U.S. Court of Appeals for the Second Circuit. Hit by the depression of the 1930s, a gambler and loser in extra-curricular activities, Manton became insolvent and was deeply in debt. Thus, he stooped to actively solicit bribes to influence his decisions in pending cases. He was indicted, convicted and spent time in the federal penitentiary.[29]

In Cook County, Illinois, nine judges and seven other men were indicted by federal grand juries after a three-year undercover investigation of corruption in the nation's largest court system—an investigation called "Greylord." Judge John M. Murphy was found guilty of accepting thousands of dollars in bribes to fix cases after facing twenty-four counts of mail fraud, racketeering and extortion. In September 1985, following Murphy's conviction, Judge Richard F. LeFevour, 54, was convicted on more than fifty counts of fraud and racketeering and sentenced to 300 years in prison and fines of $103,000. He was charged with accepting $400,000 in bribes to fix drunken driving cases and parking tickets in Cook County traffic court. In February 1986, Circuit Judge Reginald J. Holzer, 58, was found guilty of extortion and mail fraud after shaking down litigants and their lawyers for more than $150,000 in loans. Another judge pleaded guilty, one was acquitted and others are awaiting trial.

In Hattiesburg, Mississippi, on February 9, 1986, a jury convicted U.S. District Judge Walter L. Nixon Jr. of two counts of perjury. The judge had accepted $60,000 worth of oil and gas interests from a wealthy businessman in exchange for his help in trying to get state charges dropped against the businessman's son.

Reaching the top of the judgeship ladder can mean wealth. But those who get caught taking bribes surely suffer the agony of defeat and exposure.

Canon II of the Judicial Ethics stipulates: "A judge should avoid impropriety and the appearance of impropriety in all his activities. Public confidence in the judiciary is eroded by irresponsible or improper conduct by judges. He must expect to be the subject of constant public scrutiny. He must therefore accept restrictions on his conduct that might be viewed as burdensome by the ordinary citizen and should do so freely and willingly."[30]

When Justice John Todd of the Minnesota Supreme Court took the Florida bar exam in 1982, he didn't do so well, so he took the exam again in 1983, and cheated.

At age 56 Todd had been a member of the Minnesota bar for three decades and spent thirteen years on the state's supreme court—appointed by his former law partner, Wendell Anderson, who had been elected governor. Todd said he was thinking of giving up his prestigious job to move to Florida to practice law. Consequently, he took the so-called multistate portion of the bar exam, a standardized test used by most states, and had the results transferred to Florida.

When the director of bar admissions told Todd that Florida would not let him transfer his bar scores under those circumstances, Todd said he knew somebody on the Florida Supreme Court who might be able to get the rule waived. Todd would contend that it was only after he had taken the test in 1982 that he was told this; the admissions director did not remember "precisely" whether it was before or after the '82 exam.

As he had in 1982, Todd arranged to take the exam the next year, not with the hundreds of other exam-takers at the civic center, but in the private office of the bar admissions director, while the latter was occupied with the crowd at the civic center. Taking out three lawbooks and a copy of the Bill of Rights, Todd told the secretary he had the bar admission director's permission to use the books. The chief investigator for the board on judicial standards, who had an adjoining office, saw Todd using a book once, and the telephone once.

Todd's punishment? He agreed to accept public censure from his own court for violating a canon of judicial ethics that requires judges to conduct themselves in a manner that promotes public confidence in the integrity and impartiality of the judiciary.[31]

And in Miami there was an uproar over a judge accused of making a bigoted remark in court. Several lawyers said they heard Circuit Court Judge Dick Lantz use the perjorative Yiddish word *schwartzer* to describe a black man during a hearing on a lawsuit. Lantz was quoted also by the lawyers as saying the man, who was struck and killed by a car at night, could not be seen without smiling.[32]

Canon III of the Judicial Code states: "A judge should perform the duties of his office impartially and diligently. He should be patient, courteous to litigants, jurors, witnesses, lawyers and others with whom he deals in his official capacity. He should dispose promptly of the business of the court. He should diligently discharge his administrative responsibilities and maintain professional competence in judicial administration."[33]

> A woman who had sold a pound of cocaine to undercover agents pleaded guilty in Hillsborough County, Florida Circuit Court, during the fall of 1982 and was sentenced to three years in prison as provided by plea bargaining with the state. The State's Attorney's office charged her with trafficking, which carried a 15-year prison sentence. Later, the officer made a deal with the defendant's attorney and the chief judge, Arden Merckle. The charge was reduced to simple sale of cocaine, which carries no minimum sentence, in exchange for the defendant to plead guilty and accept a three-year prison sentence. Scarcely had the prosecutor left when the judge called the defendant back in the absence of the State's Attorney and without explanation, set her free on probation with a payment of $5,000 court costs to be paid in six months, and let her avoid a criminal record. Enter Judge Richard Leon from the same circuit, a lifelong friend of the defendant's father. A day or so before the sentencing, the defendant's father

> paid Judge Leon $50,000 for a piece of land appraised at $23,800. He also said he gave the judge $400 to $600 in gambling chips while the two men were on a trip to the Bahamas. This the judge denied. What added to the suspicious turn of events was a prosecutor's statement that he saw Judge Merckle having lunch that day with Judge Leon. The Judicial Qualifications Committee investigated and the findings were kept secret. Judge Merckle resigned from the bench. Before the committee Judge Leon committed perjury. He was indicted for perjury before the committee and misconduct for influencing Judge Merckle, bribery and receiving unlawful compensation. In his jury trial in Tampa he was convicted of perjury and misconduct; Judge Merckle was a state witness. Polk County Circuit Judge Oliver Green sentenced Judge Leon to five years' probation, a $5,000 fine and 1,000 hours of community service. He offered Judge Leon a chance to keep his lawyer's license—if he passed a lie detector test showing that he did not lie in court when he denied accepting gambling chips from the father of the drug defendant. To this the prosecuting attorney refused to participate in any examination.[34]

In Allegany County, Maryland, a jury rendered a $50,000 verdict for my client plaintiff, a state trooper injured on duty through the negligence of two defendants. One was a teenager who had been drinking and the other, a tractor trailer driver who had left his vehicle parked near a busy thoroughfare. Within three days after the jury verdict, the attorney representing the corporate tractor trailer company, which was highly insured, filed a motion for a verdict, notwithstanding the jury verdict. The court took the case under advisement. Five months later the motion was granted. The judge's son was a member of the law firm that represented the tractor trailer's corporate owner. The senior partner in the firm was a crony of the same judge and they spent vacations together. The case was affirmed on appeal.[35]

Speeding the Cause of Justice

Many court delays are not caused solely by the added cases filed or a shortage of judges, but due to procrastination by the judges in deciding cases, and poor court management in scheduling cases. Postponements or continuances are granted freely, especially to unprepared insurance company lawyers who request delays on the eve of the trial after a long list of witnesses have been subpoenaed, including such experts as doctors, economists and engineers. Once a case is removed from the trial docket it takes months to get back on. At the same time, the insurance company's reserves are accumulating interest while the plaintiff must continue to suffer, out of work, with bills piling up.

Too many courts have not yet learned that a key to effective justice is the operation of the courts in a businesslike manner. Justice William Brennan of the U.S. Supreme Court has written:

> There is actually no difference between the business of judicial administration and the business of running industrial or commercial enterprise in the sense that the efficient and businesslike conduct of both means better service for the public. And inefficient and wasteful judicial administration can and does result in a denial of justice, however earnestly an honest and upright judge may strive to prevent that lamentable result.

But instituting businesslike methods, thus decreasing delay, is only part of the answer as we strive to insure equitable treatment for all who come in contact with the judicial process–criminal and civil.

One way to make our court system fluid, viable and effective, and to eliminate the many delays, would be to institute court administrators in all state courts. Administrators could schedule cases and not allow scheduled cases to be postponed.

Refraining from Political Entanglements

Canon VII rules that a judge should refrain from political activity "inappropriate to his judicial office. He should not make speeches for a political organization or candidate or publicly endorse a candidate for public office. . ."[36]

I saw a classic example of abuse of this Canon in 1966. During my seventh year of practice, I tested the waters for political office by running for state's attorney on the Democratic ticket. For almost fifty years the office had been held by a Republican in a Republican county with a greater than 3,000 voter registration majority. My campaign slogan, "For clean and honest government," touched base with the rank and file because of two unsolved murders and a $100,000 bank heist. If elected, I threatened to clean house and to reopen the files to examine what shennanigans the incumbents were getting away with.

I covered the county well with a host of friends and supporters. Things looked promising as election neared; the "establishment" opposition got squirmy and called for extra help. On the Sunday prior to Election Tuesday, the two sitting judges of the circuit co-sponsored a full-page display ad in the local newspaper, featuring their photos with that of the incumbent, and declaring: "WE AGREE, ALLEGANY COUNTY DESERVES THE BEST."

Their action constituted a serious breach of judicial ethics, specifically of Canon VII which prohibited their public endorsement of a candidate. What made it worse was that it had been sanctioned by the "establishment" newspaper and later concurred in by the local bar association. I submitted the question to the state bar association grievance committee, but politics entered in and they dismissed it on short notice. I lost the election by a relatively small margin despite the involvement of the two judges. The state's attorney's office is still held by a Republican and much of the dirt that has crept into the files is still covered up.

Should a judge running for office accept contributions from a party in a pending suit? The code doesn't specifically answer that question, but accepting such contributions appears to be inappropriate. And it happened in one of my cases. A judge who receives money for a campaign must feel obligated to return the favor. There are many ways a judge can show favoritism in the course of court proceedings, such as ruling on the admissibility of evidence, granting or refusing to grant instructions to the jury, voire dire, demurrers, change of venue, granting postponements or continuances, motions, or deciding nonjury close cases, plus a host of others.

When a judge is to receive $50,000 to $80,000 annual salary, why should he look to the electorate and lawyers to pay for his campaign expenses?

Problems of Personal Bias

Do judges have personal biases which affect their performance? There's lots of evidence that they do, and many others have expressed their observations that such biases exist.

"What motivates judges to act as they do? Is it an innate and fundamental characteristic of the judicial temperament? Is it a compulsion to follow the letter of the law no matter where justice lies?" Goldberg and Levenson asked this question in *Lawless Judges*, then gave this answer:

> No! The great majority of our judges betray their judicial trust because they believe that it is one of the fundamental duties of the judiciary to protect the system of private ownership, defend property against the onslaught of

> workers' demands, and wherever possible, advance property rights at the expense of human rights. They are no longer impartial interpreters of the law. They are co-partners, conspirators as it were with their own kin and kind—the owners of property. It is their economic bias which speak.[37]

Or, as Strick would have it:

> Does the judiciary apply law to fact with elegant and unfair impartiality? Of course not. Impartiality is a judicial myth. In adversary procedure, the lawyer does not want an impartial judge. Quite the opposite. It is partiality he seeks. In truth, by adversary definition, the lawman wants as much bias as he can find on his side. The attorney tries to maneuver his client before the judge likeliest to give him a win.
>
> Lawyers make their living trying to figure out how judges will handle discretionary matter. He is paid for assisting the judge's discretion.[38]

In catering to their perception of judicial biases, our local coal mining corporate interests pick one law firm to handle their business. The law firm is a noted part of the establishment that thrives on politics and judicial appointments.

Another example: Judge Charles H. Carr of Los Angeles hated such insignia of modernity as long hair. Once, when an especially shaggy-haired lawyer appeared before him, Carr stormed, "I can't tell whether you are a man or a woman." He announced he was recessing court, "until I can decide whether to address you as sir or madam." Encouraged by the snickers of his staff or bailiffs, and courtroom hangers-on, Carr went on: "I would have you take down your pants and resolve the gender once and for all. But judging from the way you look, I'd have to rule there was not sufficient evidence to render a decision."[39]

"The particular traits, disposition, biases and habits of the judge will often determine what he decides to be the law," Frank wrote. He continued,

> In every case of actual thinking, the whole of a man's personality enters into and colors it in every part.
>
> Now the trial judge is a man, with a susceptibility to such unconscious prejudiced "identifications" originating

> in his infant experiences. Sitting at a trial, long before he has come to the point where he must decide what is right or wrong, just or unjust, with reference to the facts of the case as a whole, he has been engaged in making numerous judgments or inferences, as the testimony dribbles in. His impressions, colored by his unconscious biases with respect to the witnesses, as to what they said, and with what truthfulness and accuracy they said it, numerable hidden traits and predispositions often get in their work in shaping his decision in the very process by which he becomes convinced what those facts are.[40]

In *Lawless Judges* we read:

> Our system elects judges from those who have been purported leaders at the bar association. Such leadership generally falls to those who have been able to secure the right clients. It is natural for those who have associated with the wealthy and have defended the interests of property for a long time, to continue to look at things from the point of view after they mount the bench. We should not blind ourselves to the fact that certain powerful interests such as banks, railroads and insurance companies have had their share of influence in the selection process. It is humanly impossible for judges to get away from the bias of their limited experience and class feeling. It depends entirely on the personnel of the court as to what they will consider to be due process or within the police power. These phrases are blank checks which the judge fills in, in accordance with his personal opinion.[41]

Thomas Jefferson said, "It is not enough that honest men are appointed judges. All know the influence of interest on the mind of man, and how unconsciously his judgment is warped."

The prejudices of judges are but human. They are susceptible to, but seldom swayed by reason only. It is upon their feelings, their emotions, even their prejudices, that an advocate must play.

Seventy-nine men were laid off from their jobs at the Cumberland Brewery Company in Cumberland, Maryland. Most had worked the greater part of their lives there. They collected their last paycheck and were awaiting vacation pay that had accumulated for the year of termination. An employee had to work one year before being eligible for vacation; one year was always held back. When their jobs were terminated, they insisted they were due vacation pay for that year. "Not so," ruled the judge, a political appointee. The president of the brewery was an attorney, a member of the establishment who played a big part in the appointment of many local officials, including judges. Was it possible to find justice in this county circuit court of western Maryland? Hardly! Even the brewery union was company-oriented and did nothing, not even ask for a grievance hearing after vacation pay was denied. It was a company union with fidelity to the company corporate heads; the leaders were company controlled. Weak-kneed and powerless, the union did nothing. When unemployment compensation ran out for the seventy terminated employees, many of them in their 50s and 60s, they were out in the cold.

A suit was filed against the company, the local union and the Brewery International. The case continued for two years with the union and the company using all possible tricks of delay and influence. The politically influenced judge finally dismissed the case by summary judgment. There was no chance to present evidence, no one to testify, no documents to be admitted; plainly a decision was made for corporate management and the political wheeler-dealers of the trade. The employees' many long years of devotion to duty was forgotten. Money was the crux and political influence meant the difference. It was bias and politics in the highest degree.

The Delicate Issue of Criticizing the Lower Courts

In England it was treason to criticize the king, no matter how much he deserved it. This was one reason—among many—that the founders of the United States, who were earnest scholars of history, guaranteed freedom of speech and of the press. "The basis of our government being the opinion of the people," wrote Thomas Jefferson, "the very first object should be to keep that right; and were it left to me to decide whether we should have a government without newspapers, or newspapers without a government, I should not hesitate a moment to prefer the latter."

It was Ben Franklin who said, "Freedom of speech is a principal pillar of free government; when support is taken away, the constitution of a free society is dissolved and tyranny is erected on its ruins."

By tradition it is acceptable to criticize all public officials, including the President and his aides, members of Congress and legislatures, and the prestigious Supreme Court. Recently, a local circuit court judge bombasted Chief Justice Warren Burger for his statements regarding the lack of competency of lawyers and the bad state of lawyering. He was neither chastised nor admonished, but got much publicity for his criticism. But criticism of the lower courts is considered unpatriotic, an act of treason! Nowhere else is the power of the judiciary so great. Does a man lose his human frailties when he mounts the lower judicial bench?

Abbeville, Alabama, 1983: A judge fined a woman $100 for contempt of court after she wrote a letter to a newspaper in which she questioned the judge's fairness. Circuit Judge Billy Joe Sheffield imposed the fine and court costs on Connie Cox, 31, who said at her contempt hearing, "I just wrote a letter stating my opinion. This is freedom of speech and freedom of press." She had alluded to the sitting judge as one who found justice in letting a man who had worked seventeen years, running a very prosperous clothing business, supporting himself, his wife and three children, suddenly declare himself penniless and unable to work. Her letter urged women "to sit up and take notice of this situation because next time it could be you."

"The law of contempt is not made for the protection of judges who may be sensitive to the winds of public opinion," wrote Justice Douglas. "Judges are supposed to be men of fortitude, able to thrive in a hardy climate."[42]

Said Judge Harold Medina, "We cannot deny the fact that a judge is almost of necessity surrounded by people who keep telling him what a wonderful fellow he is. And if he once begins to believe it, he is a lost soul."[43]

Or, in the words of Justice Frankfurter:

> Judges as persons, or courts as institutions, are entitled to no greater immunity from criticism than other persons or institutions. Just because the holders of judicial office are identified with the interests of justice they may forget their common human frailties and fallibilities. There have sometimes been martinets upon the bench as there have also been pompous wielders of authority who have used the paraphernalia of power in support of what they called their dignity. Therefore judges must be kept mindful of their limitations and of their ultimate public responsibility by a vigorous stream of criticism expressed with candor however blunt.[44]

In grievance hearings it has been held unethical to criticize a judge while a case is pending. When closed, it is otherwise. However, this determination is controlled by the various state bar associations' grievance committees.

In a New York case an attorney was censured when he made public the following statement: "There are so few trial judges who just judge, who rule on questions of law, and leave guilt or innocence to the jury. And appellate judges are no better. They're the whores who become madams.

I would like to be a judge just to see if I could be the kind of judge I think a judge should be. But the only way you can get it is to be in politics or buy—and I don't even know the going price." In his case, it was reversed for the attorney when the court said, "Without more, isolated instances of disrespect for the law, judges and courts expressed by vulgar and insulting words or other incivility, uttered, written, or committed outside the precincts of the court are not subject to professional discipline.[45]

During a grievance hearing in Kansas, the lawyer was disciplined for saying, "I have very little respect for the police and courts; that is absolutely true. And I am very zealous in defending my clients but I do it very ethically." Asked by a reporter why he was disrespectful of the police and courts he replied, "The police are deadbeats and they arrest people illegally about as often as they do legally. I think they commit more crimes than the worst of our criminals. The courts are commonly prejudiced and they are much more concerned about who appears before them than what the facts are, and the law is." The court, in dismissing the action on appeal said, "The statements were general and directed broadly at all existing law enforcement and judicial institutions and not in the form of specific accusations.[46]

Judicial discretion manifests itself openly in threats against a lawyer who goes further in aiding his client than the court deems he should. A Massachusetts lawyer reports, "One of our leading judges threatened a defense attorney with contempt of court if he mentioned the Supreme Court once more."[47]

How far can a lawyer go in criticizing a judge, in and out of the courtroom? That was the question in the landmark Garrison case in Louisiana. The Supreme Court of the United States spoke out. Garrison, the district attorney of Orleans parish was convicted for remarks he made at a press conference attacking eight local judges who had refused to approve his expenditures of certain controlled funds. He told the reporters, "The judges have now made it eloquently clear where their sympathies lie in regard to aggressive vice investigations, by refusing to authorize use of the district attorney's funds to pay the cost of closing down Canal Street clip joints. . . . This raises interesting questions about the racketeer influence on our eight vacation-minded judges." He also attributed the large backlog of pending criminal cases to the inefficiency, laziness and excessive vacations of the judges.

The Supreme Court of Louisiana classified the criticisms as personal attacks upon the integrity and honesty of the eight judges, unrelated to their conduct of any case. The case was tried under a criminal libel statute of Louisiana. The U.S. Supreme Court held the Louisiana libel statute unconstitutional and in contravention of the free speech provided in the First and Fourteenth Amendments which embody our profound national commitment to the principle that debate on public issues should be uninhibited, robust, and wide open, and that it may well include vehement, caustic and sometimes unpleasantly sharp attacks on government and public officials.[48]

III

Appellate Courts—The Red Barons

To do justice and judgment is more acceptable to God than sacrifice.
Proverbs 21:3

"We must remember, too, that we have to make judges out of men and that being made judges, their prejudices are not diminished and their intelligence is not increased."[1]
Robert G. Ingersoll

The Power of Appellate Court Justices

The justices of the appellate courts: They occupy the uppermost seats in the hierarchy of the state courts—intermediate and supreme. They are the red-robed wisemen, the red barons of the court system.

Their opinions issue forth like granite tablets freighted with the highest authority in the law. They, the appellate judges, conduct no trials, suffer no witnesses, just hear metered arguments. They have traffic lights, red and green, signaling when to start and when to finish arguments. They are called the aristocrats of the bench.

They are selected as politically as their brothers in the lower courts. Their appointments come through the buddy-buddy system of politics. Governors view their appointments as patronage jobs and respond to pressures of local party bosses.

They are accessible on occasion—like their lower court brethren, the high priests—but maintain an untouchable aura. Their contacts are with people of similar backgrounds, and their attitudes and social values are likely to be representative of their social circles. A vast majority are white, male and Protestant, raised in comfortable economic circumstances.

They seldom reject or change the findings of the lower courts. The timid follow precedent; the bold ignore it. They appear as gods with limitless power, and their errors are covered up in the same fashion the physician buries his mistakes.

Justice is not their forte, but only the deciding of cases and writing of opinions. They rely heavily on staff researchers and recent law graduates who serve as their clerks for writing opinions.

Because of their privileged position they are personally immune from public and press scrutiny. They rarely step in to help out an inadequate attorney avert injustice and they are immune from civil action—even when in error or after having acted maliciously or in excess of authority. There is a code of honor among lawyers not to reveal the truth about them. Their incompetency is covered by the robe.

They usually hail from law firms that represent the corporate rich and the insurance industry. They never see the lonely misery of the poor, but give priority to the smug security of the wealthy, surrounded by learned lawyers.

They are a priestly caste, the state appellate courts, and their word is usually the final one. We look to them as the red barons of the bench.

Correcting Trial Court Errors and Developing the Law

"The function of the appellate or reviewing courts is to see that justice is done," wrote Judge John J. Parker. "It is accomplished by the correction of error of the trial court and the development of the law."[2]

Justice must serve the needs of the litigant; the law's development serves the needs of the public. The search for errors reinforces the dignity, authority and acceptability of the trial court and controls any adverse effects of personal shortcomings of the trial judge. But appellate courts fail to fulfill either function adequately. The costs of the appeals and the delays inherent in the process present additional formidable obstacles to providing equal justice under the law for poor litigants. Appeals are meant for the wealthy in civil cases.

The cast of characters in the appellate system is much like that of the trial courts below. There is the cautious and cowardly judge; the biased and prejudicial one, who reaches the level of bigotry. There's the political hack who must pay his dues and debts to the friends who put him there. There's the lazy and there's the crook—all sitting on the same bench.

Trial judges exercise broad discretion in deciding many questions—questions on which the law lays down hard and fast rules. Great weight, however, is given to the lower judge's findings.

As John W. Davis wrote in the *ABA Journal*, "A lawyer who criticizes harshly the action of a lower court runs the risk of offending the quite understandably esprit de corps of the judicial body. Rhetorical denunciation of opposing litigants or witnesses may arouse a measure of sympathy for the person denounced. Such things can irritate. They can never persuade."[3]

The Slim Possibility of Winning an Appeal

The possibility of winning an appeal is slim, Marks and Goldfarb have pointed out. "Criminal cases range from 5 percent to 10 percent; and in civil cases, from 15 percent to 20 percent. The court tries to sustain the lower decision if it can. It works out for itself some combination of a correct rule and an assumed fact which will logically justify the trial court's decision. It will assume facts if there is some oral testimony which will support it."[4]

The right to appeal does not exist unless expressly given by statute or state constitution. West Virginia, Virginia and New Hampshire do not allow an appeal as a matter of right from the final judgment. In West Virginia and Virgina, a petition for leave to appeal must be filed in the state supreme court.

During a trial, the lawyer must at all times prepare for an appeal. Errors committed must be timely objected to and made a matter of record. Failure to object constitutes a waiver of that point. Many courts hold that errors in jury instructions and admission of evidence are harmless unless the case is a close one. The appellate court will not reverse a decision simply because it would have acted differently. Charges of error must be supported by legal authority and reasoning.

Some appeals are merely delaying tactics, intended to keep the civil judgment debtor in possession of his money and out of the hands of the poor plaintiff who won the case before the jury and was granted a sizeable award.

On December 7, 1982, James Fazenbaker was killed instantly in Allegany, Maryland, when a county truck ran head-on into his small vehicle. He was survived by a young wife and four infant children. The widow retained me as counsel and I took on "The Duke" to assist me because this was considered a big case. Three years later a Washington County jury awarded her and the children $200,000. The county's liability was unquestioned and the award was not excessive, but ten days after the jury verdict the attorney for the county (insurance company, insurer now a circuit court judge), filed an appeal. The purpose was not to win on appeal, but to force the plaintiff to accept less money. Since the case could take a minimum of six months to process through the appeals court, the wife, in desperate need of financial assistance, agreed to take $170,000 in full settlement.[5]

As a general rule, an appeals court will indulge all reasonable presumptions in favor of the correctness of the judgment, order or decree from which appeal is taken. It is presumed that the lower court acted correctly and not in error. The appellate court will draw every reasonable presumption in favor of matters shown on the record and will draw every reasonable inference arising therefrom. And it will be presumed that the trial was conducted in a proper, regular and orderly manner.

In the trial court, after a jury has rendered a verdict for the plaintiff, the judge may grant a motion filed by the defendant's attorney for a judgment notwithstanding the verdict (NOV), and this motion when granted, is generally upheld on appeal. (In those situations, why hold a jury trial, many people wonder.)

In passing on the propriety of a motion for a judgment, notwithstanding the jury verdict, the appellate court will view the evidence in the light most favorable to the plaintiff.

The question of fact in a jury case is not ordinarily reviewed by the appeals court; the court is concerned only with the legal sufficiency of the evidence to sustain the verdict. The credibility of the witnesses and the weight of the evidence is left to the jury. But a jury case is generally won or lost by instructions given jurors by the trial judge when the case presentation is concluded. Before the jury is closeted, the trial judge instructs the jurors on what he believes to be the law of the case. It is here—through bias, poor attorney-judge relationship, and judge inexperience—that a trial judge can mislead the jury with improper instructions. Too, a young and inexperienced trial judge can destroy a plaintiff's case by whatever evidence he allows or doesn't allow, and by his overall conduct, especially his attitude toward an attorney for whom he has small liking. The jury usually believes the judge to be correct in his rulings; he is looked on with great respect, due more to the magnificence of the robe than his character. However, when a judge constantly badgers an attorney or is harsh with a witness, it can have an adverse effect on his client's case. On appeal, the appeals court takes the position that many of the errors made by the trial judge were harmless and don't constitute grounds for a reversal. However, in cases of large verdicts, the appeals court is quick to reduce the amount for friends, an insurance company, or to remand the case for a new trial.

In nonjury cases, a decision of a trial court is not set aside unless it is clearly erroneous. The appeals court will review the law and evidence with due regard to the judge's having had the opportunity of ruling on the demeanor and credibility of the witnesses. If there is substantial evidence, the appeals court will not touch it.

Modern science regards the mere seeing and hearing of witnesses as of little or no help in determining their veracity. Psychologists agree with Shakespeare: "There is no art to tell the mind's construction in a face."

Appearances can be deceitful. A successful swindler quickly learns to look a man directly in the face.

A trial judge can do many things during a trial that may help or hurt either side, but which would not constitute reversible error. All the appellate court gets is a cold transcript of the trial, taken from a court stenographer's notes, and this cannot reflect the judge's facial expressions or voice inflections. Since the trial judge sees the witnesses and evidence firsthand, his rulings go to any appellate court with a strong presumption of correctness.

The trial judge hears motions even after a jury verdict, and he has the power to reverse himself and the verdict if he can be convinced that he committed prejudicial error. The appellate courts are talking more and more about harmless error, which means they are becoming reluctant to reverse a case on a mere technicality. If the verdict makes sense and the judge did not do anything to interfere with the substantive rights of either party, it is likely that the decision will be affirmed.

The Decreasing Impact of "Harmless Error"

Legal procedures make it difficult for a defendant to obtain justice on an appeal once the factual record is established in the trial court. The judge or jury in the trial court determines what transpired factually, and it is at that stage that the police version of events in a criminal case usually is accepted. An appellate court, in reviewing the validity of a conviction by a lower court, is often bound by the lower court's determination of the facts, so it limits itself to reviewing the correctness of the legal principles applied to the facts. By the time a case reaches the appellate court, what was actually a blatantly illegal street search of a long-haired "hippy" type, might be determined—because of fact findings by a judge or jury—to be a perfectly legal search and arrest.[6]

Former Chief Judge of the California Supreme Court Roger Y. Traynor, after many years on the appellate court, dealt with the question in his book, *The Riddle of Harmless Error*:

> How does a judge determine whether an error is harmless or not? What is the test or standard that is to guide appellate courts in handling this matter? Did the error committed

> by a trial judge have a substantial effect on the verdict, one which caused a miscarriage of justice? The criteria must be some substantial wrong or miscarriage occasioned at the trial that affected the rights of the parties. The difficult problem of harmlessness usually turns on whether a right is substantial or technical and whether it has affected the judgment below. The emphasis should be on whether the judgment is not clearly right or wrong so long as there is a substantial chance that error brought it about.[7]

Edson R. Sunderland, for many years professor of law at the University of Michigan and one of the nation's leading authorities on judicial procedures, says:

> It would probably not be an exaggeration to say that the United States as a whole has the least efficient system of judicial review to be found among civilized people in the world today. The English system of reviewing law and facts, and thereby enabling appellate courts to render the maximum service to litigating parties...has spread over the English-speaking portions of the Empire. The nations of continental Europe have never restricted the full review of law and facts which was characteristic of the Roman law, and they have always maintained a system of appeals competent to render final and complete justice.[8]

During an interview I had with Justice Richard Neely of the West Virginia Supreme Court, he had this to say:

> In some jurisdictions the trial courts are liberal in wealth redistribution cases while the appellate court is conservative. Since the appellate court does not like the rendition of large judgments against industry and insurance companies, they will frequently reverse fair jury verdicts on minor procedural technicalities that have nothing to do with the integrity of the trial. On the other hand, liberal appellate courts may affirm all judgments for plaintiffs while judgments for defendants are often reversed for minor technicalities.
>
> The net result is that law is a chancy business at best. Going to court is like going into a chemical laboratory and

> mixing a lot of strange chemicals at random. Only after mixing, boiling, reducing and otherwise fiddling around, is it clear whether you have concocted a gooey mess or invented Saran Wrap.
>
> Obviously, some cases in the law are clearer than others. Yet more often cases appear to be clear until skilled lawyers begin to manipulate the panoply of half-hidden principles that lurk in a body of law eight hundred years old.
>
> Courts miss the point when they think of making litigation process, per se, more perfect in its justice. Far more perfect justice is achieved by designing rules that expedite settlements and encourage people to sort out their own problems on some reasonable basis. We have now had eight hundred years of experience trying to make the court system produce perfect justice, but we have just as many dissatisfied litigants today as ever before. We should always keep in mind that the cases that are actually in court are but an infinitesimal percentage of all the conflicts that the threat of going to court have settled.

Appellate courts at times are reluctant to examine the record on appeal to seek justice. Their response is that if the attorneys did not point out any error, why should they? This is done despite the merits of the cause. Should an appellate court decide an appeal for reasons not raised by the parties? They may do so, *sua sponte*, i.e., of its own motion, but rarely do.

Actually, the function of the appellate judge in raising issues *sua sponte* is akin to the increasingly recognized duty of the trial judge to be more than just a passive umpire passing upon the contentions and witnesses of opposing counsel. To assure decision on merits, rather than merely on the abilities of lawyers, the trial judge should more often exercise affirmative responsibilities with respect to pleadings, evidence, conduct of counsel, witnesses, and whatever may be reasonably necessary during trial to prevent a miscarriage of justice.

In other words, there is increasing recognition of the judiciary's responsibility to see that justice is done in each case, and to play an active rather than passive role in the administration of the judicial system, to assure that litigants' cases are decided according to general law and processed with reasonable expedition. *Sua sponte* consideration by appellate courts is simply another manifestation of this modern agreement that all judges have an affirmative duty for the prompt hearing and the correct disposition of all litigation.

The Role of Oral Argument

In many appellate courts oral argument is optional with counsel. Some courts encourage it and some discourage it. Some make it mandatory. The majority of courts find it helpful. The time period for argument can range from five minutes to two hours for each side. The principal function of oral argument is to make essential facts of issue stand out in the light of their true importance. It also tends to prevent one-man decisions because it calls every jurist's attention to the essential contentions of the parties and gives each an opportunity to ponder them and question for clarification.

Karl Llewellyn, in his book, *The Traditions of the Common Law*, has this to say:

> The function of the oral presentation is, if that be doable, to catch and rivet attention, to focus the issue into a single challenging question, to make the facts create ineluctable conviction as to where right lies, and to fit that conviction into a persuasive, even compelling legal frame. The brief can develop the frame, but the oral argument must get the case into the desired frame, and for keeps. . . . In oral argument lies counsel's one hedge against misdiagnosis and misperformance in the brief, the one last chance of locating a postern missed in the advance survey. In oral argument lies the opportunity to catch attention and rouse interest among men who must be got to read—or to reread—this brief not as a routine duty nor under the indiscriminating press of other business, but with the pointed concentration this cause merits.
>
> Finally, the oral argument is the one chance for you . . . to answer any questions you can stir any member of the court into being bothered about and into bothering with, and the one chance to sew up each such question into a remembered point in favor. By the same token, in the measure that this court has the practice of leaning heavily on either the reporting judge, or the chief, or both, or on the court's expert in the field, in that same measure the oral argument gives you your one direct access to the whole team together.
>
> In any but freak situations, oral argument is a must.[9]

Good oral argument can help the fallible judge make a better analysis of the case and contribute more to the sound development of the law with a minimum investment of time and energy. A good oral argument ensures that a court will not unwittingly go astray. Further, it may bolster a poorly-written brief. When the case is close, and all things are equal, effective argument can turn the tide.

Selecting Appellate Court Judges

The red-robed intelligensia, the jurisprudential intellectuals, are as politically inclined and motivated as their subordinates, though they would like the public to think otherwise. They probably have kissed more asses, paid more money, and sacrificed more principles to reach their higher post. They frown upon the elective system or democratic way, preferring the so-called merit or establishment system. They distrust minorities and anyone else who does not think their way. The retention system they espouse casts a long shadow on accountability.

The retention (or Missouri) system of selection is best characterized by Richard A. Watson and R. G. Downing in their book, *The Politics of Bench and Bar*:

> The business concerns most heavily involved in appellate court litigation have consistently attempted to influence the decision of the nominating commission and the governor in order to insure the recruitment of judges that would be sympathetic to their interests. They are the banks, the railroads, public utilities, insurance companies and the Attorney General's Office, which are the groups that have the largest number of cases before these courts. They play a dominant role in appellate selection. When it comes to the appointments made under the plan, both the political organizations and the lobbies put the heat on the Governor. Frequently, they get together on a candidate. But the lobbies dominate.
>
> Most appellate lawyer commissioners do not feel that attorneys with an exclusively plaintiffs' orientation should be given consideration for appellate court judgeships. . . .
>
> Lawyer members of the commission have no reservations about candidates with a defense practice. One appellate judge, commenting on his own selection, recalled that one of the lawyer commissioners was especially interested in the kind of practice that he had. "When he found out that I had represented casualty insurance companies, he became pretty enthusiastic about my candidacy," reported the judge.

> Their preferences with respect to the types of attorneys who should be recruited to the appeals bench are consistent with the lawyer commissioners' views as to the kinds of interests that deserve representation in the selection process. One lawyer commissioner observed: "The members of the business community are the ones that should be heard in the matter of judicial selection. That's because businessmen have one interest, that of getting good judges on the bench."[10]

Who Drafts the Opinions?

It's a fact that some appellate judges insist on doing all research, drafting and finalizing of opinions, however, in the majority of situations, judges are furnished with law clerks and the hard work falls on their shoulders. When an appellate judge gets lazy or is pressed for time, he shoves the full responsibility of the opinion writing on his assistant; hence, we find layman-made law from our highest courts.

Circuit Judge Lois Forer, in her book, *Money & Justice*, quotes with precision a well-respected appellate judge:

> I rarely read the record of the trial testimony and documents, usually reading only those parts that seem from the briefs or my clerk's draft opinion likely to be critical. In reviewing a draft opinion, I often accept the clerk's exposition, so that my revisions are mostly stylistic. Sometimes I do not read the record at all. In deciding whether to join the opinion of another judge, I often accept the opinion of the judge's statement of the record, on my clerk's assurance that the statement is accurate. I usually rely on summaries and recommendations prepared by the staff attorney and my clerks.[11]

"Most law clerks have not tried a case or written a brief or argued an appeal," Forer points out. "Not only are they young and inexperienced, but for the most part, they are not the most able students. They who apply for state judge clerkships are, on the whole, mediocre. Those who seek positions as permanent court staff are even less able."[12]

When a case reaches the appellate court one of the clerk's first functions is to screen the briefs and the record of the case. Here, he checks for accuracy of cases cited and brings them up to date with current precedents or law. He summarizes and clarifies important issues to be raised and adds any not mentioned. A judge may decide at the outset whether the case can be summarily dismissed, or he may determine that in-depth research needs to be done, plus the furnishing of a comprehensive memoranda. Some judges want recommendations, others don't.

Prior to oral argument and a study of the briefs, the judge may form tentative conclusions, all resting on the benefit of oral argument. The assistant attends this session for new light on the issues and further recommendation. In many instances, this is followed by post-oral conference with the judge. Further research may be required. Now the issues are firmed up, leading prior cases reviewed, and substantial agreement reached on the opinion to be written. Of course, in the interim, there is the collegiate exchange of memoranda from other members sitting in the case and the judge selected to write the opinion. Most law clerks and assistants spend over half their time preparing memoranda.

Great stress is laid on accuracy which means running the citator on each case to check grammar, spelling, correctness of case names, reports, and other authorities. The facts must be perfect, as well as the law.

The appellate judge demands that his assistants keep current on the law, legal periodicals, and all recent decisions of his court and higher courts. The assistant must also understand the philosophy of his judge and blend it into his so they can work hand-in-hand in developing opinions.[13]

Five-minute Decisions

Justice Neely was elected to the West Virginia Supreme Court at the age of 31, while in his third year of law practice. He was the youngest judge of last resort in the English-speaking world. In his book, *Why Courts Don't Work*, he wrote:

> The appellate court hears as many as three hundred appeals every four months. Their entire attention will be focused on the implications to the judicial machinery of permitting a new category of lawsuits—social torts as it were. Furthermore, since some cases involve very little money, no loss of liberty, and no economic problems like a factory closing, it is unlikely that the judges themselves will be very interested. The case will be shunted off to "central staff," a group of kids right out of law school who will summarize the case so that reading or hearing about it will take the judges no more than five minutes. The irony of this process is that the issues about which the parties thought they were arguing in the lower court will probably

> not be the issues on which the appellate court and its law clerks ultimately decide the case. In a hypothetical case, the parties believed they were arguing about whether White was unconscionably nasty to Prince. In the final analysis, however, the people who will decide the case are uninterested in either White or Prince and are equally uninterested in the "Who struck John?"of their relationship. Appellate judges and their clerks will be interested only in the world of abstraction—legal principles as it were—because with four hundred cases on the docket, abstraction is all they have time for![14]

Types of Appellate Opinions

Authors of appellate opinions may be said to fall within three general classes:

First, there are those who try to emphasize in their opinions the philosophy and literature of the law by obtaining much information from law reviews and other well-prepared articles.

In the second class are those who feel called upon to write exhaustive opinions. In every opinion they believe that all the law touching all the legal points raised, or those that could be raised, should be pursued to the minutest detail and that every case to be found in the digest or reports having any bearing, should be analyzed and quoted. Within this class are those lawyers who were precise and exacting in their practice before being elevated to the bench. Cases involving many points and fine distinctions are to their liking. They are sometimes more interested in busying themselves in the technical aspects of the case than they are in a correct decision of the case on its merits.

In the third category are the judges who decide the particular case and nothing more. They write briefly on the determinative issues, and state the facts in their own language in the light of the verdict and judgment of the lower court. They apply the law, refer to as few cases as necessary, and condense and condense.

An opinion dealing with the sufficiency or insufficiency of the evidence need not be detailed in reciting it nor need it quote at length the questions and answers appearing in the record. The judge should briefly state the evidence in the light of the verdict. That will be conducive to brevity and will be sufficient.

When a well-established rule of law is to be applied, a judge need not labor the point by discussing the law nor attempting to restate the rule. He simply should state that the the case is controlled by a well-established rule, or *stare decisis*, as announced in a certain case.[15]

The Weakness of the "One-man" Opinion Approach

Arthur T. Vanderbilt, former Chief Justice of the Supreme Court of New Jersey, was one of the most effective judicial administrators and advocates of reform in judicial procedure in this country. His untiring work bore much fruit and has continued to produce results after his death. In his book, *Improving the Administration of Justice: Two Decades of Development*, he said:

> The greatest bane of appellate courts today, in my judgment, is the so-called "one-man" opinion. I am referring to the situation where an opinion purports to be the decision and reflect the thinking of all the judges on the appellate court but which in fact represents the view and work of just one of the judges. . . . In more than half of the appellate courts of the several states, opinions are assigned in rotation in advance of oral argument. Judges, you can be sure, listen more attentively to the arguments where they are to write the opinion than they do to the arguments in other cases. There is an art, I am told, of seeming to listen. . . . The elimination of one-man opinions is not difficult of accomplishment. First of all, the rotational system of assigning opinions should be done away with. Every member of the court should read the briefs, listen to the argument and discuss each case in conference before he knows whether he will be called upon to write the opinion for the court. Only after this has been done should the opinions be assigned by the presiding judge to a member of the court who had indicated during the preliminary discussion of the case that he shares the view of a majority of the court. After an opinion has been written it should be studied by every member of the court and subjected to full discussion and frank criticism in conference, both as to substance and as to language.[16]

Precedent—Blind Adherence to the Past

Given the hierarchical system of courts, it is necessary for each lower tier to accept the decision of the highest tier. The doctrine of precedent holds a coercive force over the lower courts. This is the common concept or doctrine, called *stare decisis*, blind adherence to the past. It means: Stand by your decisions and those of your predecessors however wrong they are and whatever injustice they might inflict. Antique laws must take priority over justice. Adhere to the decision and do not unsettle things which are established. Do not muddy the waters.

The Right Honorable Lord Denning wrote: "There are courts that follow precedent which states a legal rule, even if on reconsideration it thinks it should be revised. It clings to an unjust rule until the legislature intervenes. *Stare decisis* serves the function of enabling judges to dispose of their caseload readily and turn their back on the more arduous task of re-examining the basis and soundness of every rule of law in cases that come before them."[17]

"The life blood of a healthy, vigorous, growing legal system is reasonable unpredictability," writes LeFlar. "Law is the servant of mankind but the law that served mankind yesterday may afflict it tomorrow. Law to be helpful must change as the world changes—with the customary lag."[18]

Development of the Law

Justice, not adherence to old, outmoded laws, should be the end sought by appellate courts and it should be the touchstone of the courts' thinking. The theory of precedent is that the law should be certain and stable, and that to attain that certainty, it is occasionally necessary to sacrifice justice, despite any hardship incurred.

The old slogan, "Let the legislature do it; it is not our function," was strongly opposed by the noted justice, Jerome Frank. In *Courts on Trial* he asked, "Why should that be so? Why wait for the legislatures?"

> The underlying assumption is that the legislature should and will promptly rectify the unjust judge-made rule. In truth, legislatures sometimes are extremely tardy in doing that job. But, aside from that difficulty, note the inconsistency of the court's position: It refuses to alter its own admittedly unjust rule for fear of causing instability. Yet it invites the legislature to wipe out that rule. Will not the legislature, if it accepts that invitation, cause as much instability? Why, then, should a court look to the legislature to remove an injustice created by the court itself? Legislatures repeal rules which legislatures have made. Why should not courts do the same with rules they have made?[19]

"Development of the law to conform to changing technology, newly acknowledged rights and unprecedented problems should be one of the major functions of appellate courts," wrote Forer. "We cannot say that the common law as announced by the courts is a body of rules that always keeps abreast of the needs of society."[20]

A five-year-old went to get his ball that had bounced over a fence into a yard. As he was reaching for his ball, a doberman knocked him down and an Afghan mauled him. He spent five weeks in the hospital and sustained permanent facial scars. The boy's parents thought the dogs' owners should pay for his injuries and they sued, claiming that large, vicious and ferocious animals with dangerous propensities to attack, should not be allowed to wander freely on the property. The Maryland Court of Appeals affirmed the lower court and restated the aged common law rule: "Trespassers take the premises as they find them; it extends to inadvertent trespassers and children who are trespassers."[21]

In another case, Timothy Paul Murphy obtained a jury verdict in the Superior Court of Baltimore for $150,000 damages as a result of his hand coming in contact with an electrical transformer on land owned by the Baltimore Gas and Electric Co. But the trial court took the case away from the jury and found for the defendant, the utility company.

The lower court's action was sustained by the appellate court, which ruled that "In support of the common law rule, a land owner owes no duty to a trespasser except to abstain from wilfully or wantonly injuring or entrapping a person." Strict application of the archaic common law rule resulted in cruel and severe treatment of the property entrant.[22]

Contributory Negligence

One of the more unjust rules of the old common law was that of contributory negligence, which had its origin in England in 1838. It provides that an injured plaintiff cannot collect damages from another if he is found to have contributed to the cause of his injuries. Over a time, forty-five states have changed the old rule, either by legislation or by a high court decision, to that of "comparative negligence." This allows a person to collect damages in proportion to his fault.

Maryland is one of five states that stubbornly clings to contributory negligence, which it adopted in 1847. This is because Maryland's court membership consists principally of lawyers formerly with law firms dealing in insurance and corporate defense work; they owe allegiance to their former clients. One judge came from a law firm whose sole business was insurance defense. The Maryland legislature has been trying to change the law since 1966 but in each session it gives in to the strong political action committees who wine and dine the legislators and buy their votes. Law professors and plaintiffs' organizations that want to do away with the common law rule quote actuarial studies showing that insurance rates would not be increased by application of comparative negligence.[23]

In no state in which the doctrine of contributory negligence was overturned has the legislation been challenged.

We have made great advances in science and technology; public agencies and private entrepreneurs plan enormous undertakings. But some of our men of law, having eyes to see and minds disciplined to visionary thinking, still hold to outworn precedents—despite their inequities.

Equality and justice, especially in the higher courts, are what is needed now, not sameness of treatment for those of the past, the present and the future generations.

IV

The Veniremen: Juries and Justice

But jury trial at best is the apostheosis of the amateur. Why should anyone think that twelve persons brought in from the street, selected in various ways, for their general lack of ability, should have any special capacity for deciding controversies between persons?
Former Dean Erwin Griswold

The jury system puts a ban upon intelligence and honesty and a premium upon ignorance, stupidity and perjury. It is a shame that we must continue to use a worthless system because it was good a thousand years ago.
Mark Twain

The Challenges of Jury Service

Jurors: They are transformed into lawmen overnight and imbued with great power and authority despite no training for the job. They hold reign over verdicts involving millions of dollars and decide matters of life and death.

A jury consists of at least six and not more than twelve persons, chosen at random, with no experience in weighing evidence and perhaps none in applying their minds judicially to any problem; many are unaccustomed to intellectual exercise or protracted thought. The case before them may be an intricate one, lasting months. Without taking notes they are expected, within hours, days or months, to arrive at a conclusion in unison and harmony.

Jurors are the sole judges of all the facts, as they view them, which they then apply to the law. They deliberate in secret and return a verdict without giving reasons and are responsible to no one—only to their individual consciences. After the trial they meld into the community from which they were drawn.

To the discouragement of the state, they acquit the guilty on some occasions. On other occasions, they execute the innocent on the slenderest threads of evidence. They are cowed and bullied by judges and considered the weakest link in the judicial system. They are never instructed by the court to be fair or just. They are rarely a cross-section of the community or peers of the suit parties. They frequently make decisions and render verdicts based on their feelings; they can perceive credibility in a source beyond the control of statistical analysis. Their mental workings are not known to one another—some are intellectuals, some are stupid, and some ignorant.

They are asked, after many hours or days or months, to assemble or separate fragments of evidence, including the demeanor of witnesses, and to fit them into the judge's instructions on the law. Unpredictable as spring weather, they make the orderly administration of justice virtually impossible. They will give greater credence to police testimony than to the ordinary witness's. Some doze off after a heavy lunch and snore, interfering with the court proceedings.

No two jury panels are alike. Each panel's effectiveness depends on the jurors' courage, convictions and intelligence—which many lack. They surrender their consciences and wear compromise like a halo. They are expected to agree, no matter how complex the circumstances of the case or how obscure the darkness in which it is shrouded. Often they will base their verdicts on matters having no relation to the law or facts, and call it "community law."

Justice is not standardized nor defined because it is a concept of the mind and varies with each person. Jurors' rearing, religion, environment, politics, and philosophy determine their sense of justice. They render verdicts in obedience to their prejudices or sympathies, regardless of their oath and duty to seek justice. The bias and prejudices that are inherent in most people get worked out in the jury room discussion. Corporations and the wealthy do not trust juries because a panel rarely consists of their counterpart or peers. Jurors often do not understand the judge's instructions; oftimes they are muddled and confused by them.

Juries are publicly extolled by politicians who have little or nothing to do with jury trials. Many trial lawyers esteem juries in their public utterances but scorn them in private. They are considered a sacred institution while doling out a strange form of justice.

Juries are an odd-lot of men and women chosen at random from the assessment, the registration, or other miscellaneous rolls. They come from all walks of life: the cooks, carpenters, laborers, housewives, accountants, artisans, unemployed, preachers, doctors, farm hands, custodians, nurses, industrial workers, college students, professors, salesmen, funeral attendants, engineers, letter carriers, bartenders, junk dealers, bank tellers, and who not. They are alleged to be the depository of common sense, the palladium of liberty, the community at large, and a body of one's peers. The veniremen or jury, they are the fact blenders, blending the facts with the judge's instructed law, and they can make or break you.

Establishment of Juror Rights: An English Trial in 1670

In the history of the English jury system, the trial of greatest importance was that of William Penn and William Meade for unlawful assembly and disturbance of the peace, held at London's Old Bailey Criminal Court on a Sunday afternoon in September 1670. At that trial the recorder directed the jury to find the Quakers, Penn and Meade, guilty, but after returning to the jury room on five occasions in four days of deliberation, the jury refused. The recorder likewise refused to accept their verdict of not guilty and threatened them with a variety of pains and punishments for disobeying. Finally, he kept them all night without food, drink, heat, or the accommodation of a chamber. Then each juryman was polled and again each replied, "Not guilty." For this the recorder fined them 40 marks apiece and cast them into prison until the fines were paid.

Tudor era juries were regularly fined or imprisoned for failing to return guilty verdicts. Jurors also had to fear "attaint," a procedure whereby a second jury could decide that the first jury's verdict was erroneous. In "attaint" all their land and property was either destroyed or relinquished to the king, their wives and children were left homeless, and they were declared "infamous" by the community—held not to be "oathworthy" for future trials.

One of the jurors in the Penn-Meade trial, Edward Bushnell, did not take it lying down. He filed a writ of *habeas corpus* before the court of the King's Bench. The opinion was written on November 20th of the same year by Chief Justice Vaughn and never after were juries to be punished for not finding in accordance with court's instruction. A jury's right to give a general verdict of innocent was established, and based upon their verdict, the accused could be set free.

The Penn-Meade trial is marked for posterity by a plaque hanging in Old Bailey, inscribed: ". . . that courage and endurance of the jury refused to give a verdict against them although locked up and punished; upon a review by a Writ of Habeas Corpus it was established, the right of juries to give their verdicts according to their conscience."[1]

The Origins of Trial by Jury

Man's history is a record of constant strife, dissension, invasion and war—conflicts, disputes and ambitions being a vital part of life. For centuries trial by combat, or ordeal by fire or water, were accepted means of resolving disputes. When ways to resolve disputes amicably were found, the principal method was through court trials. Only later were juries inserted into the process.

The origin of the jury has been lost in the darkness of antiquity; investigation is hopeless. But as Greece is considered the cradle of liberty, it is also considered the place of the jury's origin. The Romans adopted it but when juries became too powerful, they were abolished in 352 A.D. Still, the jury system spread across Europe, the idea carried by wanderers from group to group. When William the Conqueror conquered England in 1066 he took the system with him.

The jury was derived from the Scandinavian tribunals where the judicial number "12" was venerated. Twelve men were regarded as the proper number to establish the credibility of a person accused of a crime, and it was natural that the same number should be required when the witnesses came forward, not to speak to character but to facts. The number twelve had other significance: twelve prophets to tell the truth, twelve apostles to speak the truth, twelve discoverers sent into Canaan to seek and report the truth. In ancient days, twelve judges determined matters of law and for matters of state, there were twelve councilors of state.[2]

In England, law courts did not spring up overnight but developed over several centuries. The first courts were presided over by judges appointed by the sovereign. These judges went from town to town to hold court sessions. Each case required the judges to find the usage or custom applicable to the facts presented them. In this way they determined the validity, scope and application of the usages and customs which came before them. The determinations of the judges were called decisions.

Each decision on a point of law became a precedent to be followed in similar cases. The use of precedents allowed a consistent and uniform law to develop.[3]

The Normans, who had brought with them the seed of the jury trial system, used twelve men as a court of inquest to determine title to lands, particularly lands over which the crown could assert ownership.[4]

The Magna Charta and The Statute of Westminster, the First

In 1215 the Magna Charta was signed after a bitter struggle between King John and his nobles. The king had pillaged and oppressed the nobles—his actions legally supported by judges he had appointed. Signed by the king, twelve barons and twelve bishops, this historic document contained several provisions, one of which reads: "No Freeman shall be taken or imprisoned or be disseized of his Freehold, or Liberties, or free Customs, or be outlawed, or exiled, or otherwise destroyed; nor will we not pass upon him nor condemn him, but by lawful Judgment of his peers, or by (a) the Law of the land. (b) We will sell to no man, (c) we will not deny or defer to any man either Justice or Right."

By this provision the Magna Charta has been commonly understood to have established jury trials for all people in England. It did not. The misconception stems from two misunderstandings. The first of these is in reading the word Freeman. The freemen of that day were members of the nobility, as opposed to the common men who were known as villeins or villains and who held no free land. The other misunderstanding is in reading the phrase, "law of the land." This phrase was a guarantee to the nobility that the right to trial by combat was reserved to them, that their possessions could not be arbitrarily condemned by the king, and that judgment would precede execution. The king could continue to dispense justice to the commoners but the nobility were to be tried only by their equals. The Charta, therefore, was a compact between the nobility and the king; it did nothing to forward the development of jury trials in general.

The barons, having triumphed over the king in asserting their power, conducted their own courts thereafter, and exercised arbitrary power over their vassals and underlings, thus largely denying them justice. To correct this situation the first Parliament enacted the Statute of Westminster, the First, in 1275. This statute extended the benefits of the aforementioned section of the Magna Charta to the common man in these words: ". . .that no City, Borough, nor town nor any Man be amerced [fined or punished arbitrarily] without reasonable cause, and according to the Quality of his Trespass, that is to say, every Freeman saving his Freehold, a Merchant saving his Merchandise, a Villain saving his Gaynage [his rights in agricultural land, his tolls and the product thereof] and that by his or their Peers."[5]

The deep meaning to us of Magna Charta and the Statute of Westminster, the First, is that they established the principle of due process of law.

The statute firmly established the King's Courts which went from place to place holding court sessions, much as our circuit courts do today. When a court convened, the people of the area were required to report crimes and wrongs committed by villians and these suspects were then brought to trial. The jurors, if we may call them such, were twelve men in the area considered most likely to know the facts involved. The losing party could then call for a trial by twenty-four knights. This was the first use of an appeal system in England. If this body decided the case contrary to the verdict of the first jury, the first twelve were subject to attaint.

The next step in the development of the jury trial system was the hearing of witnesses in open court. We can assume that as the population increased it became more and more difficult to find twelve men who might know of the doings of their neighbors and know the facts sufficiently well to act as witnesses and jurors.[6]

In any event, the use of witnesses in open court was introduced and became established.

Thus, the jury trial system evolved into its present form. Jurors, instead of being qualified as men familiar with the facts, became men selected because they did *not* know the facts. This change called for new laws on the qualifications and selection of jurors, and for the formation of rules and evidence.[7]

Juries in the American Colonies

When Englishmen first came to North America, they brought with them the concept of trial by jury. The first charter of Virginia in 1606 provided that all subjects should: "Have and enjoy all Liberties, Franchises and Immunities within any of our Dominions, to all Intents and Purposes, as if they had been abiding and born within this, our realm of England, or any other of our Dominions."

The right to trial by jury was specifically mentioned in King James the First's instructions for government of the colony of Virginia. Trial by jury was introduced into the Massachusetts Body of Liberties, adopted by the General Court of Massachusetts on December 10, 1641. The Concessions and Agreements of West New Jersey, 1677, contained the guarantee of trial by jury and when the English occupied Amsterdam in 1664 and renamed it New York, they instituted the jury system. Jury trials were held in Pennsylvania as early as 1673.[8] The king, however, was not always happy with the way the colonials on juries administered the king's laws. They often found in favor of colonial defendants who were in violation of England's statutes regarding the colonies—laws deemed oppressive by the inhabitants.[9] And because some judges in the colonial courts attempted to dominate juries, other changes came about which evolved into the jury trial system as we know it.[10]

Prior to the American Revolution there was no uniformity among state juries as to the decisions of law and fact in a case. Radical changes were wrought by two occurrences: the 1734 trial of John Peter Zenger and the publication in England of Blackstone's *Commentaries on the Common Law* which began in 1765.

In 1734 Zenger published articles criticizing the royal governor, William Crosby, alleging misadministration and corruption. Zenger was charged with an act in violation of the criminal laws. His defense was freedom of the press and truth. Zenger's attorney, Andrew Hamilton, contended he was not guilty on grounds that publications are only libelous if false, and Zenger could prove the truth of what he had published. The court ruled that truth was not a defense and charged the jury to decide only on the facts, leaving the court to decide the law.

In his argument to the jury, Hamilton declared that the community well knew the facts were true; he then cited legal precedents to show the judge had misinterpreted the law and that truth was a defense. Accordingly, he argued, it would be bad law to impose criminal penalties for the publication in question. The jury quickly returned a verdict of not guilty, having determined the question of law and fact.

The jury was obviously unwilling to apply an unjust or unpopular law. It was representative of the conscience of the community. The attorney's conduct would not have been condoned in England where the accused's counsel was not permitted to address the jury. The colonies were thus molding their own idea of a jury trial.[11]

The second factor to have a great impact on the American courts was a work produced by William B. Blackstone, a judge of the Court of Common Pleas of England. At the time there was no real collation of English common law. In 1765 he began publishing his *Commentaries*, and this became the basis for molding and influencing the colonists' attitude toward the law.

As to juries, Blackstone said:

> But in settling and adjusting a question of fact, when entrusted to any single magistrate, partiality and injustice have an ample field to range in . . . therefore, a competent number of sensible and upright jurymen, chosen by lot from among those of middle rank will be found the best

> investigators of truth and the surest guardians of justice. . . . [12]

If there was sometimes doubt in theory that juries had the right to decide law, there was no doubt in practice. In 1761, a case, *Erving v. Cradock* was brought for trespass against a custom house officer for detaining a brigantine and its cargo. The defendant pleaded the general issue and the plaintiff obtained a judgment. The question had been submitted to the jury which found in favor of the plaintiff. In this case as in the Zenger case, it was not so much a matter of the court's recognizing the jury's right to decide law, but deferring to their decision of it.[13]

The importance of jury trial to the nation's earliest citizens is evident in revolutionary and constitutional documents. The Declaration of Rights of the First Continental Congress, issued October 14, 1774, stated: "The respective colonies are entitled to the common law of England, and more specially to the great and inestimable privilege of being tried by their peers of the vincinage according to the course of law." And on October 19, 1775, the first session of the American Stamp Act Congress resolved, "that trial by jury is the inherent and invaluable right of every British subject in these colonies."[14]

The Declaration of Independence, on the matter of jury trial, was brief but to the point, declaring that one of the reasons necessitating the separation of the colonies from England was, "For depriving us, in many cases, of the benefits of trial by jury."[15]

The colonists had long been dissatisfied with some of the operations of the colonial courts, and in the Declaration of Independence they expressed two specific grievances against the king regarding the operation of the courts:

> He has made judges dependent on his will alone, for the tenure of their offices, and the amount and payment of their salaries. For depriving us in many cases of trial by jury."[16]

The ordinance for the government of the Northwest Territory in 1878 provided, in Article II, that "The inhabitants of said territory shall always be entitled to the benefits of the writ of *habeas corpus* and trial by jury."[17]

Court trials in the colonies were open to the public except in a few instances. The form of jury trial in effect when the individual state constitutions were adopted has been defined in these words:

> Trial by jury, in the primary and usual sense of the term of common law and in the American Constitution, is a trial by a jury of twelve men. In the presence and under the superintendence of a judge empowered to instruct them about the law and advise them on the facts and (except on acquittal of a criminal charge), he may set aside their verdict, if in his opinion it is against the law or the evidence.[18]

Trial by Jury Today

The right to a trial by jury is exercised in this way. In criminal cases, a defendant is informed that he has the right to a jury trial and that he can elect to have a jury trial or waive it. In civil cases, any party can demand a trial by jury or waive it, as provided by the state constitution and statutes.

The state system of courts consists of courts sitting at each county seat. These courts may have jurisdiction over a whole county, parts of a county, or more than one county—according to the will of the legislature. Courts covering on or more than one county are known as circuit courts. These are circulating trial courts, holding terms of court at each county seat. In large cities there are courts having jurisdiction over the entire city. These have various names—such as city court, municipal court, or court of special sessions—and in them the legislatures usually provide for the same jury trial system used in county courts. (There are also minor courts, such as police courts and courts held by Justices of the Peace. They may or may not use juries and a jury need not be twelve in number. We are not concerned with them in this context.)

Appeals may be taken from these trial courts to the appellate courts.[19]

Despite the long history of the jury trial, its future is uncertain. Changes in American society have created new demands for justice which may not be met by traditional jury trials. Increased volume of civil and criminal trials has clogged the court system and placed unprecedented strains on the ability of the jury system to dispense high quality justice. There have been drastic increases in the length and complexity of trials. On the civil side, advances in science and engineering create complexities in disputes that challenge experts in the field and would seemingly require an unattainable level of sophistication on the part of jurors.

Traditionally, all states held to the twelve-man jury, and this too is changing. Now jury procedure differs among states, both in criminal and jury trials. For example, the twelve-member unanimous decision jury is required in both criminal and civil trials in only seven states at present. The size of a jury ranges from six to twelve members and decision rules range from unanimity, which is required in all states for six-member juries, to a two-thirds majority.[20]

The U.S. Supreme Court has determined that the traditional member jury size is not a requirement for state or criminal trials, but that juries with fewer than six are less representative, less reliable and less accurate than large juries. In a Louisiana case, the court found that lack of unanimity, however, does not establish reasonable doubt. Nationally, there is near uniformity in requiring unanimous verdicts from six-member juries in criminal trials.[21]

An Essential Element: The Judge's Instructions to the Jury

The first and most essential element in a jury trial is a wise, learned, impartial and competent judge who is qualified by character, learning, integrity and experience to preside over and control the proceedings. He advises jurors as to the law of the case and instructs them in the discharge of their duties.

The judge determines the rules of law for the jury; the jury ascertains the facts and applies them to the law before rendering its decision. The jury must in no manner encroach upon the powers of the judge. It must not concern itself in any way with the authority or wisdom of the law.

Whatever the judge announces to be the law, the jury must take as being completely authoritative. In essence, the jury is more than a fact-finding body. The application of the legal rules to the facts involves legal reasoning. The jury, therefore, is partly engaged in the role of law finding. The general verdict is a composite one—a blend of fact finding and legal reasoning. The application of the rules of law to the facts must be done intelligently and requires an interpretation and understanding of the meaning of the rules of law.[22]

One of the principal grounds for an appeal to appellate courts is error by the judge in instructing the jury. It has been said this happens in roughly 40 percent of the reversals by the appellate courts.

To render a just verdict, the jury must not only hear the applicable facts, jurors must also be instructed in the legal proposition to the case. On the whole, judges do a very poor job of instructing. Some ramble on, using legal language not easily understood (with Latinized phrases) and as a result, the jury fails to grasp some significant question of law.

"A South Carolina judge, attending the National Judicial College in Reno, Nevada (to make himself a better judge), remarked to a fellow judge that he had almost missed his plane because he had been presiding over a first degree murder case. "I made it because I had the jury instructions down so pat that I can do seven pages of instructions in fifteen minutes," he said. The jury had been given fifteen minutes to comprehend the law of murder, yet, when an appellate court reviewed the conviction there would be no reversal or retrial, because the judge had said all the right things and the words would look right in the record transcript."[23]

"The truth is that in many cases juries are neither able, nor do they attempt, to apply the instructions of the court. For all practical intents and purposes, the judge's views on the case might never have been expressed. A better instrument could scarcely be imagined for achieving uncertainty, lack of uniformity and disregard of former decisions. A wise lawyer will hesitate to guarantee any jury results."[24]

The best case in the world is at best a gamble.

A good example is my case of the cyclist proceeding through the intersection with the green light. The jury said his right of travel was not absolute, even with the green light, because he had the obligation to veer right or left to avoid the collision, even though he risked colliding with another vehicle.

"Jury-made law, as compared with judge-made law, is peculiar in form. It does not issue general pronouncements. You won't find it set forth in the law reports or in text books. It does not become embodied in a series of precedents. It is nowhere codified. Each jury makes its own law in each case with little or no knowledge of or reference to what has been done before or with regard to what will be done thereafter in similar cases."[25]

A principal claim of the jury, popularly favored, is its ability to defy, in a general verdict, the law of the land as announced by the judge. The trial court, however, may grant a verdict that overturns a jury verdict.

In many cases, jury decisions are products of irresponsible caprice and prejudice. The plaintiff may be poor, the defendant a wealthy corporation. The principal witness for one party may be a Mason or a Catholic. The attorney for one side may be a brilliant orator. Such prejudices can determine who wins and who loses.[26]

In legal literature this is a typical comment: "One of the greatest fictions known to law is that a jury of twelve laymen can hear a judge read a set of instructions once, then understand them, digest them, and correctly apply them to the facts of the case. It has taken the judge and lawyers years of study to understand the law as stated in the instructions."[27]

One of my questions to the Honorable Lord Denning in 1984 was why the English system had disposed of civil juries. His answer was crisp and immediate. "Mr. Sullivan, who are better able to decide legal questions, those who are learned in the profession or amateurs?"

Many judges' instructions are "canned"—taken from a form book entitled, *Pattern Jury Instructions*. In many instances the judge reads the instructions without explanation; the judge and the lawyers are familiar with them, but to the layman on the jury, they sound like a foreign language.

Consider this example from an Illinois book of jury instructions on the subject of damages in a civil suit:

> In computing the damages arising in the future because of injuries, medical expenses, and loss of earnings, you must not simply multiply the damages by the length of time you have found they will continue or the number of years you have found that the plaintiff is likely to live. Instead, you must determine that present cash value. "Present Cash Value" means the sum of money, needed now, which when added to what that sum may reasonably be expected to earn in the future, will equal the amount of the damages, expenses and earnings at the time in the future when the damages from the injury will be suffered, the expenses must be paid and the earnings would have been received.

Imagine this being read like a story from a book with no repeats or taking the instructions to the jury room![28]

Moving Trials: Juries' Awards Related to Community Size

Judges' instructions, notwithstanding, juries are apt to arrive at their own conclusions in determining awards. Harry Kalven Jr., and Hans Zeisel, authors of a foremost book on juries, had this to say about jury awards: "The size of awards given by juries for comparable personal injuries was strongly related to the jury's domicile. The larger the community from which the jury came, the larger the award."[29]

In a civil suit, either side—plaintiff or defendant—may move a place of trial or venue to another county at the discretion of the trial judge. As a matter of custom, cases in my county involving large sums of money were often moved by the defense to a more western rural county where the people place a greater value on the dollar and verdicts are relatively low.

It is difficult to fathom the moods and minds of jurors as to what motivates them to decide as they do. I had a case in which my client plaintiff was a 40-year-old construction foreman who had been hospitalized for a hernia operation. In pain, he asked a nurse for a sedative. She injected Demerol® into one of his buttocks but in the process, hit a sciatic nerve and in a short time he became permanently paralyzed in his left leg. It appeared to be a clear case of negligence. I took in a specialist malpractice attorney with me and we sued.

To avoid local prejudice we moved the case to a neighboring easterly county for trial. However, the defendant's attorney did us one better by asking the judge to remove the trial to the most western county of Maryland. At the outset of the trial the court informed the jury of the case removal twice, then nothing more was said about it for the remainder of the trial. Expert medical testimony was presented in abundance for both sides, but it appeared a foregone conclusion that the plaintiff would prevail; we looked forward to a six-figure verdict. After five days of testimony the case went to the jury. Deliberation went on all night and into the early morning, but the jurors could not agree, even with added instructions; hence a mistrial.

Weeks later I ran into one of the jurors, an elderly housewife. I asked her what was on the jury's mind that they could not decide the case. Her answer threw me. She and the other jurors believed the case had been tried twice before—once where the suit was filed and the second at the first removal. "Since those two courts couldn't decide, neither could we," she said.

The attorneys had believed the judge made clear the history of the case on the two prior removals; the jury had different ideas and that became fixed in their thinking throughout the trial.[30]

Theories of Jury Selection

"When John Mitchell and Maurice Stans of Watergate fame were brought to trial their attorneys prepared a profile of the type of juror they wanted to hear the case. Their ideal jurors were members of the working class who read *The New York Times* and were of Catholic background."[31]

Favored jurors for the criminally accused are the Irish, Italian, Jews, French, Hispanics and blacks. Stay away from the English, German and Scandinavian.

"Counsel for Rap Brown in Maryland described his ideal juror as white and female between the ages of 25 and 44; a people-oriented professional or married to a professional, living in the posh area of Columbia; who is Presbyterian, Episcopalian or Congregationalist. A dangerous juror, on the other hand, would be a male manager, engineer, government employee or real estate broker, over 45, Methodist or Pentecostal, living in a rural area or small, quiet town. The reason for juror research is to obtain the best possible jury from the viewpoint of the client's case."[32]

Lawyers seek out jurors who will be partial, not impartial. Nor do they seek a cross-section of the community. Finding a jury of one's peers is a myth—one among the many myths surrounding the jury system.

Don't look for a fair juror but rather a strong, biased and sometimes hypocritical individual who believes the defendants are different from their own kind rather than degree. Some commonly accepted beliefs: All Catholics are bad for any criminal defendant because they reflect authoritarianism, which leans toward the prosecution. Bankers are cold and poor defense jurors except in cases of embezzlement. Protestant sects are prosecution oriented. Liberal Protestants, like Reform Jews, make good defense jurors unless they are bankers or engineers. Older people are rigid, younger are liberal.[33]

The great criminal lawyer, Clarence Darrow, who once was tried and acquitted of bribing a juror, had a theory on jury selection: Choose a man who laughs, because a juror who laughs hates to find anyone guilty. Avoid wealthy men because wealthy men are always convicted unless the defendant has violated the anti-trust laws. Choose Methodists because their religious emotions can be transmitted into love and charity. Do not take Presbyterians because they know right from wrong but seldom find anything right. Not Lutherans because they are almost sure to convict. Never a non-drinker. Best jurors are Catholics, Unitarians, Congregationalists, Universalists, Jews and agnostics.

And then there are the wild cards in the deck. A woman shot her husband in front of three witnesses and the defense had been unable to prove she acted in self-defense. But the jury returned a verdict of not guilty. The stunned prosecutor knew why. There was something he'd known all along and chosen to ignore, hoping its vaguely occult implications would work to his advantage. The defendant was a graphologist, a handwriting analyst who'd helped her attorney select the jury according to personality traits revealed in samples of their hand writing.[34]

And then there was the prosecutor who never selected men with beards as jurors because he had found them to be nonconformists who would, in an open-and-shut case, hold out and hang a jury out of sheer cussedness.

Don't rely on hunches or other psychic impulses on *voir dire* selection. It's not uncommon for prospective jurors to conceal relationships and predelections that might affect the verdict.

"Blacks have systematically been kept off juries over the years. The perception in the black community is that justice is not working in the courts for all people. Prosecutors use peremptory challenges to eliminate potential jurors for no stated reason. Such an example is the case of Luis Alvarez in Miami who was charged with manslaughter in the killing of a young black and acquitted by an all-white jury. His attorney said blacks were dismissed from the jury in the racially-sensitive trial because a pretrial opinion poll showed nearly one-half of the county's blacks thought his client was guilty.[35]

Generally speaking, jurors are selected in a pending trial through the process of *voir dire*, an examination conducted by attorneys and the judge to determine each panel member's fitness to serve. *Voir dire* refers to an oath taken by the juror to tell the truth. Such an examination assumes that only qualified, unbiased and unprejudiced jurors will sit in the trial. In some cases, an extensive investigation is made of prospective jurors and it is then that the power of money is felt. Such jury behavior studies cost hundreds of thousands of dollars. However, in a case like the MCI Communications Corporation's anti-trust suit against AT&T in a Chicago federal court where the jury, selected according to a profile, returns a verdict for $600 million, the costs seem justified. But on appeal, the verdict was reversed.

The use during *voir dire* of preferred juror profiles and preemptory challenges, in which jurors can be struck without cause from the panel, raises profound issues of public policy. Can lawyers for a white defendant, for example, use peremptory challenges to exclude blacks because some statistics suggest they are more likely to convict? This is a sensitive issue, since the sword can be two-edged: Government prosecutors can use peremptory challenges to assemble a jury they believe is predisposed to a guilty verdict.

Samuel W. McCart, in his book, *Trial by Jury*, summarizes some characteristics which are indicated by physical features. Eyebrows meet and eyes are close together—narrow mindedness. Narrowly closed eyelids—deceit. Upper lid covering more than a third of iris—secretiveness. Round, wide eyes—credulousness. Large round eyes—perceptive. Small eyes—short on emotion. Downcast eyes—timidity and over cautious. Pointed ears with no lobes—dishonesty. Flat-topped ears—tight with money. Short upper lip—sensitive, fears criticism, loves praise and flattery, responds to charm. Long upper lip—individualist, impervious to flattery, responds to logic. Drooping corners of mouth—pessimism. Upturned corners of mouth—optimism. Wide mouth—generosity. Full lips—emotional.[36]

During *voir dire*, if the number of prospective jurors is trimmed down to fewer than the six or twelve legally required to sit, the court can instruct the sheriff, or another agent, to go into the street and summon people at random to serve immediately. When this happens, we have a different type of jury because these people have been commandeered, interrupting their daily pursuits. They do not take this lightly.

It happened in a criminal case I was involved with in a western Maryland rural community. The sheriff, under order of the court, went out and brought back farmers, industrial workers and housewives in town doing their weekly shopping. Following testimony and argument, the jury retired to reach a verdict. Hours passed into the night and early morning without their agreeing on a verdict. They became stubborn and angry with the court system. The men were being kept from their work and the women from taking care of their homes and children. As a result, they could not agree; it was a hung jury and a mistrial was declared. The commandeered jurors revenged themselves on the system.[37]

When a judge sent the sheriff into the streets of Joliette, Quebec, to round up 100 prospective jurors for a murder trial, citizens scurried for cover. The town of 13,000 looked like a ghost town. It seems that residents had heard news reports that jury duty could require a six-week separation from family and jobs. Incidentally, an initial summons of 225 candidates had provided only eleven jurors because of the number of challenges by defense and prosecution attorneys.[38]

Jury selection cannot be accomplished satisfactorily without considerable knowledge of human nature as well as a thorough understanding of one's case and the type of jurors who might be sympathetic or adverse to it. Men and women differ as jurors, not only because of their backgrounds but because of the differences in their experiences. The lawyer must determine in a very short time which jurors will be hostile or apathetic to his cause.

Selecting a jury is educated guesswork. There is no guarantee that mastery of the art will lead to victory but in the long run mastery does increase the chances for success.

Influencing Jury Verdicts

During the past twelve years the one segment of society to be worked over by prosecutors is politicians. There were the Agnews, Mitchells, Mandells and the parade of Nixon henchmen—all so-called law and order men. There were the Abscam figures who delighted in pocketing extra money. All were convicted of an assortment of crimes, but particularly obstruction of justice. All have drawn special attraction and provided material for news stories and books. At times it's hard to tell the winners from the losers or whether or not crime does pay.

No political trial has received more publicity than that of John Bowden Connally, who served three terms as governor of Texas and was Secretary of the Treasury under President Nixon. Riding in the car with John F. Kennedy when he was assassinated in November 1963, Connally was also shot. A poor Texan farm boy, he headed a respected Houston law firm and was one of the big timers to switch political parties and join the millionaire Republicans.

No one thirsted for the presidency more than "Big John" Connally. But, as he would tell it, he was a victim of the Watergate taint and "they" were out to get him. Nobody knows for sure whom he meant by "they."

Connally traveled with the high and mighty but by one stroke of a grand jury he was in court on two serious charges. He was accused of accepting $10,000 illegally and then lying in a conspiracy to conceal it. The indictment charged that while he was treasury secretary in 1971, he accepted two illegal gratuities of $5,000 each from Jake Jacobsen, a lawyer lobbyist for the Association of Milk Producers of America, Inc., a dairy farmers cooperative. In return, he was to exert influence on the Nixon administration to increase milk support prices. According to Jacobsen, he gave Connally $10,000 who, at the height of the Watergate investigation, returned it. The cash was allegedly left untouched in Jacobsen's lock box in an Austin bank for two years.

Jacobsen had been a fund-raiser for Connally's opponent in 1962 but when Big John won, Jacobsen ingratiated himself with the governor. Texas indicted Jacobsen for illegal dealings in savings and loan transactions. But when the state set out for bigger game it made a deal with Jacobsen—a plea bargain in exchange for his testimony against Connally.

Connally lost no time in retaining sportsman and big-time attorney, Edward Bennett Williams. If convicted, he faced a possible twenty years in prison and fines of more than $50,000.

A jury trial was requested and Judge George L. Hart of the U.S. District Court was designated to preside.

As the trial got underway Williams applied his great ability in picking jurors. They included ten blacks and two whites—seven women and five men. Among them were an art historian, a cafe worker, three clerks, a retired clerk, a receptionist-secretary, a retired printer, a cook, a maid, and two unemployed persons. A motley group, but hardly a jury of Connally's peers.

The best array of talent was yet to come. They were Williams' witnesses, who were to play an important part. Ten jurors were blacks and most of them Baptists—they generally are identified as to religious denomination. And among the witnesses was Dr. "Billy" Graham, renowned Baptist evangelist who was to extol the many virtues of John Connally.

The government's case went well. Jacobsen's testimony never varied, although there was little corroboration of it. But when Connally took the stand and denied all the allegations, it was a case of the tainted Jacobsen against respectable Connally. Then there was the parade of character witnesses: Robert McNamara; Lady Bird Johnson; Dean Rusk; James Towe, the FDR brain truster; Robert Strauss, an old friend and Democratic National Chairman; Barbara Jordan, the black Congresswoman from Texas; and then the star, "Billy" Graham. How was it possible to defeat this combination of talent? None of the witnesses knew anything about the alleged offense, the real issue, but as they put it, "We just wanted to lend a helping hand for an old friend."

Williams joked to make jury contact and develop rapport. But he was at his best trampling down the sad character of his client's old pal, Jake Jacobsen. It was a year of anguish, humiliation and assault upon Big John's integrity.

The jury's deliberation was not done in haste. It came out once for a breath of air and inspection of the exhibited documents. As instructed by the judge, they had to find the defendant guilty "beyond a reasonable doubt."

What that constitutes can be different to each juror. Does it mean beyond a shadow of a doubt, or according to the greater weight of evidence? When jurors are confused about this, they lean toward the accused, particularly one with the stature of a John Connally.

After six hours and twenty-two minutes of deliberation the jury returned its verdict: not guilty.

The celebration party was held at the Mayflower Hotel and Dick Nixon called his old nemesis, Williams, to congratulate him on a good professional job. Jacobsen was given a two-year suspended sentence. The judge could hardly be tough on a man who had pleaded guilty to giving a bribe which a jury determined had not been received![39]

"Ridiculous" Jury Verdicts

Juries are called upon to reach verdicts in civil cases involving injuries through auto accidents, product liability, medical malpractice, and other alleged sources. In these, the plaintiff must prove his case by submitting the greater weight of evidence, what is termed "the preponderance" of evidence. Subsequently, complaints are filed about some of the ridiculous jury verdicts.

Insurance companies pay awards with money paid by policy holders, who in turn, pay their premiums from the fees and charges to their customers and patients. The premiums paid by individuals, doctors, hospitals and chain stores are buried in the cost of their services or products.

Where substantial verdicts are at stake, a high degree of expertise is needed by both the plaintiff and the defendant. The initial outlay in preparing for trial can run into thousands of dollars and is normally advanced by the plaintiff's lawyer. The defense is usually furnished its funding by the insurance companies, which spend exhorbitant amounts to defend even a lesser claim.

The facts on which a jury must render a decision must come from the evidence presented. If substantial justice is to be meted out, close attention must be given during every minute of the trial. A long trial can dim jurors' memory of events taking place in the courtroom. In view of this, a juror tends to guess.

In some instances a "risk" stamp is placed on a jury. That is, they are sent out to begin deliberation after four o'clock in the afternoon, in hope they'll return a verdict quickly, clearing the court deck for the next day. The jury often comes up with a hasty verdict to get home in time for supper. This is considered a judge-forced verdict for his convenience.

Other juries may spend months listening to evidence only to have a settlement reached out of court after the final argument. Let's examine some extraordinary verdicts:

A three-and-one-half-year-old girl who suffered brain damage in a beating by a babysitter won a $1.5 million negligence suit against her parents. The babysitter pleaded no contest to a charge of aggravated assault when the infant was eighteen months old. The insurance company that issued the parents' homeowner's policy had defended the couple and was obligated to pay the sum in a trust fund for the child.[40]

Two soft drink companies were ordered to pay $1.4 million to a police officer who was blinded in one eye when a bottle cap exploded in his face in March, 1982.[41]

In Hialeah, Florida, a jury awarded $162,000 in a wrongful-death case against paramedics who reported a 66-year-old man to be drunk and left him alone and naked. He died of a heart attack.[42]

There was a doctor whose girlfriend tossed an egg on him at a lakeside party and he dived into the water to clean himself off, breaking his neck and spinal cord. A jury awarded him $1.02, or 17 percent of $6.00. His medical expenses alone were over $8,000 and he had a lifetime disability that meant permanent care and loss of income.

A traveling salesman who was robbed and sexually assaulted at a motel was awarded $750,000 in damages.[43]

In the *Pennzoil v. Texaco* jury case, the plaintiff was awarded over $10 billion for interfering with a proposed merger of Pennzoil and Getty oil companies. A Texaco vice president claimed the jury was not intelligent or sophisticated enough to rule on the case. The jurors included a letter carrier, homemakers, a warehouse foreman, nurses, a county employee, an industrial salesman, clerical workers and a city employee—all people who work for a living. Some say a jury consisting of workers may constitute a deprivation of one's property without due process of law.

In one case in Escondido, California, it was after a twenty-one month trial that the judge announced an out-of-court settlement.

The trial had consumed 288 days, 115 witnesses and 38,000 pages of testimony. It had cost taxpayers an estimated $2 million. Then it was dropped; a settlement of $10 million was announced the day the plaintiff's attorneys were to begin final argument. The judge turned to the jurors and told them they were exemplary and dedicated citizens and thanked them for the one year and nine months they had spent away from their jobs and families.

One juror climbed onto his bike and rode fifty miles, as hard as he could. "It was either that or punch someone in the nose," he said.

The marathon trial left almost everyone in court blistering mad, except for the plaintiff and the attorneys who could look forward to a big payday."[44]

V

The Criminal Law Jungle

"The accused is treated like a piece of meat on its way to dressing and processing."

Clarence Darrow

The Complex Problems of Criminal Law

The Criminal Law process is exceedingly complicated, wrote Howard James. "A person caught up in it—whether guilty or not—feels bewildered and alone." Once put through the wringer, even if acquitted, you become tainted and are never the same. The accused's reputation is immediately damaged, usually irreparably.

"Anguish and anxiety become daily presence for the accused and his family and friends," Freedman pointed out. "It destroys marriages and alienates children. The financial loss is burdensome with loss of employment, sickness and even suicide."[1]

The reasons were outlined by James:

> The defendant faces investigation, arrest, police questioning, finger printing, and press publicity; there's financial chaos at home, jail unless he can raise bail, preliminary hearings, the grand jury, arraignment, strange and stilted formalism of the court procedure and disdain for him as a human being. Witnesses swear to his guilt sometimes falsely; and there's the skeptical judge and jury.[2]

He must seek out a lawyer according to what he can afford; if he is poor he takes what he gets from the state.

> The poor sit in jails for months awaiting trial. It is easy for a policeman or other officer to swear out a warrant and have a person arrested on information from an informant or on a grudge. The charge may be totally unfounded and ultimately dismissed.[3]

Nor can the defendant rely on justice to prevail in the courtroom, Gregg Barak asserts: "Opposing lawyers are not equal in ability or competence. When one side is much stronger than the other, a correct determination will not come out of the conflict but only the answer that power can impose. Anything that tends to build up one side as opposed to the other, or anything that tends to weaken one side is detrimental to the adversary system."[4]

A respectable, young married factory worker came to my office on a Monday morning. He had been in jail since Friday night for playing his radio too loudly. An irate neighbor had called the police to complain and he was immediately jailed, instead of being released pending trial. After a formal investigation the prosecutor found no evidence of criminal behavior, and the case was dismissed. The young man sued for malicious prosecution and false arrest. The case was tried before a jury in the "low bucks" western county and he was awarded $300 against an insolvent defendant.

"There has been a charge over the years that the public knowledge of fixed cases, corrupt judges, crooked bail bondsmen, shyster lawyers, dishonest and economically motivated corporation lawyers and political influences in the judicial process causes a general disrespect for law and order," wrote Barak. "Trial judges are not exempt from contributing to national dissatisfaction with the administration of criminal justice. Sentence disparities bring about an unwarranted power that is highly dangerous."[5]

The amount of justice one receives largely depends on money, power, influence, and position, as well as many other circumstances. Presidents get pardons, vice presidents get unsupervised probation, persons of rank, office and wealth rarely go to jail or prison. It is "white collar" supremacy.

Barak found that "More than 90 percent of convictions are upon pleas of guilty made on bargain days in the assured expectation of nominal punishment as the cheapest way out, and amount, in effect, to license to violate the law."[6]

The entire criminal law system of justice or jungle boils down to the powerful state with all its weapons: police, prosecutors, courts, prisons and probation officers, going after the poor, uneducated, stupid persons.

Police routinely lie, particularly to save their own skin. If you are arrested on a serious charge and cannot make bail, you may wait months for your case to come up. The rich can get out at once, but the poor must suffer. We have a lazy and politically oriented judicial system. Equal justice under the law is a blatant lie. For years in the South, black offenders received heavier punishment and averaged longer sentences than white offenders, regardless of the race of the victim. To be both black and poor is almost a guarantee of unequal treatment under the law. Delays and postponements are a part of the system.

One study concluded: "Defendants who are in jail because they have not been able to make bail are more likely to be coerced into plea bargaining; more likely to plead guilty when they are not, more likely to be convicted of a crime and more likely to receive a severer sentence than those out on bail."[7]

Eighty percent of those accused cannot afford counsel and must accept state-appointed counsel. Most defendants don't trust an appointed counsel to be on their side. As part of the folklore, the judge is usually portrayed as all-wise, compassionate, neutral and knowledgeable in the law, but many defendants see him as a rubber stamp for the wishes of the prosecutor. Many judges are former prosecutors who have never relinquished the prosecution complex. The public defender and the prosecutor are viewed as state men who are not to be trusted. In the prosecutor's eyes, a high record of convictions is the measure of his worth.

"Lawyers outside corporate law firms lack power and influence," Barak argued. "Most lawyers of reputation and skill concern themselves less and less with community problems. The miscellaneous interests of society are becoming subservient to the interests of the high paying clients."[8]

In another passage Barak explains why:

> The dollar becomes the symbol of success and the mercenary attitude of the corporation lawyer permeates the bar. The number of competent and honest lawyers willing to struggle for civil liberties and personal rights, rather than property rights, and to care for the interest of the poor and of the persons of inadequate means is distressingly small. There is no other professional so self-satisfied and at the same time so lacking in social obligations. Here and there you may find some obscure lawyer battling for the poor, the needy and oppressed without regard for the pecuniary awards that spell professional success.[9]

Justice is not well-served, as evidenced by these cases: Bradford Brown, convicted of murder, spent four years, from 1975 to 1979, in a federal prison. William Jackson was locked up from 1977 until 1982 after an Ohio jury found him guilty of two rapes. Lenell Geter was in a Texas prison for fourteen months, following a 1982 conviction for armed robbery. Each man's conviction rested on eye-witness identifications by strangers. In each case the eye-witness was wrong.

As the *St. Petersburg Times* noted in an editorial:

> The injustices in these cases were corrected—but not because of some built-in check or protection in the structure of the criminal justice system. Chance intervened, saving Brown, Jackson and Geter from prison sentences of 50 years to life. But our criminal justice system ought not to depend on chance to avoid such errors. Eyewitness identification by strangers, with no additional proof of guilt, is too fragile a base on which to rest a long prison term, or the death penalty. In three-quarters of the states, Brown could have been executed for his "crime" long before the error was discovered.[10]

The idea of the blindfolded lady with the scales, who treats both rich and poor alike, is a figment of the imagination.

The Prosecutor's Awesome Discretionary Power

The head of the criminal system in any state is the prosecutor, commonly called the district attorney or state's attorney. It is he who sets in motion the criminal process following arrest, by exercising the awesome discretionary power to seek an indictment against a fellow citizen.

Rosenblatt has described him as "the most powerful man in the criminal law system. A politician first and a law enforcement officer a distant second; the fact that he is intricately hooked up with local politics is the major reason for the pitiful state of American law enforcement."[11]

A *Pennsylvania Law Review* article stated:

> The discretionary power he [the prosecutor] exercises in the accusation and discontinuance of prosecution gives him more control and clout over an individual's liberty and reputation than any other public official. It enables him to eliminate or defer criminal prosecution as part of a tactical move. However, the future of many individuals and

> the protection of the community may hinge on his judgment, who through bias, inability or inexperience unwisely exercises the responsibilities of his office. Since he is usually an elected official, questions of political expediency may affect both the diligence with which he carries out his functions and his choice of assistants. Personal enmities or friendship may have a similar effect.[12]

In essence, James agreed:

> It is common practice for a prosecutor to try a few men for assault with intent to kill, drunken driving or murder. Then for the sake of expedience or for other reasons, he reduces charges for others (who have broken the same law) to simple assault, reckless driving, or manslaughter. Still others are released by the prosecutor, who may be convinced of their guilt but feels he lacks evidence to convict.[13]

On the same topic, Rosenblatt wrote:

> Publicity and favors are at his disposal. He can dismiss a case or hold it in abeyance as he pleases. Judges exercise little or no power over him in their discretionary roles, although the judge becomes important during the trial of specific cases. Most judges are happy to see cases dismissed since this lightens their case load and seldom would they have reason to question the prosecutor's discretion in this regard. . . . He can turn a deaf ear to gambling and prostitution enterprises from which he can expect handouts at election time. He is hardly a part of any reform movements in the community. His raw power is hardly understood by the American people. He is untouchable by the ethics committee of the bar associations and is rarely cited for misconduct.
>
> It is unbelievably easy for him to throw a case, even in front of a jury, because there are many stages at which a technical goof may be contrived. He can assign a particular file to a raw beginner assistant who is not capable of handling it. Many assistants are weak and lazy. Many

> practice law on the side and here they can be retained to handle some of the large moneyed civil cases involving serious injury and death through negligence in automobile cases. He refers them to his friends but cuts in on all the fees, unknown to the client.
>
> He is expected to be a little crooked so as to work out some of the deals of his cronies. Who wants a puristic prosecutor? With a prosecutor involved in some fashion in a civil suit, forced settlements are a part of the game.[14]

"Many appear arrogant, aggressive, overzealous and unscrupulous," we read in *Verdicts on Lawyers*:

> He has at his beck and call the local police, the FBI, investigators, the power of the grand jury which he controls, the expert scientist, psychiatrist and medical doctors and economists. In doing all this he need not concern himself with expenses. At the other end of the spectrum, his opponent—many times the lowly public defender or young lawyer—is lacking in experience and funds to properly prepare his case which come naturally to the prosecutor.
>
> He can secure cooperation with the courthouse crew and he practices before judges whom he knows well and who often themselves were once prosecutors. He controls the court calendar and can call up cases for trial in order to suit his convenience. He can obtain extension of time for late briefs and default judgments are not enforced against the government.[15]

When the state possesses information that could well exonerate a defendant, it has an affirmative duty to disclose same. A burden is on the state to do justice. This burden is the essence of due process. It is the state that tries a man and it is the state that must insure the trial is fair.

Former US Attorney General and Justice of the Supreme Court Robert Jackson said:

> The prosecutor has more control over life, liberty and reputation than any person in America. He can dismiss a case before trial in which case a defendant never had a chance to be heard. He has a fair chance of finding a technical violation of some act on the part of most anyone.

> It is in this realm, in which the prosecutor picks some person whom he dislikes or desires to embarrass, or select some group of unpopular persons, and then looks for an offense. This is the greatest danger of the prosecutorial power. His job is to protect the innocent as well as to convict the guilty; to guard the rights of the accused as well as to enforce the rights of the public. This he rarely does.[16]

"Conscientious prosecutors," Freedman points out, "do not put the destructive engine of the criminal process into motion unless they are satisfied beyond a reasonable doubt that the accused is guilty. He should not seek charges that he cannot reasonably support with evidence at trial."[17]

"Another abuse," noted Freedman, "is the practice of deferred sentencing which permits the prosecutor to maintain a powerful coercive hold on a witness who has pleaded guilty, but who will not be sentenced until after having testified in a manner satisfactory to the prosecutor in a trial of another defendant."[18]

And there is the practice of the prosecutor insisting to the judge that the defendant be jailed following a plea and awaiting sentencing. In many instances the defendant cannot make bond and the prosecutor knows that.

Every lawyer who practices in the criminal court knows that perjury flourishes on the part of the state witnesses. Committing perjury that contributes to a guilty verdict and the death penalty is the most abominable.

"And there are those covering up police abuses such as brutality, perjury, unlawful arrests, unlawful searches and seizures and unlawful interrogation," said Freedman. "It has been the latter that has brought disrepute to the office."[19]

Barak speaks of a federal judge "who stated that his greatest challenge is to discern when a law enforcement official is lying [saying] this is crucial to doing justice."[20]

"And there is a further abuse," Freedman wrote, "when the prosecutor leaks information to the press as to the guilt of the accused, particularly where the accused is tried in the vicinage. The well known principle of criminal law is that a defendant is presumed innocent and that is to follow him throughout the trial until contrary evidence is adduced. This is one of the many myths that has been part of the legal system. Neither the court nor jury believe in this principle."[21]

From time immemorial in our country, prosecutors have used peremptory challenges to remove blacks from the jury when blacks are on trial. It would be hard to estimate how many blacks have gone to the execution chamber because no one of their race was sitting either on the grand jury or the petit jury. The proponents of capital punishment never give this a thought.

"It is most unusual that the prosecutor is disciplined for even the grossest misconduct," Freedman charged. "The attitude seems to be that an occasional reversal of a conviction on appeal is an adequate sanction, although it is not." Wrote Freedman:

> Take the trial in a rape-murder case where the prosecutor introduced into evidence a pair of man's shorts, allegedly the defendant's, and described them as being heavily stained with blood. The dramatic stains that the prosecutor described to the jury were red brown paint, a fact unknown to the defendant's attorney because the prosecutor blocked efforts to examine the shorts. Despite a finding by the Supreme Court that the prosecutor had deliberately misrepresented the truth in securing the conviction, the grievance committee failed to recommend disciplinary action.[22]

"Most prosecutors are part of the electoral process and have no inhibitions in taking money for election purposes. In other words, 'they are for sale,'" the *St. Petersburg Times* editorialized, citing as an example that in the November 1984 election in Hillsborough County, Florida, the incumbent state attorney, E. J. Salcines, received about $227,000 in contributions from members of his staff, lawyers, Tampa businessmen and corporations. His successful opponent, Bill James, received about $97,000. "In common terms, they were selling favors," the Times concluded.

"Should a prosecutor take the Fifth Amendment when asked to testify before a grand jury?" the newspaper asked. "The same E. J. Salcines took the fifth as he refused to testify before the grand jury who was investigating corruption in his office. The Fifth reads: 'No personal shall be compelled in any criminal case to be a witness against himself.' Salcines, who was a public official, was obligated to account to the public through a grand jury for the way he conducted his public business," the Times contended.[23]

"In 1932 William Fisher stopped at a Harlem speakeasy and dance hall for a drink and dance. He wound up being convicted of shooting a man to death. Fisher recalled that a brawl had ensued at the bar and he was stabbed and shot in the left leg, then carried out the back door. Two men were killed by the gun fire. He was paroled in 1944 after eleven years in prison but it was not until 1958 that his manslaughter conviction was overturned because misconduct was uncovered on the part of the prosecutor at the trial. The New York State legislative assembly approved a special bill in June 1983, saying, in effect, that the state was liable for damages if Mr. Fisher was unlawfully imprisoned."[24]

Weaknesses of the Grand Jury System

Each county or series of counties have a grand jury, whose prime function is to determine whether a crime has been committed and, if so, whether there is reasonable probability that the accused committed a crime. At common law the panel consists of not less than twelve members or more than twenty-three, but this is regulated by statute or the constitution of the respective states.

When the proper number are in agreement as to the accused committing a crime the grand jury is said to have returned a "true bill" or indictment. Where there is no agreement a "no bill" is returned. In cases where the body feels that while there is insufficient evidence to warrant an indictment, but there is some reprehensible conduct or neglect or malfeasance of duty, they make a report or presentment calling for action by some governmental administrative body or agency, such as the inadequacies of jails and other places of detention. It may inquire into corrupt misconduct in the office of public officers of every description except sitting judges who are immune. Prosecutions are brought in the name of the state versus the accused. The indictment shall be signed by the jury foreman in a plain, concise and definite written statement of the essential facts constituting the offense or offenses charged. The prosecutor examines witnesses and advises upon legal points in framing the indictment.

The grand jury must take an oath to conduct its business in an honest and prudent manner and then the local judge charges them concerning their duties. Following the first series of meetings it may be recalled at the order of the court as the occasion arises. Where the first grand jury does not indict a person or persons for crimes alleged, a second sitting grand jury may reinvestigate and return an indictment. It shall not share or disclose the nature or substance of the deliberation or member vote to the public nor allow to testify in court where an indictment is reached. No person shall be present at any of its sessions except the grand jury, witnesses under examination, the court reporter and a member of the prosecutor's office.

Witnesses are subpoenaed by the State's Attorney to appear and testify as to what they might know concerning the facts of the crime. Witnesses may challenge, among other things, this inquisitorial and accusatory body as to the substance of the crime, for lack of qualification of the members, prejudicial members due to blood relationship of juror and accused person or other reasons that might lend itself to bias or discrimination. All challenges must be made before the jury is sworn.

> for a capital or otherwise infamous crime, unless on the Presentment or Indictment by a Grand Jury."[26]

There are some, however, who are quick to point out the limitations of the Grand Jury system:

> England from whence it came, abolished it in 1933. In this country there has been a discernable trend toward its non-use. Among the twenty-two states that require a Grand Jury indictment in felony cases, three require it only when the crime is punishable by death or life imprisonment. In [others] a prosecutor launching a criminal case may elect whether to seek an indictment or simply to file an Information. The Grand Jury has been assailed as inefficient, an obstruction, and a rubber stamp for the prosecutor. It has been held to harass the unpopular, to chill free expression, to trap unwary witnesses on perjury charges and to oppress those summoned to its secret chambers. . . .

The reasons for criticism of the Grand Jury system have been outlined by no less a body than the U.S. Supreme Court:

> The Grand Jury may probe broadly and investigate on the basis of tips, hearsay and speculation. It is an arm of the Executive Branch. As the U.S. Supreme Court has observed in *Blair v. US*, 250 US 273, 282 (1919): "Traditionally the Grand Jury has been accorded wide latitude to inquire into violations of criminal law. No judge provides to monitor its proceedings. It deliberates in secret and may determine alone the course of its inquiry. It may compel the production of evidence or the testimony of witnesses it considers appropriate, and its operation is generally unrestrained by the technical procedural and evidentiary rules governing the conduct of the criminal trial. It is a grand inquest, a body with powers of investigation and inquisition, the scope of whose inquiries is not to be limited narrowly to questions of propriety or forecasts of the probable result of the investigation, or by doubts by any particular individual will be found properly subject to an accusation of crime."

From the Desk of

JOHN C. SULLIVAN
ATTORNEY AT LAW
52 Linden Street
Frostburg, MD 21532
1-301-689-9326

5-15-89

Preferential treatment!!
(O.J. Simpson)

Dear Stan,

Thanks for the letter and enclosed check.

Glad to hear you are living it up and enjoying life.

Things are fine with me. Have not heard anything more of your brother.

If I get to Cal. I'll look up your whereabouts.

Sincerely,

John

To this we would add Rosenblatt's observations:

> A closely guarded secret is that it is a myth and a fraud. A sharp prosecutor can take the average Grand Jury, put it in his hip pocket and make it work his will. The accused does not have the right to be heard by the Grand Jury. If he is subject he must appear though then he may take the 5th Amendment and refuse to testify unless given immunity; then he must testify or be held in contempt of court. He may be indicted without even knowing the Grand Jury is in session on his case, without a lawyer to examine the witnesses against him, or even to know the witnesses against him. Probable cause that a crime was committed will be sufficient for a Grand Jury to return an indictment. The prosecutor decides if the evidence is sufficient, decides what witnesses to call and explains the legal significance of the testimony.[25]

Concludes Rosenblatt:

> Without question, it is unfair and is used as a political tool for the moving-up prosecutor in his quest for higher office, trampling on the backs of hapless defendants caught in the system.
>
> If one Grand Jury fails to bring an indictment on the same set of facts, the prosecutor may try again a second time with a new Grand Jury. There is no such thing as double jeopardy. The media is used to support the Grand Jury's findings and promote the welfare of the prosecutor.[26]

"From this secret conclave leaks are common," James G. Abourez maintains. "The cloud of suspicion resulting from such leaks has destroyed businesses, political careers and community organizations whose existence depend on credibility in the community."[27]

"Sometimes the somewhat complex and technical language of indictments is drafted by the prosecutor and handed to the Grand Jury foreman or forelady for the signature which is almost invariably affixed. In the Grand Jury room there is nobody to object; there is no adversary. Rules of evidence do not customarily operate. A prospective defendant does not have the right to compel the Grand Jury to hear witnesses.

who may testify favorably to his case, nor is he allowed to be present when witnesses testify against him."

The selection of grand juries is much like that of the selection of civil or petit juries and sometimes from the same rolls. However, there is no *voir dire*, that is, the right to select and dismiss jurors. Over the years the blacks have been intentionally kept off the panel, particularly in the deep South.

In a Mississippi case, described by David Mellinkoff, a defendant was indicted by a grand jury on a murder charge arising out of a shooting death. On the advice of counsel, the defendant pleaded guilty and was sentenced to life imprisonment. "He sought a writ of *habeas corpus* and among other things he alleged blacks were illegally excluded from the Grand Jury which indicted him," Mellinkoff wrote. "The court held that his counsel's action of entering a plea of guilty for him constituted a valid waiver to the jury composition and that his plea of guilty foreclosed his assertion of the constitutional claim."[28]

The US Supreme Court reversed a black man's rape conviction in a Texas case. Justice Black, speaking for a unanimous supreme court, said:

> What the 14th Amendment prohibits is racial discrimination in the selection of grand juries. Where jury commissioners limit those from whom grand juries are elected to their own personal acquaintances, discrimination can arise from commissioners who know no negroes as well as from commissioners who know but eliminate them. If there has been discrimination, whether accomplished ingenuously, the conviction cannot stand.[29]

Justice White, speaking for the US Supreme Court, stressed the importance of seeking a true cross-section to the degree possible:

> We accept the fair cross section requirement as fundamental to the jury that is guaranteed by the 6th Amendment and are convinced that the requirement has solid foundation. The purpose of a Grand Jury is to guard against the exercise of arbitrary power—to make available to the common sense judgment of the community as a hedge against the overzealous or mistaken prosecutor and in preference to the professional or perhaps overconditioned or biased response of a judge. . . . Community participation in the administration of the criminal law, moreover, is not

> only consistent with our democratic heritage but is also critical to public confidence in the fairness of the criminal justice system. Restricting jury service to only special groups or excluding identifiable segments playing major roles in the community, cannot be squared with the constitutional concept of jury trial.[30]

"Nobody is literally entitled to a jury of his peers. Their absence does not invalidate the group chosen to serve. The qualifications are much like that for the civil jury, namely, at least 18 years old, a resident of the geographical area, ability to speak and write English, no conviction of felonies, etc."

The Supreme Court has shown itself extremely sensitive to the opportunities for oppression that examination of witnesses provide, raising the possibility of 'secret inquisitions."

> In the case of *In re Groban*, Justice Black said, "Secret inquisitions are dangerous things justly feared by free men everywhere. They are the breeding ground for arbitrary misuse of official power. They are often the beginning of tyranny as well as indispensable instruments for its survival. Modern as well as ancient history bears witness that both innocent and guilty have been seized by officers of the state and whisked away for secret interrogation or worse until the groundwork has been securely laid for their inevitable conviction. [31]

Plea Bargaining Used in Ninety Percent of Criminal Dispositions

"The primary purpose of plea bargaining is to assure that the jury trial system established by the Constitution is seldom used," a *Harvard Law Review* article charged. Describing the criminal justice system as "a complex bureaucracy preoccupied with its capacity to apprehend, try, convict and dispose of a high proportion of criminal offenders," the article goes on to say:

> Plea bargaining is a process of negotiation in which the prosecutor offers the defendant certain concessions in exchange for a guilty plea. His reason: an overwhelming workload the broad discretion overcharging and sentencing by the prosecutor and judge enables the prosecutor to

> induce many defendants to bargain for a more favorable disposition.
>
> Plea bargaining is inherently destructive of the values of the trial process, for it is designed to prevent trials. It forfeits the benefits of formal public adjudication; it eliminates the protection for individuals provided by the adversary system and substitutes administration for judicial determination of guilt; it removes the check on law enforcement authorities afforded by exclusionary rules. It distorts the sentencing decisions by introducing non-correctional criteria.[32]

"Plea bargaining is a bureaucratic expediency by whose use 90 percent of criminal dispositions are currently made in America," Jan Gorecki wrote. "Our entire criminal law system lives and moves and has its being in the plea bargain institution. Very often judges when distributing 'negotiated justice' make severity of punishment dependent on bargaining position and skill of the defendant rather than in degree of guilt. Penalties are imposed for crimes different from those committed by the defendant."[33]

Wrote Gorecki, "The negotiated penalties differ in like cases from case to case, judge to judge and court to court. The basic requirement of justice—treat all cases alike—is gone, and thus gone is the just character of criminal dispositions."[34]

The prosecutor makes sweeping charges in anticipation of plea bargaining. When the defendant cannot make bail, the prosecutor enjoys a substantial bargaining advantage. If the state's evidence is weak, the prosecutor will propose generous bargaining terms to overcome his inclination to go to trial. When it is strong, he offers few concessions. He wants to protect his conviction record.

A wealthy defendant can hire a top-notch attorney who is usually free from the administrative pressure which plagues both prosecutor and public defender.

The American Bar Association has sanctioned plea bargaining and the U.S. Supreme Court has lent its imprimatur, calling plea bargaining an "essential component of the criminal justice process." Former Chief Justice Warren Burger, writing the opinion in a New York case, had this to say:

> Disposition of charges after plea discussions is not only an essential part of the process but a highly desirable part for many reasons. It leads to prompt and largely final disposition of most cases. It avoids much of the corrosive

> impact of enforced idleness during pretrial confinement for those who are denied bail release pending trial. It shortens the time between charge and disposition, and it enhances whatever may be the rehabilitable prospects of the guilty when they are ultimately imprisoned.[35]

Law school won't prepare you for plea bargaining. A lawyer with any criminal practice must get used to it. Given that it is universal, economical and flexible, it yet is somehow not quite a respectable legal practice. Its fundamental weakness is that it takes place behind the scenes even though its results are validated in the courtroom.

"Copping a plea also has extra-legal coloration because it involves lawyers doing what they are not empowered to do—fix sentences," Milton Neuman argues. "This added authority may be a drawback. Their clients may blame them for the sentence their attorney plea bargained them into serving."[36]

Plea bargaining also distorts ideas of right and wrong, justice and injustice. The guilty may assume that the crime they committed was no worse than the lesser crime to which they ultimately admit. Conversely, those who have committed no crime may plead guilty to a lesser offense to avoid prosecution for a more serious crime with which they were originally charged. This possibility is perhaps the most serious objection to plea bargaining.

Many defendants plea bargain for a lesser charge, assuming the judge will be more lenient. Some judges even will state that under certain circumstances a defendant should be penalized for wasting the court's resources by trying an unmeritorious case.

Sentencing—Equalization of Penalty is Sorely Needed

Edward Strother pleaded guilty to second-degree murder for shooting Carol Renee Gray three times in the head while her 80-year-old grandmother watched. Judge H. Carl Moultrie sentenced Strother to 146 weekends behind bars, ordered him to pay $200 a month in child support to Gray's six-year-old daughter, provide for her continuing education, and establish a life insurance policy payable to Gray's mother. The verdict shocked the mother. "He got nothing but a slap on the wrist," she said. "Judge Moultrie should be ashamed to sit on the bench. He's a judge, not a social worker."[37]

On January 7, 1983, Adam (Archie) Novak, a 64-year-old longshoreman, went to his son-in-law's house and killed him with four shots at close range. He then shot himself in the chest. When he'd recovered from the self-inflicted wound, Novak, who admitted shooting the son-in-law, pleaded guilty to second-degree murder. In exchange, the state agreed not to charge him with first-degree murder, which carried a possible life sentence. Instead, the state asked for only ten years. The case went before Baltimore City Circuit Court Judge Elsbeth Bothe who decided that even ten years in prison was too much for Novak. She sentenced the confessed murderer to three years of community service and residence in a local halfway house where residents are free to come and go in the daytime and are not locked in or guarded at night. Novak was eligible for parole in nine months.

The way the victim's brother saw it, "You can kill somebody in cold blood if you're 65, and get off just about scot-free." The judge insisted her decision was reasonable and just, taking into account Novak's age and what she called his "sterling-pure" record and the circumstances surrounding the murder.[38]

A businessman, found guilty of violating probation of a drunk driving death conviction, was sentenced to three years in the state prison. Found guilty of killing a 25-year-old woman, he was placed on probation. In another drunk driving case, a defendant was found guilty and sentenced to fifteen years in prison. No probation, no second chance. He had not been able to obtain a lawyer of his choice.

The St. Petersburg *Evening Independent* commented, "Equalization of penalty for the sake of justice and the credibility of the judicial system is sorely needed. Disparity in sentencing was never more apparent."[39]

A Tallahassee babysitter who killed a seven-and-a-half month old boy was sentenced to two and a half years in prison after being allowed to plead "no contest" to third degree murder, which carried a maximum penalty of fifteen years.[40]

In California, public anger still simmers over Doug White's voluntary manslaughter conviction and the brevity of his sentence for the November 27, 1978, slayings of San Francisco Mayor George Moscone and Supervisor Harvey Mills. Freed after five years, White was paroled for one year.

Vincent Chin, a 27-year-old Chinese-American, was dining with friends in a Detroit tavern on June 19, 1982, when Robert Eben, an auto worker, and his stepson, Michael Nitz, became incensed at Chin's presence in the tavern, mistaking him for a Japanese. "It's because of you we are out of work," one of them snarled, referring to the auto industry. They were asked to leave but returned with a baseball bat and cruelly hammered Chin who died four days later. Charged with second degree murder, they entered a plea bargain agreement and accepted a plea of guilty to manslaughter for which the top penalty was fifteen years. The judge, after remarking that these were not the kind of people you sent to prison, sentenced them to three years on probation and a $3780 fine.

"It is sometimes called the sentencing wonderland," wrote Howard James:

> Except for police practices, sentencing may be the most flawed of all. More often than not, it is based on tradition rather than on reason, and whim rather than fact. Prison officials across the nation consider the most pressing court-related problem is disparity in sentencing. Young Dave—from northern Wyoming— received 10-12 years in the Wyoming State Penitentiary for a $750 armed robbery. John—who committed the same crime took $124 in the southern part of the state got 2-3 years.
>
> As lawyers make their rounds in the criminal courts of their state, they become aware of the many incidentals that enter into the sentencing process. Politics, money, and one's social standing is the name of the game.[41]

"How do sentences come about?" asked James:

> Some judges are hard on those charged with violent crimes like rape and robbery. Another judge may be incensed when property rights are violated. He may be tough on those charged with burglary and auto theft and lenient on those charged with assault and rape. Sometimes the judge's decision is based on his reaction as to how a man is dressed, the length of his hair, the color of his skin, his nationality and even his religion. Take the judge with KKK sympathies or indirect membership. In this situation the black defendant has one foot in prison as he walks inside the purported hall of justice.[42]
>
> The lawyer's duty is to get the best deal for his client. The better the deal, the more money he makes. The interest of the victim or the victims, can play second fiddle. Judges owe their jobs to political leaders. A telephone call can change things. Unfortunately, there are too many judges who pass sentences according to how the wind is blowing from a press or public angered by a crime. The American system of justice should, among other things, protect the minority from the aroused majority. It should bring reasons and balance to impassioned emotional situations.
>
> When judges pass sentences, they often do not realize what a prison sentence means to the man convicted. If only

> a new judge could spend his first thirty days incarcerated so as to get the taste, feel and smell of the jail.
>
> Prosecutors and defense lawyers influence the outcome of a trial, the sentence and other court business by getting next to the judge. Some attorneys set up a judge on a pedestal, they invite him to their functions such as for dinners, picnics and other social functions. They honor him and bow to him. They know this personal relationship gives them the edge over other lawyers and they get continuances and other advantages when they want them.[43]

Don't criticize the judge in public or private. There's nothing to compare with a judge's scorn for the outspoken lawyer who criticizes the system. It's called self-crucifixion.

The Death Penalty—An Eye for an Eye?

"The easiest positions to espouse in society are those that tug at people's prejudices, biases, emotions and sometimes bigotry," said Tony Anaya, former governor of New Mexico. "The most difficult are those rooted in reason, humaneness, justice and courage. Such is the debate over the death penalty." Continued Anaya:

> It is easy to clamor about eliminating the "scum" from society, for everyone believes in retribution against those who commit crimes, especially heinous crimes. Yet a calm, reasoned evaluation leads to the conclusion that the death penalty is not only inhumane and immoral, but it is applied arbitrarily and disproportionately and is extremely, costly, slow and uncertain.
>
> A penalty to be justified must be compatible with an enlightened society and must be swift and certain. The death penalty fails on all counts. It has been declared inhumane and immoral by virtually every religious order; yet these unbiased and learned teachings are ignored by individuals clamoring to be God fearing men and women of good will.[44]

In November 1984 an ecumenical movement got underway in Florida as religious leaders, Protestant and Catholic, joined offices to denounce the death penalty. Florida holds the dubious distinction of being the execution capital of the U.S. Also, Florida is one of two states where a presiding judge may countermand a jury recommendation for a life sentence.

Harry Fogle, a Florida circuit court judge and a leader in criminal jurisprudence, said, "In my own experience I know of four persons convicted of first degree murder and sentenced to death who were later found to be innocent."

The twenty-six leaders of a movement representing 2.5 million Christians, in a historic letter to their fellow Christians, proclaimed the barbarism and futility of the death sentence, saying: "The impact of the death penalty is inconsistent with our efforts to promote respect for human life, to stem the tide of violence in our society and to embody the message of God's redemptive love."[45]

"The only western democracy, the U.S. stands alone, followed by dictatorial Russia and South Africa, among the so-called civilized industrial nations allowing the death penalty," Anaya noted. "In South Africa out of every 100 executions, 99 are black citizens. In Russia, individuals are executed for such crimes as making a profit, a goal we encourage in the U.S."[46]

Myril G. Alexander, retired director of the Federal Bureau of Prisons, said, "After thirty-five years in prison administration, I am fully convinced that execution of criminals is a vestige of those ancient and barbaric punishments which are grossly inconsistent with the growing knowledge of the human behavioral sciences."[47]

Charles L. Black contends in his book, *Capital Punishment, the Inevitability of Caprice and Mistake,* that "the system by which we choose those who are to die as penalty for crimes is so much mistake prone and so saturated with standardless and arbitrary discretion that it cannot decently be used for this terrible of choices.

"All white grand juries are commonly quite heavily under the influence of the prosecutor to bring about an indictment. It is the discretion, in one way or another, the offer of choices—by the prosecutor, judge, juries and governors—that divide those who are to die from those who are to live, under standards not meaningful and clear."[48]

"It is the luck of the draw in the petit jury," Black wrote. "Those who are to die have been chosen by a process, which at every trial stage proceeds on no clearly articulated or understandable criteria. This starts with the stage of charging and pleading; the decision of the prosecutor as to what to charge, and as to whether to offer a plea bargain, is not only unfettered and unreviewable, but also without any clear and authoritative standard for the exercise of discretion."[49]

McCafferty cites one example: "Charles Bernstein was due to be executed for murder in Washington, D.C. The testimony in the case before a jury was very weak and it was convenient for a fall guy with a prison background to take the rap. President Franklin Roosevelt, on the eve of the execution, commuted his sentence to life imprisonment. Not long after, the prosecutor was told through the underworld grapevine, that Bernstein was a patsy and that the murder had been committed by a small town thug for pay. Roosevelt then commuted his sentence and set him free."[50]

How many others have died in similar circumstances and miscarriages of justice? We may never know. Queen Elizabeth II of England pardoned Edward B. Evans on the grounds of innocence fifteen years after he was hanged. Dozens of pardons have been granted condemned men on grounds that their confessions were coerced, mistaken identifications were based on perjured testimony, they were given inadequate counsel or in some instances, no counsel.

Edward B. Williams, author of *One Man's Freedom*, listed several cases:

> In the famed English case of *The Crown v. Evans*, Evans was an illiterate truck driver who vigorously denied his guilt and accused John Christie of killing his wife and infant daughter. The jury disbelieved Evans and believed Christie, a state witness. Evans was hanged March 9, 1950, protesting his innocence. Three years later Christie was arrested and charged with murdering his wife. In searching his apartment and outbuildings, the bodies of six women were found. He confessed to the murders, including those of Mrs. Evans and his wife.
>
> On August 12, 1925, a paymaster in Buffalo, New York, was robbed and killed by a bandit wearing dark glasses. Edward Lackman was arrested and charged with the crime. An eyewitness to the crime swore that Lackman was the man. Lackman denied his guilt, but the jury deliberated forty-three hours and convicted him. He was sentenced to the electric chair. The conviction was affirmed on appeal. Governor Al Smith commuted his sentence to life imprisonment. Two years later a Buffalo gangster named Anthony Kolkiewicz confessed to the crime.
>
> In another English case, prostitute Olive Balchin was killed with a hammer on a bombed site in Manchester on October 9, 1946. Walter G. Rowland was arrested and charged with the murder. He was convicted and sentenced

> to die. After exhausting his appellate rights, Rowland, like Evans, was hanged while still protesting his innocence. Four years later, David John Ware walked into a police station in Bristol and told the police he killed the prostitute.[51]

England abolished the death penalty in 1965, having learned through the sad experiences of hanging the innocent. As the death penalty is irrevocable, no amount of money can atone for the execution of an innocent man; no one can restore his life.

Several cases of innocents condemned to death in this country deserve closer attention:

In Massachusetts, Santos Rodriguez, a penniless Puerto Rican bus boy, was freed after thirty-nine months in prison for a murder he didn't commit. In 1954 he had been found guilty of second degree murder for killing a woman. In January 1957 another prisoner confessed his guilt in the murder. He had withheld his confession until after his mother's death. Rodriguez was released and given $12,500 compensation.

In Georgia, James Fulton Foster had been twice sentenced to death, then a former policeman confessed he was guilty and Foster was freed in July 1958. He had spent twenty-six months in prison.[52]

In the U.S. Army, Private A. B. Ritchie was convicted of murder by a court martial and was sentenced to hang July 1, 1945, when another man confessed. Mrs. Ritchie reached President Harry S Truman at a homecoming celebration in Independence, Missouri. Ritchie's death sentence was commuted and he was pardoned in 1947.

In Pennsylvania, David Almeida was granted a second trial after six years because the prosecutor had withheld evidence at the first trial. Almeida had had thirty execution dates! In the same state, Paul A. Pfeffer was serving a sentence of twenty years to life when John F. Roche, who had taken at least three other lives and wanted to die, confessed his guilt.

The New York *Journal-American* of July 24, 1961, reported that Pietro Matera had been released from New York prisons after serving thirty years for murder. He was originally sentenced to die but Governor Franklin Roosevelt commuted his sentence. Then, in the winter of 1960, the real culprit's wife, Adalgisa Lo Cascio, confessed on her deathbed that she had "fingered" Matera to save her husband.[53]

James V. Bennett, former director of the Federal Bureau of Prisons, said: "Over the years I found myself increasingly appalled by the nature of the [death] penalty. I was often responsible for carrying out the death penalty." It was only seconds before the execution of Charles Bernstein that Bennett was able to reach the prison to tell of the commutation by President Roosevelt of the execution. He went on, "There is little question in my mind as my experience increased that the death penalty was revolting, susceptible to miscarriage of justice and ineffective, in the sense that it was not a deterrent to murder. I was affronted by the macabre methodology of capital punishment. I was shaken by the fact that men sentenced to death were generally penniless, friendless and disproportionately black. The death penalty also lent itself to erratic procedures in the courts."[54]

Lewis E. Lawes, warden of the New York prison at Ossining (Sing Sing) in the 1920s and 1930s and a witness to over 150 executions, was irrevocably opposed to the death penalty:

> I am opposed to the death penalty because the evasions, the inequality of its application, the halo with which it surrounds every convicted murderer, the theatrics which are so important to every court proceeding where the stake is life and death, the momentary hysteria, passion and prejudice aroused by the crime which often make it impossible to weigh the facts carefully and impersonally and, finally the infrequency of its application—all tend to weaken our entire structure of social control.[55]

The eminent criminal lawyer, Clarence Darrow, long a foe of capital punishment, had this to say: "We teach people to kill and the state is the one who teaches them. From the beginning procession of the poor, the weak, the unfit have gone through our jails and prisons to their deaths."

Former Justice of the Supreme Court Felix Frankfurter opposed the death penalty for this reason: "When life is at hazard in trial, it sensationalizes the whole thing, almost unwittingly."

Former Attorney General and Governor of California Edmund G. Brown, declaring the death penalty "a gross failure," said: "Beyond its horror and uncivility, it has neither protected the innocent nor deterred the wicked. The recurrent spectacle of publicly sanctioned killing has cheapened human life and dignity without the redeeming grace which comes from justice meted out swiftly, evenly, humanely." His son, Edmund G. Brown Jr., was elected governor although disavowing the death penalty in the heat of the election in which the citizenry voted 2 to 1 for it.[56]

Ramsey Clark, former U.S. Attorney General and a strong abolitionist of the death penalty, stated that most capital crimes are committed on impulse in a moment of passion without thought of gain or loss. "Seventy-five percent of all murders are crimes of passion upon loved ones, neighbors and friends," he said.[57]

The two principal arguments commonly advanced in favor of the death penalty are retribution and deterrence. The public feels a need for retribution and vengeance which the death penalty satisfies. The deterrence influence of the death penalty has occupied the forefront in criminal research for years. The preponderance of evidence indicates that capital punishment does not act as a deterrent to murder. Murder rates have remained constant despite some trends away from the use of capital punishment.

"The deterrence argument is based on the premise of what a reasonable man would do," Bedau and Pierce wrote. "Killers are not reasonable men. The vast majority of killings are crimes of passion not subject to rational secondary process thinking and reality testing and are rooted in overwhelming rage in the face of inadequate ego control. Relatively few murders are carefully planned."[58]

Wrote McCafferty:

> The thrust of the abolitionist's argument is it brutalizes society and it is rooted in revenge. It does not deter but increases the level of serious crime because those who have already committed a capital crime will not hesitate to commit others since they feel they have nothing to lose. Where judicial errors occur it is irrevocable. Swift and certain punishment is more effective. Killers are also victims. Their lives are filled with alcoholic parents, physical sexual abuse, divorce, parental deaths, tough neighborhoods and the jail doors are closed behind them as they enter society. They have little idea of the answers to chaotic society's questions and demands. Capital punishment degrades the society that inflicts it.[59]

Murderers are more likely to be sentenced to death if their victims are white, according to a Stanford University study of more than 17,000 homicides in eight states: Georgia, Florida, Illinois, North Carolina, Oklahoma, Mississippi, Arkansas and Virginia. The study also concluded that the death sentence was more likely when the victim was a woman.[60]

Death Row and Women: When Margie Velma Barfield was killed by lethal injection in North Carolina on November 2, 1984, it had been twenty-two years since a woman was executed in a U.S. prison. *The St. Petersburg Times* predicted: "As capital punishment gains increasing public acceptance, the grim exercise of legal murder is becoming more frequent and more routine." The editorial further stated:

> Mrs. Barfield was put to death in the last days of a vicious election campaign as North Carolina Governor Jim Hunt confronted U.S. Senator Jesse Helms, a bigoted right wing extremist. How many careers will be advanced by the number of death warrants signed. The Barfield execution drew a large crowed, not only because a woman being put to death is still a novelty, but because her fate had become a part of politics. About 300 death penalty opponents stood in silent prayer near the prison and extinguished candles as lethal drugs were pumped into her arms. Eighty champions of the death penalty cheered and applauded as some of them shouted, "Burn the Bitch!"[61]

The scene is reminiscent of that described by McCafferty of executions in England during the reigns of Henry VIII (1509-47) and Queen Elizabeth I: "Death was enacted in public with thousands looking on so as to deter witnesses from breaking the law. They were hanged, cut down while still alive, castrated and then disemboweled and then cut in pieces."[62]

"There have been 307 women executed in the U.S. prior to the Barfield execution," the *St. Petersburg Times* of November 2, 1984, noted, tracing the history of women executed in this country. "Jane Champion was the first hanged in the Virginia colony in 1630 for murdering a child conceived outside of her marriage. The last woman to be executed prior to Barfield was Elizabeth Ann Duncan, 58, in a California gas chamber August 8, 1962. From 1930 to 1968, 30 women were put to death for committing murders, one for kidnapping and one for espionage."

By 1967 an effort was well underway to persuade the U.S. Supreme Court that the death penalty violated the Constitution, in particular the 8th Amendment forbidding cruel and unusual punishment.

Executions were stayed by court order, pending the outcome of several suits. Then, on June 29, 1972, the Supreme Court, ruling on *Furman v. George* and related cases, rendered a 5 to 4 decision that spared the lives of 631 death row inmates and invalidated all capital punishment legislation then in effect. One was my client, Gary Lee Miller, 16 years old at the time of his arrest in 1967.

Each of the three petitioners in the Supreme Court cases—*Furman v. George, Jackson v. Georgia, and Branch v. Texas*—was a black convicted by a jury in a state court in which the states allowed juries the discretion of determining whether or not to impose the death penalty. One petitioner had been convicted of murder and two of rape, and all convictions had been upheld by the states' highest courts.

The justices each wrote separate and diverse opinions; however, it was the showing of infrequency, arbitrariness and discrimination of the death penalty that united the five justices—Douglas, Brennan, Stewart, White and Marshall. Although eight of the nine justices indicated opposition to capital punishment, only five agreed that the death penalty as then administered violated the constitution, and only two, Brennan and Marshall maintained that the death penalty in any form would be unconstitutional. In reaching these conclusions, all members of the majority made use of empirical data.

In summary each justice said:

DOUGLAS, J. (concurring) stated that it is cruel and unusual to apply the death penalty selectively to minorities, outcasts of society, and who are unpopular, but whom society is willing to see suffer though it would not countenance general application of the same penalty across the boards, and that because of the discriminatory application of statutes authorizing the discretionary imposition of the death penalty, such statutes were unconstitutional in their operation.

BRENNAN, J. (concurring) stated that the 8th Amendment was not limited to torturous punishments...; that a punishment was cruel and unusual if it did not comport with human dignity; and that since it was a denial of human dignity for a state to subject a person to an unusually severe punishment which society indicated it did not regard as acceptable, and which could not be shown to serve any penal purpose more effectively than a significantly less drastic punishment, death was a cruel and unusual punishment.

STEWART, J. (concurring) stated that the petitioners were among a capriciously selected random handful upon whom the sentence of death was imposed, and that the 8th and 14th Amendments could not tolerate a death sentence under legal systems which permitted this unique penalty to be so wantonly and so freakishly imposed, but that it was unnecessary to reach the ultimate question whether the infliction of the death penalty was constitutionally impermissible in all circumstances, under the 8th and 14th Amendments.

WHITE, J. (concurring) stated that as the state statutes involved in the present cases were administered, the death penalty was so infrequently imposed that the threat of execution was too attenuated to be of substantial service to criminal justice, but that it was unnecessary to decide whether the death penalty was unconstitutional per se, or whether there was no system of capital punishment which would comport with the 8th Amendment.

MARSHALL, J. (concurring) stated that the death penalty violated the 8th Amendment because it was excessive and unnecessary punishment and because it was morally unacceptable to the people of the United States.

Chief Justice Burger, joined by Blackmun, Powell, and Rehnquist (dissenting) stated that the constitutional prohibition against cruel and unusual punishments could not be construed to bar the imposition of the punishment of death; that the 8th Amendment did not prohibit all punishments which the states were unable to prove necessary to deter or control crime; that the 8th Amendment was not concerned with the process by which a state determined that a particular punishment was to be imposed in a particular case; that the 8th Amendment did not speak to the power of legislatures to confer sentencing discretion on juries, rather than to fix all sentences by statutes; and that to set aside the petitioners' death sentences in the present cases on the ground that prevailing sentencing practices did not comply with the 8th Amendment involved an approach which fundamentally misconceived the nature of the 8th Amendment guaranty and flew directly in the face of controlling authority of extremely recent vintage.

BLACKMUN, J. (dissenting) stated that although his personal distaste for the death penalty was buttressed by a belief that capital punishment served no demonstrable useful purpose and although the arguments against capital punishment might be a proper basis for legislative abolition of the death penalty or for the exercise of executive clemency, the authority for action abolishing the death penalty should not be taken over by the judiciary in the modern guise of an 8th Amendment issue.

Powell, joined by Burger, Blackmun, and Rehnquist (dissenting) stated that none of the opinions supporting the court's decision provided a constitutionally adequate foundation for the decision, and that the case against the constitutionality of the death penalty fell far short, especially when viewed from the prospective of the affirmative references to capital punishment in the Constitution, the prevailing precedents of the Supreme Court, the limitations on the exercise of the Supreme Court's power imposed by tested principles of judicial self-restraint, and the duty to avoid encroachment on the powers conferred upon state and federal legislatures.

Rehnquist, joined by Burger, Blackmun and Powell (dissenting) emphasized the need for judicial self-restraint, and stated that the most expansive reading of the leading constitutional cases did not remotely suggest that the Supreme Court had been granted a roving commission, either by the Founding Fathers or by the framers of the 14th Amendment, to strike down laws which were based upon notions of policy or morality suddenly found unacceptable by a majority of the Supreme Court.[63]

Within days after the court announced its decision in Furman, it became obvious that the political reactions to the decision would keep the death penalty controversy alive for some time. In November 1972, California restored a mandatory death penalty for several crimes and to prevent judicial review of such legislation. In December the Florida legislature met in special session and enacted into law several new death penalty statutes. The Nixon administration made overtures to ask Congress to pass legislation for mandatory death penalties covering several categories of crime.

"As legal killings increase, executions will become so commonplace that they will no longer draw crowds or headlines or morbid curiosity," the *St. Petersburg Times* opined. "But as the killings lose attention and concern, America will lose part of its soul. Capital punishment degrades the society that inflicts it."[64]

"The law of capital punishment seems to be almost where it was in the years preceding Furman," Gorecki has concluded. "Whenever plea bargaining occurs arbitrariness and inconsistency are allowed to prevail.

"In capital cases arbitrariness means that some are spared while others are pushed on along the road to execution without any rule to govern the choice. In two cases of a capital crime, where the degree of guilt is undistinguishable, one defendant is sent to confinement and the other to the gas chamber."[65]

Justice and the Press

Injustice and lack of due process do not always take place in the courtroom. The press convicts even before the grand jury votes on an indictment. A determined editor can turn the public against a defendant. Howard Felsher and Michael Rosen in their book, *The Press in the Jury Box* show how police frequently tell the public about a crime that's been solved, overlooking the fact that a crime is not solved until the accused is found guilty. Prosecutors play footsie with reporters to promote their selfish interests when climbing the political ladder to a judgeship or legislative office.

Trial by newspaper is as old as the printed press and is now expanded to radio and television. The media can destroy an individual's right to a fair trial by reporting inflammatory details about a suspect and the crime, even before trial. Regardless of a judge's instructions to a jury about disregarding what they have read or heard in the media, juries can be prejudiced against a defendant before hearing testimony. There is no way of estimating the number of persons sent to prison or death because they were convicted before trial.

The function of the criminal process is to determine criminal guilt with the intent of imposing a penalty. Nothing in the 6th Amendment to the U.S. Constitution guarantees the right to a fair trial. It provides, in part, that the accused shall enjoy the right to a speedy, public trial by an impartial jury of the state and district where the crime was committed. The judge never announces at the outset that the trial is to be fair and just, nor is the jury instructed that it will be.

The press contends the public has a right to know what is going on when a person becomes a suspect. It relies on the 1st Amendment right to the freedom of the press without considering how this may affect due process and the trial. When an accused is charged, the press goes to work reporting every aspect and allegation, true or untrue, that comes to its attention. How can the prospective juror forget what was reported earlier about the case? It's been said that a brain is like a sponge and that much of what it absorbs is subject to recall.

Three cases in which the press played a part were the Sacco-Vanzetti case, the Bruno Hauptman case involving the Lindberg infant killing, and that of Dr. Sam Shepperd. The convictions of these men included an overzealous prosecutor whose goal was to satisfy the public and achieve his personal advancement, and the cautious, timid and callous judge, but principally, it was the biased and oppressive media whose goal was to promote their business ends, not see justice done.

On August 23, 1927, Nichola Sacco, a shoemaker, and Bartholomew Vanzetti, a fish peddler—both aliens and anarchists—were executed in Massachusetts for murder. Their trial had been the object of controversy from its beginning and had reached international proportions. It was not two anarchists on trial, but justice and injustice. ABA President Charles S. Whitmun, in his annual address to his colleagues, delivered after the executions, declared it was an ABA policy to remain aloof from controversial matters of a political nature and to avoid purely local questions.

Ludovic Kennedy, a British author, in his book, *The Airman and the Carpenter*, described how Richard Hauptman was framed in the Lindberg case and substantially convicted by the press. Hauptman refused to plead anything other than not guilty and went to the execution chamber calmly declaring his innocence.

On July 4th, 1954, Marilyn, the attractive wife of Dr. Sam Shepperd, was murdered in their suburban Cleveland, Ohio, home. Not long afterward the press began to convict her husband. Among the press headlines were: GETTING AWAY WITH MURDER, TIME TO BRING BAY SLAYER INTO OPEN, GET THAT KILLER. In editorials, the press continued to point the finger at Dr. Shepperd throughout his trial. It became the judge and the jury. The grand jury was influenced by the campaign to convict him. In October 1954 Shepperd's trial was a mockery of justice as he was convicted, then sent to prison. Only through the enterprising efforts of a newcomer to the criminal defense ranks, Lee Bailey, was Shepperd's conviction overturned in the U.S. Supreme Court and a new trial ordered. He was acquitted, but ten years of his life were wasted and his profession destroyed by the press, which had refused to exercise its responsibility.

The English press is forbidden to publish anything that might in any way interfere with a defendant's right to a fair trial. Newspapers are subject to large fines for committing contempt of court by printing prejudicial stories. Publishers, editors and reporters are subject to fines and also risk jail sentences. English law is so strong that it cares not only about actual harm but also about the possibility of harm resulting from prejudicial publicity. A story need only tend to interfere with the due course of justice.

Psychiatric Justice—the Insanity Plea

Rich criminals can buy high-priced lawyers and experts; the poor are stuck with public defenders and court-appointed counsel who have no investigators and no budgets and who often plead their hapless clients guilty. It's justice for sale.

Many go free because their lawyers successfully pursue a plea of "not guilty by reason of insanity" by hiring experts and psychiatrists and psychologists to examine the defendant and who then testify as to his mental incapacities. The client's handicap indicates he cannot be held responsible for the crime with which he is charged. Such defendants go free because some lawyers and experts are willing to manipulate juries and the criminal justice system precisely in the area where judgment is most difficult—judgment based upon imagining what was in a person's mind when he committed the act.

The psychiatrist provides us with his own confusion but presents it in an appealing way with esoteric language to validate his "special" knowledge.

The insanity plea asks if the defendant could knowingly choose to fire the gun. It asks about an internal subjective phenomenon, about a state of mind which cannot be observed by others, photographed or tested retroactively.

The bulk of psychiatric testimony does not rest on any kind of testing. Instead, it is the psychiatrist's impressions after interviewing the defendant.

How can a psychiatrist determine what was in the defendant's mind three months after the criminal act was committed? How can the defendant's mind be explored as a matter of fact? It consists only of a series of presumptions which may be factually true or factually false. It is the psychiatrist who is fooling the public and causing judgmental errors among judges and juries and allowing the criminal to go back out on the street instead of behind bars.

When my client, JM, pleaded not guilty by reason of insanity on two separate charges of attempted murder it was not because he was insane at the time the event took place but because he was trying to beat the rap, which he did. Prior to the incident he had made threats to kill his wife and an employee. He had committed overt acts toward that end. He took his loaded gun to where he knew the victims were and pulled the trigger, intending to kill them. He was not under drugs or alcohol but was having a mean streak when he decided to get rid of them. Following a not guilty plea he was sent to a state psychiatric hospital for thirty days of interviews. The director of the hospital, who probably did little or no interviewing personally, testified in court of the sad mental condition of the defendant at the time of the shooting, and expressed his opinion that the suspect should not be judged guilty of his brutal act. One of his victims, his wife, became totally disabled; the defendant was released after a short stay in a mental hospital and returned home where he could commit the same act again. For ten years until his death, he terrorized his then ex-wife, causing her much fear and mental anguish. Without question, JM belonged behind bars.

And there was a second case of mine. JK was in his early twenties when he brutally assaulted a 15-year-old female and left her nude in the woods with a pen knife in her stomach. Boy Scouts, hiking in the area, found her and rushed her to the hospital. She survived but with severe injuries, including partial loss of eyesight. At a jury trial it was a battle between two psychiatrists with the state's prevailing. The defendant was sentenced to twelve years in a mental criminal institution. Many efforts made for his release were to no avail. After serving just over half his sentence he was released and sent home. Within a year he criminally assaulted another young girl. At trial and represented by another attorney, he pleaded guilty and was sentenced to ninety-nine years in prison. This man did not belong behind bars, but in a mental hospital. He was mentally deranged and should not have been held responsible for his criminal acts.

When a Washington, D.C., middle class jury found John Hinckley not guilty by reason of insanity for the attempted murder of President Reagan and the shooting of three other men, it was a confused jury. Of course, six experts testifying in behalf of the defendant helped. Hinckley's parents had millions to spend for lawyers and experts; there was a big burden on the part of the government to prove Hinckley sane beyond a reasonable doubt, before an inexperienced, fearful and excited body of jurors.

Young Hinckley, an oddball and spoiled brat, had everything going for him in his early life. Infatuated with a girl, Jodie Foster, a Yale student who knew little or nothing of him and was not interested, he was trying to be a hero in her eyes by committing a dastardly act. He purchased a handgun, took target practice, stalked the president on other occasions, and then appeared at the critical place to kill him. This is premeditation in cases of first degree murder. It was up to the jury to decide whether the defendant had the capacity or ability to understand that his act was wrong or if he had the capacity to contemplate the act.

The Hinckley jurors were manipulated by experts. Some jurors who spoke to the press were almost incoherent in attempting to explain the outcome. They did not seem to know why they voted not guilty by reason of insanity.

VI

Justice Denied

Justice is the end of government. It is the end of civil society. It has ever been, and ever will be pursued, until it be obtained, or until liberty be lost in the pursuit.
Federalist, No. 51

For that which is done by right is justly done, and what is unjustly done cannot be done by right.
St. Augustine, City of God

Equal Justice Under Law?

Emblazoned on the portals of the great edifice that houses the Supreme Court of the United States are the words, *Equal Justice Under Law.* This is a pretty slogan carved in marble, but it was an unrealistic goal when the marble palace was erected in the 1930s, and it is still unrealized. Equal justice under law is a myth and a blatant lie.

For three thefts that totaled $229.11, the U.S. Supreme Court ruled 5-4 on March 19, 1980 that William James Rummel's life sentence was not cruel and unusual punishment. The callous injustice of that decision gave the fifty state legislatures virtual freedom to decide how long any convicted person should serve in prison.

Rarely are the wealthy and powerful imprisoned for high crimes, while the less fortunate seldom escape harsh punishment for lesser offenses. To balance the scales of justice and rectify such inequities, Americans have looked to the Supreme Court for ultimate fairness. In Rummel's case, public reverence for the high court was seriously undermined.

Writing for the majority, Justice William Rehnquist rejected Rummel's constitutional challenge of the Texas law that imposes a mandatory life sentence on "whoever shall have been three times convicted of a felony."

For the Supreme Court to second guess the length of sentences imposed on repeat offenders would be an intrusion of the legislature's power, said Rehnquist, with the concurrence of Chief Justice Warren E. Burger and Justices Harry A. Blackmun, Potter Stewart and Byron White.

"We are construing a living Constitution," countered the four-member minority in a dissent written by Justice Lewis F. Powell Jr. "The sentence imposed upon [Rummel] would be viewed as grossly unjust by virtually every layman and lawyer. In my view, objective criteria clearly establish that a mandatory life sentence for defrauding persons of about $230 crosses any rationally drawn line separating punishment that lawfully may be imposed under the Constitution."

The quality of justice in America or any other nation must be measured by that line of rationality. Unconditional, hard-line "justice," untempered by mercy and fairness, demeans all humanity and diminishes this nation's high principles.

Certainly Rummel's crimes during an eight-year span merited punishment. In 1964, when he was 20, he illegally bought four tires for $80 with someone else's credit card. In 1969 he forged a check for $28.36 to pay a motel bill. In 1972 he was convicted for accepting $120.75 as payment for air conditioner repairs he never made. Under Texas law, the third conviction made him a "habitual offender" and brought the mandatory life sentence.

Rational fairness, of course, has rarely been a consideration for Burger, Rehnquist and Blackmun—all appointed by Richard Nixon. But the Supreme Court's majestic power is seriously stained by the hard-line injustice imposed upon William Rummel.[1]

The spirit and words of Daniel Webster nearly a century ago ring out yet today:

> Justice is the great concern of man on earth. It is the ligament which holds civilized beings and civilized nations together. Wherever her temple stands, and so long as it is duly honored, there is a foundation for social security, general happiness and improvement and progress of our race. And whoever labors on this edifice with usefulness and distinction, whoever clears its foundations, strengthens its pillars, adorns its entablatures, or contributes to raise its lofty dome still higher in the skies, connects himself

> in name and fame and character with that which is and must be durable as the frame of human society.

Justice is the permanent passion of public life. When you speak of justice you are reaching for the foundations of human existence. It is the cornerstone of human togetherness. When we deny persons justice, we declare men worthless. Justice means giving to each what each deserves. To each according to his merit and earned entitlements.

Injustices Perpetrated on the Southern Blacks

In *Southern Justice*, published in 1965, the injustices perpetrated on blacks in southern states were fully enumerated:

> It was not constitutional law that the southern black was faced with but underlaw or local white custom. They called it southern justice. White lawyers rarely raised constitutional issues or provided aggressive representation for their black clients. Black lawyers avoided practicing law in the south and instead remained in the more affluent centers like Washington and New York. They contented themselves with a few hours of volunteer work in urban ghettos as part of their big city practice. There were literally hundreds of blacks in the south whose property was stolen from them in phony deeds and mortgage foreclosures and forged wills. Millions of blacks were deprived of their personal liberty and rights.
>
> Arrested by a member of an all-white police force, or sheriff's department or highway patrol, the Negro defendant was brought, perhaps for the first time, into the lonely world of the white South. The warrant for his arrest, if there was a warrant, was sworn out by a white man and issued by a white magistrate or commissioner. Then, transported to jail in a racially segregated patrol wagon, he was fingerprinted, photographed and assigned a number by a white clerk, and detained in a racially segregated cell in a jail run by white men. Later he was indicted by a white grand jury and pressured to confess or plead guilty. If he refused, he was brought to a courtroom presided over by a white judge, provided a white defense lawyer, tried before a segregated audience, referred to with first-name

> condescension, and convicted by a white trial jury in a courthouse with segregated restrooms and drinking fountains.
>
> The all-white state supreme court, some of whose justices are as well known for their bawdy Negro stories as for their attacks upon the Supreme Court of the United States, then viewed the appeal. The white lawyers wrote their briefs, the law was studied by white law clerks, and the jury's verdict was approved.
>
> In any society, democratic or totalitarian, unbalanced instrumentalities of justice are weapons of repression. The racially exclusionary system of southern justice, its white juries and white lawyers, judges, sheriffs and deputies, police and clerks, stenographers and segregated facilities, was the sophisticated and effective guarantor of the southern way of life.[2]

In her book, *Money & Justice*, Lois G. Forer, trial judge in the Common Pleas Court of Philadelphia, states:

> The legal system is divided into two separate and unequal systems of justice: one for the rich which the Courts take limitless time to examine, ponder, consider and deliberate over hundreds of thousands of bits of evidence and days of testimony, and hear elaborate, endless appeals and write countless learned opinions; the other for the poor, in which hasty guilty pleas and brief hearings are the rule and appeals the exception. Appellate judges who write opinions for the rich and the poor do not see the litigants. They do not see the lonely misery or the smug security of the rich surrounded by learned deferential counsel. They do not hear the inarticulate pause of the semiliterate or their dubious affirmations that they understand the rights they are relinquishing.[3]

In his commentary and book for reform of the courts, Leonard Downie Jr. had this to say:

> Chaos, confusion, compromise, and bureaucratic expediency and inadequacy are the ugly realities behind every "justice myth" on which most Americans have been

> reared. Speedy trial, for example, does not exist except in courtrooms where the poor and downtrodden are quickly deprived of their legal rights through pretrial deals (plea bargaining) that disregard the client's guilt or innocence and trials that are assembly-line travesties of justice. Court fees for filing suits and appealing adverse rulings shut many poor people out of the courthouse entirely, while involvement in a long case can bankrupt a middle-income person. The law and its interpretation by the courts often give those with economic power special rights not enjoyed by debtors, tenants, or consumers.[4]

"The myth of equal justice under which the legal system for all operates in the U.S. has become a cruel joke," wrote Downie:

> The poor including a large proportion of urban blacks find they are treated as second class citizens in court with laws and procedure favoring the rich, the landlord, the creditor, the insurance companies and the corporate giants and the predatory merchants, The very poor and the ordinary working man are denied basic rights including even the opportunity to confront those who victimize them. The local courthouse is a haven for the incompetent lawyers and judicial hack appointees, clothed in the robes of justice, destroying lives through prejudice, whim and limited legal ability.[5]

He further states:

> The landed rich and the captains of industry have always been able to buy the best legal representation. Often, they also can negotiate their way to favorable legal settlements without even stepping into the maelstrom of the courts. They can pay their lawyers to wait, or even to prolong the law's normal delay until they wear down opponents with fewer resources. The lawyers for the rich and the big corporations work on a fixed retainer fee that is paid no matter what kind of case they handle, so long as they maintain strong allegiance to their client.[6]

The same viewpoint was taken by Jerome E. Carlin in his book, *Lawyers on Their Own*: "The best trained, most technically skilled, and ethically most responsible lawyers are reserved [for] the upper reaches of business and society. This leaves the least competent, least well-trained, and least ethical lawyers to the lower-income individuals."[7]

Lack of Due Process of Law Brings Injustices

Justice in the courts is closely linked with due process of law. Wherever there is lack of due process there is injustice. When we speak of due process we look to the 5th and 14th Amendments of our Constitution which guarantee to all: "No state shall deprive any person of life, liberty or property without due process of law." It is the settled doctrine that due process embodies a system of rights based on moral principles so deeply embedded in the traditions and feelings of our people as to be deemed fundamental to a civilized society as conceived by our whole history. Due process is that which comports with the deepest notions of what is fair and right and just. Brief historical review indicates that "due process" has been with us since well before the "shot heard round the world" was fired. The Magna Charta in England contained the first class conception and famous exposition of the law of the land: "No free man shall be taken or imprisoned, or disseized, or outlawed or exiled, or in any way harmed...save by the lawful judgment of his peers or by the law of the land.[8]

When we speak of due process we think of that process wherein a person is accorded fair and unimpeachable treatment. It may not be in the criminal courts alone but the civil as well. It could be any administrative hearing, a small court trial or intermediate court or appellate court. Notice and opportunity to be heard in orderly proceedings adapted to the case before a tribunal having jurisdiction of the cause meets one of the tests. If not, justice is denied.

The Right Honorable Lord Denning has this to say in his book *Due Process of Law*:

> By due process of law, I mean the measures authorized by the law so as to keep the stream of justice pure; to see that trials and inquiries are fairly conducted, that arrests and searches are properly made. That lawful remedies are readily available; and that unnecessary delays are eliminated.[9]

Kermit Clay "Pinky" Twigg, who could not read nor write and who needed direction and assistance, was a laborer in one of our local breweries when he came into my office in 1965, in my early days of lawyering. On his first visit I knew he was the type of client for whom I had labored in law school and entered the practice of law.

After thirty-one years, Pinky had been discharged from his job at the brewing company, allegedly for insubordination and wearing dirty apparel to work. Pinky's job was to clean out the sudsy beer kegs and large drums. His uniform was mostly of rubber and cleanliness of dress was not a prerequisite, according to Pinky. Taking a shower at the end of the work day was not his regular habit; the beer fumes stayed with him. Pinky could not understand why he had to come to work in clean clothing when at the day's end he was dirty and drenched with beer fluid. In any event, his superiors ordered him to keep clean or hit the road. Pinky believed they could not do this and he gave them a piece of his mind.

The president of the brewery, a local lawyer and politician, issued his mandate that Pinky had to go.

Following his discharge, a grievance was reluctantly filed on his behalf by the company oriented Local No. 265 of the International Brewery Union. The arbitration was set up in the local courthouse but the local union president and general secretary told Pinky he was not to appear at the hearing and that if he did they would walk out. Nor could his attorney be present during the arbitration, he was told.

As the arbitration got underway the brewery president-attorney presented his case, followed by the weak and unprepared defense of the four union representatives. It was grossly unbalanced and unequal. The Washington based arbitrator, however, saw nothing out of the ordinary and in two weeks following the arbitration affirmed Pinky's discharge. Pinky, dumb and illiterate, the butt of many jokes at work over the years, ridiculed and humiliated, lost his job.

In the interest of justice I filed an appeal to the circuit court for Pinky, joining in the local brewery, with the brewery president as defendant. The grounds for the case was lack of due process and I requested a new arbitration hearing.

In a daylong trial with Pinky as his lone witness, the evidence was unquestioned that the claimant was not adequately represented at the arbitration hearing, that Pinky was not accorded due process, and that his fundamental rights of job security were abridged. The corporate powers defense headed by a Baltimore based attorney who represented the brewery, stifled the local judge. The arbitrator's decision was affirmed. There was no money for appeal and the case ended.

For the next twelve years Pinky knocked about for employment without seeking government assistance. From time to time he visited my office when harassed by landlords, exploited by local police, and a host of other unsympathetic persons. He was finally laid to rest on May 9, 1977, a victim many times over of injustice.[10]

Marvin Frankel wrote, in *Partisan Justice*:

> People yearning after ideal justice have dreamed over the centuries of quiet halls where the truth is effectively discovered and the wise application of fair rules of law automatically leads to just results. Like other ideals, this one is not regularly achieved. A chief obstacle is in the nature of things, the hostile clash of selfish interests. At center stage is the egotistical, prejudicial and arrogant judge. A purported know-it-all whose greatest desire is the protection of private interests. Next comes the all-purpose mercenary warrior, the shyster and many times bumbling lawyer; and then the ruthless, self-seeking prosecutor who is willing to convict the innocent for personal advantages or gratification regardless of perjurious state witnesses; and then the untrained, biased jury.[11]

Erroneous Criminal Convictions

Wrote Edwin Borchard: "Among the more shocking and glaring of injustices are erroneous criminal convictions of innocent people. When it is discovered after conviction that the wrong person was condemned, the least the state can do to right the irreparable injury is to reimburse the innocent victim by an appropriate indemnity for the loss and damage suffered. This is rarely done.[12]

A New England prosecutor claimed: "Innocent persons are never convicted. Don't worry about it, it never happens in the world. It is a physical impossibility." Borchard has cited a collection of cases refuting this claim—cases in which innocence was established in various ways, such as the allegedly murdered victim turning up alive, subsequent conviction of the real culprit, discovery of new evidence, or a pardon granted by the president or a governor on grounds that the wrong man was convicted.

Wrote Borchard:

> The sixty-five cases include in the main, mistaken identity, circumstantial evidence or perjury or a combination of these factors; the major source of the tragic errors is the improper identification of the accused by the crime victim of violence. Juries seem disposed more readily to credit the veracity and reliability of the victims of an

> outrage than any amount of contra evidence by or on behalf of the accused, whether by way of alibi, character witnesses or other testimony. The emotional balance of the victim or eye witness is so disturbed by his extraordinary experience that his powers of perception become distorted and his identification is frequently most untrustworthy. Erroneous conviction on circumstantial evidence exclusively involved charges of murder in the first and second degree. Juries not only weigh certain facts but draw conclusions from them. In doing so they are led by prejudice and partiality or want of due deliberation and sobriety of judgment to make hasty and false deductions; a source of error not existing in the consideration of positive evidence.
>
> In many cases the prosecutor takes the evidence as presented to him, including the uncontrollable perjury of vengeful witnesses and he lays it before the jury without realization of its worthlessness.
>
> And then there is the perjury of the police or private detectives or the gross negligence of the police in overlooking or even suppressing evidence of innocence, or the overzealousness of the prosecutor to convict. It is common knowledge that the prosecuting technique is to regard a conviction as a personal victory calculated to enhance the prestige of the prosecutor.[13]

"Evidence of a prior conviction is usually fatal to an accused," wrote Borchard, then continued:

> The prejudice this is calculated to create in the minds of the jury is one of the principal reasons the prosecutor insists on such evidence. Such evidence should be reserved for the judge after the jury brings in its verdict.
>
> No one is compelled to take the stand under the constitutional privilege of self-incrimination, the 5th amendment, by refusing to testify. Refusal to take the stand—under circumstances where an explanation from the accused is naturally expected—inevitably affects the jury unfavorably; in addition, the accused's known privilege of refusing to testify influences the police to obtain

> confessions, which, whether true or not, stigmatizes the system of obtaining them as public disgrace.[14]

"Criminal trials take place sometimes under conditions with respect to which public interest and passions are easily aroused," Borchard submits. "Public opinion is much to blame for miscarriages of justice and is excited by the crime and moved to revenge; a demand which juries and prosecutors are susceptible to public opinion."

Contending that the media "has not shown the problems of justice as they really are," Borchard wrote:

> They have rarely told the public about correction institutions, judicial delays, reduction of sentences of the rich, unfair treatment of the poor. Nor has the media told of inept judges, unethical lawyers, or the many other facts contributing to the present failures of our judicial system. Criminal justice is swayed by the constant and continuing interaction of press and public officials on each other. The press has long been controlled by the whims of the police and prosecutors rather than the impartial treatment of the facts.[15]

"In the majority of cases, the accused are poor, unable to retain experienced counsel and for that reason their defense is inadequate," Borchard maintains. "In many instances, the system of assigned counsel to represent an accused is a total failure and creates a disrespect for the administration of the criminal law. Justice is not promoted and it places an innocent prisoner at a disadvantage in obtaining that fair trial which is guaranteed by all our laws."[16]

In Palatka, Florida, J. B. Brown was convicted of first degree murder and sentenced to hang. On the eve of the hanging his sentence was commuted to life by the governor. Twelve years later, in a deathbed confession, another man admitted to the crime, absolving Brown of any blame. The murder conviction had been obtained by perjured testimony, circumstantial evidence and the excitement of the heinousness of the crime and the zeal of private interest. When released, the prisoner was aged, crippled and destitute.[17]

Charles F. Stielow and Nelson Green, farm laborers were tried and convicted of first degree murder in Olean, New York. The victim was an elderly respected resident. A written statement of confession was placed before Stielow but he refused to sign, saying it wasn't true. Based on the unsigned statement, both men were indicted. At Stielow's trial the unsigned confession was admitted; the jury found him guilty and sentenced him to execution. Green's attorney advised him to plead guilty to a charge of second degree murder; he was sentenced to a term of twenty years to life. Following Stielow's ineffective appeals he was sentenced to die, but a stay was granted on the eve of the execution. Eventually a second execution date was set, then one hour before it was to take place another stay was granted by the governor in the face of new evidence. A suspect was found who admitted the killing, but a grand jury refused to indict him. However, based on extensive investigation, Stielow and Green were released as innocent men. Compensation was never made to either man.[18]

In more recent times, the saga of Gary E. Dotson presents an interesting story. Dotson, at the age of 20, was convicted of the 1977 rape alleged by 16-year-old Cathleen Crowell Webb in a Chicago suburb. Eight years later, Webb, then a born-again Christian wanting to make amends, sought the release of Dotson. A new trial was conducted before the same judge (Samuels) who suspected the recanted testimony and affirmed the conviction.

Prior to the first trial, Webb had picked out a photo of Dotson, whom she had never seen before, and identified him in a police lineup because he bore an uncanny resemblance to her phony description. Dotson had been sentenced to twenty to fifty years in the Illinois penitentiary.

The repentant Webb said her new faith had "had to grow like a baby" until it overcame her fears. Dotson's second ordeal turned into an extraordinary legal melodrama which took place before national television audiences and reached the office of Illinois Governor James Thompson who commuted Dotson's sentence to time served notwithstanding his disbelief of Webb's recantation. It was the Illinois justice system that was being examined. Justice prevailed but in retrospect we can see how the system fails an innocent person. Over eight years of a young man's life were wasted because of perjury.[19]

The Butternut Hollow Murder— An Example of Miscarried Justice

No criminal case in mountainous western Maryland brought more publicity to Allegany County than the Butternut Hollow murder[20] of Sunday, May 28, 1967. *Time* magazine, the *Washington Post*, the *Baltimore Sun*, and a host of weeklies covered the case, including the antiestablishment *People's Guardian* from Frostburg, Maryland.

Sixteen-year-old Gary Lee Miller was in his ninth grade English class at the Meyersdale, Pennsylvania, high school when a state trooper asked for him. That spring day, Monday, May 29, 1967, was to close out Miller's freedom. Within months he was to be tried as an adult in the Circuit Court of Allegany County, Maryland, charged with the first degree murder of 20-year-old Judy Lee Ziegler, found brutally murdered in the early hours of Sunday, May 28, in an area called Butternut Hollow, about a mile east of Frostburg. Ziegler, a pretty, local factory clerical worker, had been returning to her home in the village of Pocohantas, Pennsylvania, ten miles away, after attending a Saturday night movie with three teenage companions.

It was 2:00 p.m., the day following the murder, when Miller was taken into custody by a Pennsylvania state trooper and probation officer. The school principal advised Miller his parents would be notified at once, but this was not done. He was taken to the Meyersdale police station to await the Maryland investigators. At 2:10 p.m. they took over and closeted Miller in a room called the council chambers.

For an hour and thirty-five minutes they questioned him but received only non-incriminating statements as to his whereabouts the night before the killing. After a five-minute break he was told to undress, his body was examined and photos taken. At 5:00 p.m. he was placed in custody of the Somerset County sheriff while the investigators visited the Miller home, ten miles away. Miller was given a lunch after which the sheriff attempted to coerce Miller into confessing. At 6:10 p.m., according to the investigators, they returned to the Meyersdale police station to be told that Miller was willing to give a statement. After purportedly reading Miller a second Miranda warning, they began questioning him again.

Typing on an unfamiliar typewriter for the next hour and fifty-five minutes, one county investigator took a confession from Miller consisting of three pages, single spaced, in which Miller admitted everything. He was then asked to sign it and refused. Outside the interrogation room, were police officers and Miller's parents who arrived at 7:40. At 8:50 they were allowed in to see their son and were urged by the two investigators to persuade him to sign the statement. He refused. At no time during the incommunicado proceeding had anyone been allowed to enter; seven hours had elapsed. Miller was then removed to the Somerset jail while the two investigators searched the Miller home, room by room. They found nothing there to incriminate young Miller.

The trial began on October 25, 1967. Most everyone in the tri-state area of Maryland, Pennsylvania and West Virginia knew of the crime and trial through the media. To get a fair trial in Allegany County was impossible; the case had to be removed to another county. A change of venue was a guaranteed right to Miller for the asking but Miller's court-assigned attorney felt otherwise.

Thirty-eight witnesses for the state were to take the stand during the four-day trial. None had witnessed the killing. The case was built on the unsigned statement attributed to Miller, convicts with long prison records who testified that Miller had admitted the killing to them, and circumstantial evidence.

To fully appreciate the scenario of the kangaroo trial court, it is necessary to examine the profiles of the chief participants:

Gary Lee Miller: Born September 27, 1950, the second of four children, he hated his alcoholic father but had not himself turned to alcohol or drugs. His waywardness had propelled him into serious crime at the age of fourteen. In November 1965 he had been convicted of raping a young woman after hiding in her car and forcing her to drive to an isolated wooded area—a crime to which he confessed. Represented by a court-assigned lawyer, Gary was sentenced to four years in the Maryland Institution for Males. He served two years and was paroled with the stipulation he attend the Cumberland Health Center for psychiatric treatment. Upon his release he returned to his studies as a ninth grade student.

Prior to that trial he was sent to Clifton Perkins Hospital for psychiatric evaluation. The report stated he was suffering from "a transitory reactive depression" but was declared competent to stand trial. He knew at the time of the offense "of the rightness and wrongness of the act," the report concluded.

From time to time Gary would leave home to stay with friends because he did not get along with his parents.

Harold Miller, father of the accused: Age 47, a tenant farmer of 220 acres, he was short on work and long on the bottle. He had been confined for treatment of alcoholism. On one occasion he was jailed for assault and disturbance of the peace. His farm, on Red Dog Road, produced little and the dairy business he operated was closed down in 1964, condemned for health reasons. He had no control over Gary, who despised his father for beating the three other children: Roger, 20; Kay, 13: and Gail, 11.

Virginia Elsa Miller, mother of the accused: Age 43 with ten years of education, she worked as a domestic, a waitress, and a beautician for family support. Small, stout, and rosy-cheeked, she was the typical farmer's wife. She was a highly religious woman, successful in having all her children attend church regularly, except Gary.

Chief Judge: In his mid-fifties, he spent four years on the bench as a political appointee before being elected to a fifteen-year term in an uncontested election. He was a former substitute trial magistrate and a lawyer of sorts. When a *Time* photographer tried to photograph him leaving the courthouse during the appeal period, the judge hurled hard snowballs at the camera.

Court-Assigned Defense Attorney: Sixtyish, much of his practice was assignment in criminal cases, along with divorce work and estates. Court-assigned attorneys notoriously urge clients to plead guilty to make it easy on all concerned.

Chief Prosecutor: In his mid-forties, he had been on the public payroll since entering law practice in the early 1950s. He was elected to the office for four years in 1966 after one of the most unethical campaigns ever undertaken. He was a favorite of the establishment which was able to control and direct his course of action.

Associate Judge: Age 47, he was a Republican politico of the first order and an appointee of a Democrat governor. Unopposed, he was elected to a fifteen-year-term in 1966.

County Investigator: Age 46 and on the job five years. Formerly in law enforcement 25 years.

Sheriff of Somerset County, Pennsylvania: He was 57 and had been sheriff twelve years. He had learned the techniques of psychological coercion—undue influence to get a confession short of beating a suspect. He promised Miller that if he confessed he would be taken care of. "That is the way your parents would like it," he told the boy. "I know your grannies and for their sake, come clean."

County Medical Examiner (Coroner): An open and honest physician, he was obliged to view and to testify to what he'd observed but despised the participants in the proceedings against Miller. He was on their hit list to remove from office but they weren't able to accomplish it.

Prior to Gary's trial the grand jury which had indicted him published a statement saying, "We wish to specially commend all law enforcing agencies, namely the Maryland State Police, the county investigator, the sheriff's office of Somerset County, Pennsylvania, the Pennsylvania authorities who cooperated and worked diligently to solve a recent homicide case. We were greatly impressed by the excellent preparation and presentation of evidence to us in the case by the Maryland State Police criminal investigator and county investigator. A county is indeed fortunate to have such capable and experienced criminal investigators." By this statement, Miller was convicted before his trial!

No direct evidence linking Miller with the murder was introduced at the trial, but the unsigned statement of his confession was admitted into evidence. The county investigator was allowed to read its entirety into the record as part of his notes taken following Miller's apprehension. The statement was challenged by Miller's court-assigned attorney but he failed to have Miller take the stand to refute it, which he could have done without subjecting Gary to cross examination by the state on the merits.

Also read into evidence, despite its incriminating testimony, was a psychiatric evaluation of Miller made at the Clifton Perkins state hospital. The report stated: "The defendant had a sociopathic personality...his selfish, ungrateful and exhibitionist attitude, the lack of feelings of remorse and guilt and his inability to profit from past experiences...led him to the commission of repeated criminal or otherwise antisocial acts."

At the opening of the trial the defense attorney made a motion for the case to be dismissed, based on the inflammatory statement made by the grand jury. His argument was cut short and his motion denied on the grounds that while the report might have affected a jury, this was a nonjury trial and would have no effect on the two judges.

The state's witnesses included two elderly ladies living in the vicinity of Butternut Hollow who said they heard screams during the early morning hours of May 28. Photos of the victim were shown and of the area where the body was found—a site encircled by a two-strand barbed wire fence that would have made it difficult to enter in the dark without being severely scratched. The photos taken of Miller in the nude were shown for close checking of cuts and bruises. None were shown.

On cross examination the investigator admitted that Miller was held incommunicado from 2:10 to 8:50 p.m. after being taken into custody and that he had broken down and cried several times. The trooper testified that Miller's parents weren't notified because Miller did not request it. Mrs. Miller stated she learned around 4:15 that her son had been apprehended but did not know where he was being held. She testified that she and her husband had waited from 7:40 till 8:50 p.m. at the Meyersdale police station to see Gary and when allowed to see him were asked to have him sign the confession statement. She said the Somerset County sheriff asked Gary to sign the statement, saying, "Now you have had your telephone call"—referring to a call to his grandparents.

When Gary's alleged statement was read into evidence over the objection of the defense attorney, the chief judge said, "The court is satisfied from the testimony that the statement given to the investigator by the defendant was given voluntarily and that the defendant knowingly and intelligently waived his constitutional rights."

The statement submitted at the trial was six pages of single-spaced typewritten copy amounting to approximately 3,000 words. It was a perfect confession relating all incidents of the crime, covering the travel to Butternut Hollow, the killing, the race home in the victim's yellow Nova, and the submerging of the car in a pond one mile from the Miller home. Because the statement was unsigned there was nothing to prevent the state from amending it into the form as read at the trial.

But the confession was suspicious in that a farm-bred boy with a ninth grade education would respond in such formal manner with perfect grammar and perfect organization of thought. The number of pages and 3,000 words, indicating additional pages after the day of interrogation, contradicts the assumption the confession was made by Gary rather than created by the two state authorities.

Neither the trooper nor the investigator had considered it important to notify Gary's parents, yet both Maryland and Pennsylvania statutes protect juveniles charged with crime by providing that a law enforcement officer taking a child into custody shall immediately notify, or cause to be notified, the child's parent, guardian, or custodian. That this was not complied with was not emphasized by the defense attorney.

State authorities ignored the law and such flagrant violation indicated bad faith in the interrogation. The police station environment was oppressive with no friend, relative or counsel on hand, only the arm of the state at all times during the nearly seven-hour period. It would appear the police were highly motivated by the fury of the public after learning from the media of the horrendous crime and desired a media conviction before trial to satisfy the public.

Thousands of criminal cases are appealed to the federal courts each year and decisions reversed because the presiding trial judges gave little or no respect to constitutional law pertaining to due process. Appellate courts have said that the interrogation atmosphere carries with it its own badge of intimidation. If an adult needs the guiding hand of counsel at each stage of proceedings against him, how great the need for a juvenile. For Miller to waive his rights, he had to do it knowingly, voluntarily, and intelligently with an understanding of the import of the warning. He must know the consequences that flow from a voluntary statement of the commission of a serious crime. Lengthy interrogation and incommunicado incarceration before the statement is made is strong evidence an accused did not validly waive his rights. This is the so-called Miranda rights as established by the Warren Supreme Court.

In a Supreme Court case predating Miller's by nineteen years, *Haley v. Kellerman*, it was stated that in dealing with juveniles courts must use the highest standards of due process and fundamental fairness. When a child is involved "special care scrutinizing the record must be used and he cannot be judged by the more exacting standards of maturity. While an adult might not be affected by police tactics, such tactics would overawe and overwhelm a juvenile, mainly because of the great instability that the crisis of adolescence produces." That's the law of the land, but not in the Miller case.

The state's prime witnesses were the police officers, the investigator and the trooper whose persuasive testimony was Miller's confession. Added to this was a conversation Miller was said to have had with a jailmate at the Somerset County jail, in which Gary admitted the killing—an admission overheard by the trooper and both sheriffs. Their testimony as to the jail conversation was admitted without objection. Then another prisoner of the Garrett County and Cumberland city jail testified that Miller had admitted the killing to him. The prisoner had nothing to lose as he came forward with this additional evidence.

There followed six buddies of Gary's who testified he carried a knife much like the one found at the crime scene. The three teenagers who had attended the movie with Ziegler testified as did fourteen witnesses who said they saw Miller hitchhiking a ride the night prior to the murder. A Frostburg police officer said he saw a yellow Nova speed through town early that morning and two young men testified to seeing Miller's hand bandaged that night. Another testified about the yellow Nova being submerged in the pond and another, who lived along Miller's route home, said he heard a car stop to pick someone up. In all, no direct testimony, but the confession heaped on by statements from convicts and circumstantial evidence.

The defense called seven witnesses, but none were of any help; no character witnesses were called. At the outset of the defense, Gary was told by the court that he had the right to testify, but he refused. The case closed on the fourth day.

Defense counsel made little effort, providing a defense that was weak and most inadequate. It's unexplainable why he did not move the case to another county and seek a jury trial. It's hard to understand why he sought psychiatric evaluation by a state institution without countering with a private psychiatric evaluation made at state expense. Or why he allowed all the state exhibits to be introduced into evidence without objection or proof. On overview, it would seem the job was bigger than the man and he had no assistance in trial preparation.

He neither owned nor drove a car, which made it difficult for him to travel to find witnesses and new leads of defense. He misunderstood his mission and the defendant's right to attack the confession from the stand. The court was equally unresponsive to Miller's rights by failing to warn him to take the stand as to the purported confession. Possibly overawed by the authority of the court, the defense lawyer refused to stand tall. He received an $800 fee for the trial and $38.68 for expenses.

The two-judge panel went to their chambers and returned in twenty minutes with a verdict of guilty of first degree murder. Next day a motion for a new trial was denied. All that was left was the sentencing. That came seventeen days later: Miller was to die by lethal gas the week of January 1, 1968.

The death sentence brought instant reaction. Nineteen Catholic friars at the local Capucian monastery wrote the governor: "The stately figure of justice has become a vicious and vengeful animal."

Further protests rang out from a vocal minority outraged by the manner in which the trial was conducted. Publisher Dorothy Martin of the *People's Guardian*, whose previous attacks drew a series of contempt of court citations, printed a list of twenty-one questions which she charged Miller's trial failed to answer and which, in her opinion, threw the verdict in doubt. Among her questions: Why wasn't blood found in Miller's hair, shoes or clothing when the public has been led to believe that crime labs can find microscopic traces even weeks after blood has been scrubbed away? Why couldn't fingerprints be found on the car, knife, or anything the state presented? The steering wheel of the car had blood on it, but no fingerprints.

On the day of sentencing, the defense attorney filed an appeal to the Court of Appeals, along with a petition for a review of sentence. A four-judge panel was appointed by the chief judge of the Fourth Judicial Circuit. Upon review, the sentence was upheld. Gary Miller was destined to be the youngest death row inmate in the state's history.

But on December 13, 1967, Gary directed a letter to the chief judge saying, "I no longer want or desire the defense attorney to represent me in my suit, *State v. Miller*, as of this date, December 6, 1967. I have requested my parents, Harold F. Miller and Virginia Miller, to ask John C. Sullivan to represent me in all further court action, Sincerely, Gary Lee Miller."

On the day previous, I had accompanied Gary's parents to the chambers of the chief judge at which time they told him they wanted me to represent their son on appeal. "Your boy has an attorney whom I appointed," the judge said, "and he does not need another lawyer."

Gary's father replied, "We wanted Mr. Sullivan to represent Gary in the original trial but you told us he was too political."

The irate judge shouted, "Get the hell out of here!"

For the next ten years I was to take this case through the higher courts. A stipulation was that I would receive no fee for all work on appeal; in all I would spend over $4,000 and hundreds of hours researching, preparing briefs, and traveling to court appearances. The case was processed through the state's Court of Appeals, the U.S. Supreme Court, the U.S. District Court of Maryland; then back to the Allegany County trial court for a post conviction hearing, then to the state's highest court, to the U.S. District Court, and thence to the U.S. Fourth Circuit Court of Appeals.[21]

The principal concern was the interrogation atmosphere which was created for no purpose other than to subjugate the defendant to the will of his examiners. The incommunicado interrogation, the removal of clothing and photographing of the defendant, the compiling of a confession by the county investigator—all were at odds with one of the nation's most cherished principles: that the individual may not be compelled to incriminate himself in violation of the 5th and 6th Amendments of the U.S. Constitution as applied through the 14th Amendment.

The Maryland Appeals Court in a lengthy 23-page opinion, affirmed both the conviction and sentence. The court ignored the principle set down by the Supreme Court of the "totality of circumstances" as noted in Miranda and held that age was not important in a juvenile confession; that the state had met its burden in establishing that the statement was freely and voluntarily given and that Miller knowingly and intelligently waived his constitutional rights. It said that the determination of whether a confession is admissible is ordinarily a matter for the trial court to decide and its determination would not be disturbed on appeal unless there was a clear abuse of discretion. The Maryland court, like the Arizona high court in *Miranda*,[22] was truly out of step with current Supreme Court past decisions and the Miller case was just another of the court refusals to interfere with a trial court's decision, however lax and out of date it was in application of constitutional law.

The death warrant was again stayed as an appeal by *Writ of Certiorari* was filed May 6, 1968, to the U.S. Supreme Court. A member of the American Civil Liberties Union joined in the brief, which was one of 431 other capital cases on appeal to the Supreme Court.

Miller remained on death row for three years, until July 16, 1972, when the Supreme Court vacated the death sentence in the wake of *Furman v. Georgia*.[23] The court did not touch on the merits of the writ, that being the unsigned confession of Miller in the isolated police station, its involuntariness and any violation of his Miranda rights. The attorney general's office sought a review of the decision, but was denied.

The case was remanded to the Maryland Court of Appeals, *Miller v. Maryland*, pursuant to the Supreme Court's decision in *Bartholomew v. State*.[24] Then the court of appeals remanded the case to the circuit court of Allegany County, Maryland, for resentencing, where, in January 1973, Miller was sentenced to life imprisonment.[25]

My next step was a petition for a *Writ of Habeas Corpus* to the U.S. District Court of Maryland, asserting among other things, that Miller was being incarcerated unconstitutionally in that the confession used against him at the trial was not voluntary and therefore its admission into evidence violated his constitutional rights under the 5th, 6th, and 14th Amendments. The writ was summarily dismissed by the court for failure to exhaust state remedies under Maryland Rules of the Annotated Code of Maryland.

On February 19, 1975, a petition was filed for review in the Circuit Court of Allegany County under the Post Conviction Relief Act and on July 24, 1975, Miller was granted a hearing before a judge of the Circuit Court of Washington County, Maryland, with the hearing to be conducted in Allegany County.

For the first time Miller was having his day in court. However, it was short-lived and of no effect. The state witnesses regrouped and came on as strong as ever. In addition, the state had admitted into evidence, an unsigned statement (over objection) of a third prisoner who shared a cell with Miller which added credence to the other two convicts' hearing Miller tell of his killing the girl. That unsigned statement by a prisoner who did not appear and who was serving thirty years for kidnapping and robbery, was an example of the tactics the state employed. At the hearing, Miller denied making the statement while in the custody of the Somerset County sheriff.

On September 30, 1975, the petition for relief was denied and on October 29, an application for Leave to Appeal was filed with the Maryland Court of Appeals. This appeal was denied and in February 1976, a *Writ of Habeas Corpus* was again filed in the U.S. District Court of Maryland.

At the prior post conviction hearing, a professional stenographer testified she had typed Miller's unsigned confession and that it had taken one hour and thirty minutes as opposed to the county investigator's taking one hour and fifty-five minutes while at the same time proposing the questions to Miller.

Judge Joseph Young of the U.S. District Court of Maryland, in answer to the *Writ of Habeas Corpus*, acknowledged there was no indication the police investigators had made any attempt to explain in detail the meaning of the Miranda warning, however, he found that irrelevant since Miller steadfastly maintained he was never given the Miranda rights.

On July 28, 1976, the judge denied relief.

The case was then appealed to the Fourth U.S. Circuit Court of Appeals in Richmond, Virginia, on November 16, 1977, with my son, Paul, joining in.

Justices Butzner and Widener held in a one-page majority decision, affirmed by the U.S. District Court, that Miller's confession had been freely, knowingly, and voluntarily given. A strongly dissenting opinion was filed by Justice Lay: "As voluntarily as the confession may otherwise seem, however, there is nothing in the record which demonstrates that this 16-year-old boy made an effective and intelligent waiver of his right to counsel at the time of the police interrogation." Quoting U.S. Supreme Court case, *Gallegos v. Colorado*,[26] he further said, "The juvenile arrestee cannot be compared with an adult in full possession of his senses and knowledgeable of the consequences of his admission. A lawyer or an adult relative or friends could have given him the protection which his own immaturity could not. Adult advice would have put him on a less unequal footing with his interrogators." And further, Court says, it was incumbent upon the state to show that any waiver of those rights was fully understood and intelligently made. The courts must indulge in every reasonable presumption against waiver. The mere litany of formal questions and answers is not sufficient." He went on to say that Maryland law requires parents be notified when a child is apprehended.

"I basically abhor the proposition that an immature and emotionally disturbed youth can be interrogated in custodial surroundings without the presence of his parents or counsel. Law enforcement personnel know full well that incriminating statements may be more readily obtained from any accused if counsel is not present. Police know that once a confession is obtained, appointed counsel may thereafter serve only a perfunctory role." In an aside and footnote, he said: "I have heard at least one state attorney general argue before me that 'every law officer knows that you must engage in a little trickery to obtain a good confession.'" He closed by adding, "I would reverse, grant the *Writ of Habeas Corpus* pending a new trial by the State of Maryland."

Thus ended the saga of the Gary Lee Miller case for the Sullivans. My days of active practice were drawing to a close. The Burger court had been creating waves against principles of due process of law established by the Warren court. New faces appeared on the court: Chief Justice Burger, Rehnquist, Blackmun and Powell, and there was a calculated risk in another appeal to the U.S. Supreme Court in hope of reversing all prior appellate courts. Miller was by then twenty-seven years old and an established "lifer" with some hope of parole at the end of fifteen years.

Miller was sent to the House of Corrections at Jessups, Maryland, and while serving on a security detail in 1981 he escaped. He enjoyed seven months and sixteen days of freedom before being apprehended in a telephone booth in San Diego, California, making a call to Pennsylvania.

No public institution should be beyond study and examination. Justice is not a cloistered virtue; she must be allowed to suffer scrutiny and the respectful, even though outspoken, comments of ordinary men. The judiciary is not so frail it should be shielded from criticism or its weaknesses of the past not recounted.

The Gary Miller case was another example of injustice and lack of due process of law in the American criminal system. the state's prosecution abounded with heavy talent in the state's attorney and his assistant, two investigators, a Maryland and Pennsylvania sheriff, Pennsylvania and Maryland state police, while for the lonely defendant was an incompetent lawyer whose main aim was to cater to the whims of the judges and not the demands and protection of his client, the son of a poor Pennsylvania farmer. The grand jury report reached thousands as it was published in the local morning and evening newspapers prior to the trial. Young Miller was under psychiatric treatment since his release from prison due to his previous encounter with the law. A private psychiatrist was available to him at state expense, but this was overlooked by his attorney who rendered no objection to all documentary evidence adduced.

I was unconcerned when I took the case as to the guilt or innocence of the youngster. My prime interest was to seek a new trial and have Miller tried in the atmosphere of due process and fair play. Case No. 911, Criminal Trials of Allegany County, Maryland, will haunt forever the principals of the state officials who participated in this trial that can be truly titled, "trial by a kangaroo court." So runs the gamut of the system.

Part II

THE PRACTICE OF LAW

VII

Legal Education in America

"Whatever incidental purposes are cherished by particular law schools, the main end of legal education is to qualify students to engage in the professional practice of law."

A. Z. Reed[1]

"Education which is not modern shares the fate of all organic things which are kept too long."

A. N. Whitehead[2]

Today's Legal Training—A Cruel Hoax

It is a fact that a student can graduate from some law schools lin the United States without ever having written a simple deed, will, power of attorney, contract, or drawn a pleading. Some have never entered a court room to understand the workings of court procedure. After passing the state bar examination they become certified as competent to render advice and represent others in court. In effect, this creates a fraud upon the general public and further creates a cruel hoax.

There is still too much stress on the theoretical or academic and not enough on the day-to-day professional life. Law schools must come to grips with the learning of the economist, the statistician, the historian, the psychiatrist, the psychologist.

Do faculties present role models for future lawyers? Do they offer an image of a Clarence Darrow or an Edward Bennett Williams or a Lee Bailey? Do they bring practical experience into the classroom? Are law schools committing fraud on students when the teachers are congenital frauds? Do they lack the know-how?

The inept law professor may not have passed the bar, yet holds himself out as an expert. His view of legal education many times ignores the nuts and bolts of the trade.

"It's been held by many authorities that poring over excerpts from judges—appellate opinions and trial courts' mistakes and old English cases focusing not on the human aspects of the case but on the intellectual dissection of the logical issues therein is no real preparation for the dog-eat-dog competition of lawyering," said Dr. Barnard L. Diamond, who has served as psychiatrist at the University of California Law School. "Somehow in the preoccupation with legal logic the humanity of the participants is lost. Doctrinal analysis of faculty reasoning of judges' decisions has always severely restricted the range and scope of professional inquiry."

Legal Training in Colonial Days

To understand present day law education and practice, one must go back to the days of Colonial America. Not many people in the colonies brought legal training with them to the new world. Consequently, opportunities for legal instruction were scarce. Lawyers were not a chosen breed; they were looked on with suspicion and distrust; they were ridiculed and despised as scoundrels in many instances (as some are today). Northeast America did not welcome them where the Pilgrims settled. The ancient English prejudice against lawyers secured new strength in America; mistrust of them prevailed. Thomas Morton, the first Massachusetts attorney, was failed and expelled for his behavior. But however much an evil, in time lawyers became a necessity.

There were no law schools. Sons of many well-to-do southern plantation owners and New England mercantile businessmen went to London and the Inns of Court—these being nothing more than living and eating places yet—a part of the English legal culture where the Americans could absorb some ideas of English law. Before the Revolution, some 200 American law students had been at the Inns of Court, pursuing their legal studies at the Middle Temple while acquiring the polish travel confers. They read English law, became apprentices of the masters and returned home to the colonies as "professionals."

Other aspiring lawyers either learned the trade through self-study of the meagre collection of books they could get their hands on or by a combination of self-study and apprenticeship. This was a control device as well as a method of training since the apprentice frequently worked as a copyist or assistant in the office of the clerk of court. This system kept the bar small and under the control of the older lawyers. How much the apprentice learned depended much on his master. The apprentice's interest was subordinated to the interest of the master. He went through a haphazard course of drudgery and copywork. The system was an outrage upon common decency, horrid and base and infamous to the last degree. It was a type of servile labor, suitable for a slave. A few lawyers were honest and good teachers, however, and one such was George Wythe, whose students included Henry Clay and Thomas Jefferson.

The principal texts of learning were Blackstone's *Commentaries* and Coke on Littleton, both English products. Only the more affluent attorneys possessed libraries containing reports and texts, and each colony set its own standards for the bar. The legal profession was one road to wealth, social position and success in the 18th century, but the poor lawyer was out grubbing for action, soliciting wherever he might find business.

Legal apprenticeship was similar to that in the common trades. Trade apprenticeship placed primary emphasis on practical application rather than book study. A perfunctory recommendation to the bar by an established attorney was all that was needed to enter practice.

Legal Schooling in the Post Revolutionary Period

In *A History of the Inns of Court* W. R. Richardson writes:

> The post-revolution brought changes in all aspects of life including lawyering and legal education. Two types of law schools developed—proprietary or self-owned, and those affiliated with universities. They grew out of specialized law offices where teaching and apprenticeship was part of a lawyer's business. Law schools were a display of independence from England where legal education had not yet escaped its formal attachment to the Inns of Court and where apprentice ship was growing in importance.

The first university law school was established at William and Mary College in 1779 in Virginia by George Wythe. Its curriculum comprised an analysis of the three branches of the new government, and its purpose was to provide training for citizenship and public service, as well as the practice of law. Other law schools to follow were: King's College, now Columbia Law School, in New York in 1793; Harvard in 1817; Maryland in 1817; Virginia in 1826; Cincinnati, 1833; and Carlisle, 1836.

The dominant law school was Harvard when Chief Justice Isaac Parker, Chief Justice of Massachusetts, was selected to be its first professor of law.

The curriculum included lectures, examinations and moot courts. An ample law library gave support to this curriculum. In 1829 the course of study led to the formal awarding of law degrees.

Supreme Court Justice Joseph Story held reign as the law school dean. An author of note, he published eight treatises on American law between 1832 and 1843 and his writings had a great impact on law schools which were founded during and after his tenure at Harvard. The law school continued to have great influence throughout the country as its graduates spread out and became the leading professors of law at other law schools.

The earliest privately-owned law school was founded in 1784 by Judge Tapping Reeves at Litchfield, Connecticut. The lecture method, fashioned on Blackstone's *Commentaries*, attracted students from all over the United States. However, with university competition its popularity declined and it closed its doors in 1833. But the Litchfield school record was impressive; many of its estimated 1,015 students distinguished themselves in public office.

There were other proprietary law schools. Between 1810 and 1851 there were six unaffiliated law schools in Virginia alone. These schools freely experimented with various teaching methods. Most of the teachers were judges who combined practical experience with a part-time devotion to academics. As the 19th century progressed, the proprietary law schools declined in status and importance, and more university schools were founded.

But among all the lawyers practicing in the U.S., the overwhelming majority had to be trained in private law offices or educate themselves by a course of reading. Abe Lincoln wrote in a letter that "the cheapest and quickest and best way into the legal world was to read Blackstone's *Commentaries,* Gritty's pleadings, get a license, go to work, and keep on reading." But he added that lawyering was "more simple and less tiring than rail splitting."

The gap between the two methods of legal preparation, law school and clerkship, closed slowly. A law degree was not required for admission to the bar between 1850 and 1900. The rise of the prestige lawyers was linked to a social change in the character of the bar—from strongly aristocratic to middle class in family background. Law school growth and development in the period prior to 1870 was poor—qualitatively and quantitatively.

It has been stated that the period between 1850 and 1870 represents the dark ages of legal education in America. After the death of Story in 1845, Harvard adopted the textbook method which required constant reading, recitation and explanation. There were no further changes in method or curriculum at Harvard until 1870.

Lawyers themselves were reluctant to accept the idea of university training, according to Robert Stevens. "The public seemed to have grave doubts as to whether the lawyer's trade should even be distinguished as a craft."

There was was no respect for formal education or for educational prerequisites for admission to the bar; all male citizens, it would seem, had an inherent right to practice law. This stagnant period of training did not convey a connection between law and life. Within the lectures was a fundamental shallowness. It was in 1870 that a new system was to take over at Harvard and that was to have a tremendous effect on law preparation with the indoctrination of the case system.

The year 1870 was a milestone in legal learning, separating the past and present in legal education. The trend toward a liberal education as prerequisite to the study of law was underway.[3]

The Introduction of Langdellianism —the Case Study Method

A new system was inaugurated called the case method. The essence of this method was to eliminate text books, substituting the study of reports of actual cases carefully selected and arranged to illustrate the meaning and development of principles of law. The classroom tone was profoundly altered; there would be no lecturer expounding the law from prevailing texts. The teacher had been a Socratic guide leading the student to an understanding of concepts and principles hidden as essences among the cases. The teacher showed how those concepts unfolded, like a rose from its bud, through a time series of enlightened cases.

The new method was to be a science that had to be studied scientifically—that is, inductively through primary sources. These sources were the printed cases. They expressed, in manifold dress, the few ever-present and ever-evolving principles which constituted the genius of the common law.

Until the 1870s there had been no uniformity in the curriculum of a law school. There were no modern universities in America—only colleges where Greek, Latin, moral philosophy and mathematics were taught through lectures and recitations. Harvard University, under Charles Eliot, a scientist who was appointed president in 1869, set out to conquer new worlds. He believed in an aristocracy of talent and declared open season on all subjects, claiming virtually everything as suitable for university study.

To head the Harvard Law School, an adjunct of the university, Eliot chose Christopher Columbus Langdell as dean in 1870. Langdell, a law grad in 1853 with an L.L.B, had practiced law in New York for sixteen years but seldom tried any cases. He hated the courthouse atmosphere and spent most of his working hours preparing briefs for other lawyers. He had an obsession for books and sought the living fonts of knowledge of law in libraries. Attorney-client relationship, persuasion of juries and judges—these meant little to him. To this cloistered, bookish man, law school came to mean library law.

The fundamental tenet of his system was that all available materials are contained in books. The printed opinions of judges, he believed, were the exclusive repository of wisdom which law students must acquire to make them lawyers. He blindfolded himself to the realities of practice in the belief that what was needed to teach was not practice but experiences in learning law. Legal doctrine and skill of legal analysis was, for him, the total of one's preparation for law practice.

He published a book, *A Selection of Cases on Law of Contracts*, in which he noted:

> Law considered as a science consists of certain principles of doctrine. To have such a mastery of these as to be able to apply them with constant facility and certainty to the ever tangled skein of human affairs is what constitutes a true lawyer. And hence to acquire the mastery should be the business of every earnest student of law.

The case method was carried to other law schools, either by members of the Harvard law faculty or by men trained there. By 1900 it was being followed in several leading institutions and case books had been prepared for classroom use in practically every division of civil, criminal and constitutional law and procedure. The system was employed as if ordained by some hierarchical judge— absolute in form and not subject to change. The system became the almost exclusive tool of American legal educators. Langdellian logic held that the law student must learn to think like a lawyer as method provides.

The ABA was an early critic of the case system. However, after pondering it for some time and forming a committee on legal education and admission to the bar, and realizing that the new system contributed to this elite club, the ABA eliminated its expression of all serious doubt concerning its effectiveness. Instead, the ABA called for the establishment of an organization of reputable law schools.

Organization of the Association of American Law Schools (AALS)

Thus, in 1900, came into being the Association of American Law Schools (AALS). The purpose of the ABA and the AALS was to tighten the requirements for admission to law school, improve pre-law requirements and to establish a set length of period of law school education. Movements continued to do away with part-time law schools which were designed for the poor immigrant, among whom were the Jews, Irish and other Europeans.

Before 1917 no state required law school graduation or attendance to be admitted to the bar, despite the efforts of the ABA and the AALS. However, progress was being made. A majority of states did require a period of either law school or apprenticeship before a student could qualify to enter the legal profession. Through 1920 the AALS continued to oppose part-time legal education, fighting to establish fulltime university law schools as the exclusive portal to the legal profession. In 1921, the ABA, joining with the AALS to improve law schools, set forth the following recommendations: law school a must to be legally educated, two years pre-law, three years fulltime, four years for night school, fulltime professors, no diploma privilege to enter practice, and the ABA to be given power to accredit law schools.

The ABA did little or nothing to assist women to enter law schools. The first woman to graduate from a law school was Ada Kepley, who graduated from what is now Northwestern University. Her degree was of questionable value because states were permitted to refuse women a license to practice even after they had passed local bar association requirements.

The ABA reached out its tentacles to the respective state courts and legislatures that control bar admissions through its lobbying efforts; state bar associations were formed in all states along the same lines of professional responsibility as ordained by the ABA. Both the ABA and the AALS insured that Langdell's method of teaching was firmly established and uniformly administered across the country. However, dissatisfactions arose from time to time. Some schools were considering what should be the next step in advance of the case method; a large proportion of law schools had not yet discovered what it was devised to accomplish or how it should be used. Experience was showing that by the third year of law school students became so restless that a different approach to school was essential.

The Case System Meets Its Critics

Albert Harno, former dean of the University of Chicago, pointed to the growing conviction that "the case method tended to produce lawyers who are too narrowly prepared for the heavy responsibilities which today are laid upon them. It generally fails to give students sufficient perspective for viewing the place and function of law in the social structure. A legal system must be ever changing if it is to adapt itself to the evolving social scene. Thus conceived, the law is a form of social and economic expression.

The late Edward S. Robinson, Yale University professor of psychology and law lecturer, held that "opinions of judges of higher courts, which students study so carefully, are of great importance but they rarely give an adequate factual picture of the primary dispute or the psychological and social forces that give rise to that dispute. It is necessary to go behind the utterances of the judge to the psychological, sociological and economical details of the case at bar."[4]

Karl Llewellyn, noted professor of Columbia University Law School, attacked Harvard as being "blind, inept, factory ridden, wasteful, defective and empty."[5] He asserted that "Doctrinal analysis of appellate decisions has always severely restricted the range and scope of professional inquiry. The general knowledge acquired in law school," he said, "is only part of the knowledge required for competition to under take an assignment in a defined area of practice."

Among the more avid and constructive critics of the case system as far back as 1933 was Jerome Frank, a respected lawyer, judge of the First Circuit Court of Appeals, and a former member of the Securities and Exchange Commission. He articulated his complaint in a thorough and forceful manner. It was the most remarkable essay of fifty years of lawyering. "The lawyer-client relation, the numerous non-rational factors involved in a trial, the face-to-face appeals to the emotions of juries, the elements of what is loosely known as the atmosphere of a case—everything that is undisclosed in upper court opinions was virtually unknown (and was, therefore, quite meaningless) to Langdell. Many of the realities of the life of the average lawyer were unreal to him. The actual varied experiences of the practicing lawyer were, to Langdell, improper material for the teacher and student."

The neurotic, escapist character of Langdell soon stamped itself on the educational programs of our leading law schools. Unavoidably, their acceptance of the Langdell-Harvard method meant that most of the university law school teachers were men who had never practiced or practiced briefly. In the case system students are supposed to study cases. They do not. They study almost exclusively upper court opinions. Any such opinion is not a case, but a small fraction of a case—its tail end.[6]

The case method is primarily a doctrinal exercise placing undue emphasis on the appellate level. The appellate judge's role is generally confined to review of questions of law and not of fact. The law teacher's focus is on the analysis of law. It is not concerned as a general rule with the correctness of the factfinder's determinations or the problems involved in arriving at the fact. The law teacher is not normally a practitioner in any real sense, nor does he provide a role model for his students. Many have little or no experience at the bar and many have not passed the bar examination; they deal with the subjects abstractly. The case method provides little occasion for any emphasis on counseling skills, is totally litigation oriented and it fails to give direct experience in what so much law is about: resolving problems in the context of a real-life client. The next link is that to modern days.[7]

Legal Education in Recent Years

Despite pleas for over thirty-five years from noted lawyers, judges, and faculties, the ABA and the AALS stood firm with the case system as the standard curricula for law study. Judge Frank spoke convincingly of a need for change or a supplement. As he journeyed about in his lecture tours to the leading law schools including Harvard, Yale and Columbia, he learned that few law students ever entered a courtroom or attended a trial. They received nothing but Langdell. Yet it remained for a later generation of legal educators and crusaders to take Jerome Frank seriously by putting his words into practice.

Deans of law schools opposed any change. Tired old faculties opposed change because they were too entrenched with case law and not capable of teaching anything else. Large classes could be taught without much expense to the school and little effort by the teacher. Above all, most faculties were unfamiliar with the practical aspects of lawyering. Some never passed the bar. Some loved the Socratic dialogue which gave them the opportunity to embarrass the student with senseless questions.

The Introduction of Clinical Studies

Once again it was the AALS in front, again pacing the ABA, which in turn was the pacemaker for state bars and legislatures. The AALS developed the Council on Education for Professional Responsibility and obtained $950,000 from the Ford Foundation to sponsor experimental clinical work. The Ford Foundation announced the establishment of the Independent Council on Legal Education for Professional Responsibility (CLEPR) to be funded by a grant of $6,000,000 during the first five years of its ten years of life. The grant encouraged all types of law schools to experiment with a limited form of clinical studies. Within a few years almost one-half of all law schools had some form of clinical study programs. There arose a new breed of law faculty members, the clinical professor.

Vital in this new crusade was the possibility of credit for clinical studies. With the advent of clinical study there was increasing hostility on the part of the more sophisticated academics toward the less sophisticated clinical approaches. The 1970s were to prove a testing time for clinical legal study.[8]

It had taken many years for law schools to respond to the pleas of Judge Jerome Frank and others for clinical study. Not until 1968 was clinical study accepted by many of the law schools.

Judge Frank sought a unified approach to teaching students what courts and lawyers do, as well as what their clients' needs might be. This methodology raised questions as to whether Langdellianism and the case method were valid means of legal training.

The high cost of clinical programs was provided by the Ford Foundation and CLEPR funding, so that by the 1970s half the nation's law schools had at least one clinical program. As an incentive, some schools rewarded participation with graduation credit. Today, all ABA-approved law schools have some clinical programs.

The fruitful bearing of clinical programs and their acceptance by students notwithstanding, they have been received reluctantly and without enthusiasm by law school faculties and administrators because they are expensive and create administrative problems. Administrators contend that with the case method they can reach hundreds of students at once and less expensively, using the case book, horne book and the library. Only a small group can be reached at one time in clinical projects, they say, and the principal funding agency has exhausted its contributory funds. Also, the student is prevented from accepting outside employment because of the clinical work, they argue. Other problems exist concerning divergent faculty salaries and the adverse interest of factions on the faculties, including clinic providers, clinic educators, regular full-time faculty, writing faculty and advocating faculty.

On the positive side, clinics expose students to the realities of law practice. They allow students to adapt the legal principles developed in the classroom to the specific facts of a case. Rules of procedure are illustrated within the context of a particular case. Clinics present the law school communities with contemporary research issues and opportunities for law reform. They attempt to teach students to deal professionally with clients, other lawyers, nonlawyers, co-workers and courts, legislatures and administrative personnel.

Outreach clinical programs attempt to expose students to the rigors of practice. Problems in ethics arise every day. Communicative writing skills are stressed; students are required to rewrite documents based on the criticism of experienced practitioners. Some clinics teach systems of analysis to help students cope with the bore of law office routine. Teaching students to evaluate and use the research and administrative technology of the 21st century is being done.

Clinics have gone a long way in preparation for lawyering; however, are law school clinics enough? The dominant forces of our law school system, the ABA and the AALS, must move forward with added plans to prepare students for practice.

The Problems of Law School Admissions

As a pre-law student, one may be overzealous in his desire to become a lawyer for questionable reasons—because his father is a lawyer or he's always admired Perry Mason, because he wants to make a lot of money, or because he couldn't make it at medical school and thinks law school is the next best. He might be thinking that law school leads to lawyering, and lawyering is a channel to politics. Who knows, he might become governor!

Desire is one thing, getting into law school is another. Never before have admission requirements been more difficult. Prior to the 1950s, almost everyone who applied and had proper minimum credentials was admitted. At the top was money. Getting in is no longer that easy, and the root of the problem is the Law School Admission Test (LSAT). The LSAT is said to measure power of analysis, recognition of the crucial point in a mass of facts, ability to memorize quickly and the ability to assimilate what has been learned. Alertness, verbal facility and the possession of a large vocabulary are also important.

Law school enrollment since the early 1960s has jumped almost threefold. This is partly due to the influx of women and minorities seeking admission. Approximately 80,000 students apply each year; about 35,000 are admitted.

In 1948, for many reasons, a new system of admission to law school was formulated—namely, the requirement of taking the LSAT and weighty consideration of the Grade Point Average (GPA). Not all schools complied or took part, but the ABA strongly urged many to participate and a strict law school accreditation took place. Some say the law deans strove for uniformity in admission; others say the giant monopolistic ABA lobbied in the state legislatures and courts to compel compliance. Many World War II vets had come home braced for more education and law school presented them the hope of a career in politics and political office—a chance to change the nation and the world.

The College Entrance Board, with its testing services, took over for the interested law schools. The admission heads became more concerned with the type of students applying and how well they scored the first year in examinations, rather than what kind of lawyers they might be. The emphasis then and now is on being a good tester. The test of lawyering was out and that is the way things went.

In 1978 the newly-formed nonprofit corporation, the Law School Admission Council (LSAC), took over and joined forces with the law schools, the ABA and the AALS. It began working with the Educational Testing Services for all tests. In 1982, the LSAC in association with another nonprofit corporation, the Law School Admission Service (LSAS), took charge of facilitating and enhancing the law school admission process and providing services to legal education and the legal profession to do their own testing. All ABA-accredited law schools and AALS members comprise the voting membership of the council.

The Law School Data Assembly Service (LSDAS) was created to organize, analyze and summarize biographic and academic information for law school applicants. By providing law schools with standardized summaries of an applicant's academic work, copies of college transcripts and LSAT scores, the LSDAS minimizes the routine aspects of the admission process. The reports are not considered substitutes for reasoned judgment of administrative officers, however. The LSAS receives an applicant's college transcripts from school registrars pursuant to the applicant's request, then coverts the transcript information to a uniform format to make it compatible with various college grading systems. It produces a year-by-year, college-by-college, summary of an undergraduate's record by converting the grades, if possible, to a standard 4.0 system and the credits into semester hours. The LSAS then calculates a GPA for each year and a cumulative GPA for all years at the college that issued the transcript. The LSDAS summarizes in uniform fashion the undergraduate records of law school applicants, converting grade notations and systems to the 4.0 system.

Candidates must ask every institution listed on their LSAT/LSDAS Regulation Form to send LSAS an official transcript. Graduate school transcripts are not summarized unless such work contributed to the undergraduate degree. A course will be excluded from the LSDAS summary only if it is classified as physical education, practical art, practical music, or if it is assigned no measure of credit by the granting institution regardless of the grades. Grades implying a failure, such as "no credit," "not passing," "incomplete/fail," "withdrew/fail" are treated as failure and given a value of zero on the 4.0 scale.

Schools that use pass/fail, honors/pass, etc., are not converted to the 4.0 scale but credits for the work are totaled on the LSDAS summary in an "Unconverted Credit Hours" area. The score scale of the LSAT had been 200-800 since 1948, then in June 1982, a new scoring system was established: 10-50. The revised system consists of seven sections, including six 35-minute multiple- choice sections and one 30-minute essay section. The change to a percentile 10- 50 was to achieve a greater level of precision. In June 1983 it became 10-48 and since June 1984, photos must accompany applications.

Recommendations from former college professors or people of substance can enhance chances for admission, but astute candidates stay away from influential politicians if they want to play it square, although the right one can substantially improve their admission chances. Some admission committees consider the diversity aspect and admit women and minorities in keeping with affirmative action, as potential lawyers for the poor. Women students have increased from 4 percent in 1963 to 37 percent in 1984. Race is taken into account beyond the consideration of LSAT and GPA in many instances. Some schools make room for a minority member in preference to a top-quality applicant. Some schools give special consideration to applicants who show evidence of overcoming significant disadvantages. Fair or foul, that is the way it goes. Honest law school admission committees should judge on the basis of the whole person.

Disabled persons cannot be discriminated against. Special consideration is given under the new test rules of 1983 for the handicapped. Under certain conditions a reader may be employed to assist a test taker. LSAC/AALS recommend that a member law school consider each handicapped applicant's individual needs and abilities when deciding whether to require the LSAT. Many will waive it. This is a good sign of fairness.

Interviews with prospective students are out—too time consuming. That is unfortunate because there is nothing like sizing up a person by personality and character traits—two of the most important assets in lawyering.

Paying for it all is another matter. Unless students have funds available, they must seek a scholarship, loans or work. All are available and in most instances, go to the needy. Law school is really for the wealthy or those willing to put themselves in debt for many years.

VIII

The Ethical Challenges of Lawyering

To treat a bar certificate of admission to practice law as a passport to try any and every kind of case in any court makes no more sense than to say a medical school degree qualifies the holder to perform any kind of surgery.
Warren Burger, Chief Justice U.S. Supreme Court, Retired

Truth in Lawyering

Law practice is complicated, ultrahazardous, difficult, and intellectually demanding. No one can be either too honest, too truthful, or too upright to be a thoroughly good lawyer and an eminently successful one.

"A lawyer is not an officer of the court," said the late U.S Supreme Court Justice Hugo Black. "Contrary to the bar men, he is engaged in a private profession. He makes his own decisions, follows his best judgment, collects his own fees, and runs his own business."[1]

In *Lawyer's Ethics* we read: "Advocacy is not a skill simply learned and applied. It is an art and its mastery can only be learned by those who possess talent. The talent must be learned from the techniques of those who have mastered advocacy in the past and by diligent practice of those techniques.[2]

"The training is long and arduous. In achieving effective advocacy, there is simply no substitute for careful preparation. Thorough pretrial preparation can hardly be overemphasized; it comprises only about half of the foundation underlying masterful advocacy. The remaining groundwork consists of establishing a good rapport with the judge and jury, being able to think on one's feet, and possessing a basic understanding of human nature. Good trial lawyers must be able to communicate on the level of the person on the street.[3]

"The advocate in the courtroom is not engaged much more than half the time—and then only coincidentally—in the search for truth. The advocate's prime loyalty is to the client, not to truth, as such. Many rules and devices of adversary litigation, as we conduct it, are not geared for, but are often aptly suited to defeat the development of truth. . . . There is no duty to the truth or duty to the community in the adversary system. In cross-examination you try to destroy a witness who you know is telling the truth. You put a witness on the stand when you know he will commit perjury.[4]

"The struggle to win, with its powerful pressures to subordinate the love of truth, is often incidentally or coincidentally (if at all) a service to the public interests."[5]

"The American system puts a premium on skill, adroitness, even trickery, on both sides."[6]

"The lawyer's professional obligation may well be to advise the client to withhold the truth, to keep silent. Any lawyer worth his salt will tell the suspect in no uncertain terms to make no statement to police under any circumstances."[7]

Justice Harlan noted, "The lawyer in fulfilling his professional responsibilities of necessity may become an obstacle in truth-telling."[8]

The Divisions or Strata of Lawyering

The legal profession is roughly divided into two main levels or strata with subdivisions in each. At the top level is the large elite corporate law firm which handles the work of the large corporations, such as railroads, utilities,industries, banks, and insurance companies. They are the high priests, rich in their own right. Their members are usually graduates of the correct law schools and have family ties to place them in lofty positions. They are the big boys of the profession—fashionably dressed, driving the Caddies and Mercedes and wearing the white hats. They help select the legislators and judges and, in turn, receive appointments to the dignified positions: serving on bar exam committees and grievance committees, as municipal attorneys, and in other offices which carry influence. Their only concern is the welfare of their rich clients. Community service is out. Their vacations are taken at bar association gatherings and on junkets with corporate heads and judges.

Subdivisions of the top level are the specialists who deal in tax, zoning, personal injury, insurance defense, unions and estate work. Their plush, push-button offices attract the affluent. They accept referrals and are known to split fees. They have ambulance chasers running in all directions and employ part- and full-time solicitors disguised as investigators. They are the experts of the trade and many get their start at the lower level.

The lower level or strata, with its various subdivisions and types, consists of the smaller law firms and solo practitioners who generalize in practice.

Among them you'll find the timid who cannot tolerate the courtroom—trying cases is not their cup of tea. There are the nine-to-fivers with a day off midweek for golf and card-playing and, on occasion, are known to tip the bottle for midday relaxation. Too, there are the hard workers who came up through the ranks and don't mind working weekends and late nights.

And there are the courageous few who take on all comers, including the poor, the criminals, and the questionable divorces. This type of lawyer stays away from bar association functions, works long hours, and carries his own lunch; luncheon dates with bar cronies are a waste of time. And also there is the know-it-all kind who claim expertise in all fields, but, in many instances, will shirk the courtroom and rush settlements. Among this group are former insurance adjusters.

Many of the lower levelers have to wash the dirty linen of the trade, such as divorce and criminal cases, and are victims of bar association grievance committees.

When you find an upper leveler making an appearance in the court and huddling in court chambers before trial, you know the fix is on. They use the telephone extensively to reach a judge prior to the official case proceedings. Winning cases on the merits is most difficult for them, so they use the other more effective indirect methods.

The Lawyers' Fees

One aspect of the business of lawyering that has brought the three "Ds"—Disrepute, Disrespect, and Discredit—to the profession, is the assessment of charges or fees for representation. Fee disputes are a major source of complaint by clients to bar associations and disciplinary agencies. How fees are assessed is a mystery to the layman who, on occasion, has hard times raising money.

The 675,000-plus lawyers—up 153,000 in five years in America—have a monopoly on legal services and a hold over every citizen, particularly those in the middle-income bracket. Roughly six percent serve the needs of the nation's poorest, while many citizens are priced out of the market. Because the U.S. Supreme Court ruled in the *Goldfarb* case that bar associations cannot set minimum fees, lawyers have gone hog-wild in gouging the ordinary person. In many jurisdictions, $750 to $2,000 is a minimum for an uncontested divorce and is higher for defending a drunk-driving case that is a sure loser. Ridiculous! Young lawyers today think nothing of charging $100 to $150 for an hour's interview, and as they get older and smarter, the tab goes up.

Rule 1.5 of the ABA Model Rules of Professional Conduct passed in August 1983 provides that "a lawyer's fee shall be reasonable." Incidentals to be considered are: "time, labor, novelty, difficulty, results obtained, conventional charges of the block, experience, reputation, and ability."[9]

A fee may be contingent on the outcome of the matter for which services are rendered, such as personal injury cases, social security, and collections. Exceptions are made in domestic cases (divorce, alimony, and property settlement) and criminal cases in which contingent fees are not allowed.

The domestic case is one where a contingency should apply. The wisdom of these prohibitions continues to be a subject for debate. Consider the wife of many years whose husband meets a young gal and wants an immediate divorce. For the wife to get her share of the family bankroll and property, she must have a lawyer. The court normally will award her attorney a sum, but one that is hardly adequate. Frequently the breadwinner husband retains a top-quality attorney so he can obtain more than his fair share. What is wrong morally or legally if a lawyer takes the case on a win/lose basis? Nothing. But the bar association says, no, it cannot be done.

Or take the situation of the accused in a criminal case who has a chance at winning but cannot pay a big fee. He must settle for legal aid which, in many instances, provides second-rate lawyers. The client knows that and doesn't want a public defender, but he has no alternative. What is wrong with a contingent fee if you hit the win column? It's unethical, says the bar association's model rules of conduct.

Counseling and Coaching

No aspect of lawyering can bring more success or abject failure for a client than counseling and coaching. Experience in human affairs and knowledge of the subject are prerequisites. Otherwise, it is the blind leading the blind. The accident victim visiting the young lawyer may become a further victim—one of poor counsel. The signing of a contract, the purchase of a business, the settlement of domestic affairs, the handling of a personal injury case—all require sound judgment.

Advocacy is largely the practice of reconciliation. Most litigation turns out to be appropriate conciliation. Ninety percent of lawsuits are settled. More than two-thirds of criminal cases are resolved by plea bargaining. Most disputes between citizens never even reach the stage where lawyers go into court.[10]

Lincoln's advice given over 100 years ago is still true: "Discourage litigation; persuade your neighbors to compromise in civil cases whenever you can. Point out to them how the nominal winner is often a real loser—in fees, expenses, and waste of time. As a peacemaker, a lawyer has a superior opportunity of being a good man."

Monroe H. Freedman wrote: "No lawyer dreams of calling his client and witness to the witness stand who has not been previously interviewed and counseled." Coaching is a better word. "The lawyer must elicit all relevant facts to help the witness marshall and to express his or her testimony as persuasively as possible. The poorly educated laborer who has suffered an injury and who can only say, "It hurts bad," must be helped to articulate what the pain is like, when it is present, and how it interferes with work, sleep, family life, and recreation. The witness must be sufficiently rehearsed and counseled to assure that no important evidence is overlooked in testimony at trial where leading questions will not be permitted."[11]

"An untrained and perhaps inarticulate person," said Freedman, "cannot be expected to relate all that is relevant without a substantial amount of direction. That is why one of the most important functions of the lawyer is to provide an awareness of what legally is relevant. What prompting can do is to trigger recognition, which is a less complex process than remembering."[12]

Said Freedman, "The lawyer who helps the client to save a losing case by contributing a crucial fact is acting from a personal sense of justice."[13]

"Valuation of a case," wrote Henry H. Miller, "generally flows from our projections of what a given jury will do and what a given court will permit under the circumstances of a case. Valuation is difficult for even the seasoned and prudent advocate. The most frequent sin of the young lawyer is over-evaluating the case because of misguided zeal. A ridiculous demand freezes all efforts of settlement. The most important component which constitutes value is the nature of the liability. When liability is good, we give it full value; we seek a premium if there's punitive liability. If liability is questionable, we take a discount; if weak, we accept an offer. Another important factor is who are the attorneys for each side. Many cases are settled because the insurance company does not want to come to grips with the specialist.[14]

Miller warns: "Coaching can be risky business; liability can attach perjury. Malpractice suits against attorneys are common these days. Communication between all interested parties is most important. The client has the last word; make no final move without his acquiescence. The attorney who breaches his fiduciary duty to the client can be held liable for a healthy sum. The attorney has a duty to exercise his knowledge, skill and ability. . .

A malpractice action is generally viewed as a negligence action and possibly one in contract."[15]

The Division of Fees

Another aspect of contingent fees is that of a "finder fee" or the division of fees in personal injury (PI) cases. It is a division of a fee in a single billing to a client covering the fee of two or more lawyers, who may not be in the same firm. And it can involve a non-lawyer. The latter is frowned on by the bar associations and grievance committees. The prohibition of sharing of fees is contrary to custom and the realities of practice. Why not allow attorneys to strike their own bargains as to the sharing of fees? Isn't the practice of law partly business and partly service? What other business inhibits the sharing of fees or commissions? It is unethical because the bar associations say it is unethical unless it meets certain criteria as set down in the model code. This is another example of how the bar associations unfairly control the practice of law. What difference does it make who shares in a fee as long as the client is satisfied? Why does the law specialist instruct at seminars? For the referral of cases and the splitting of fees.

The genesis of such referral or finder's fees in America may well be traced to the practice of countryside solicitors in England who, when faced with litigation, would associate with London solicitors as agents.

A poll responded to by lawyers from thirty-five states indicates that a forwarding fee of one-third is not considered unprofessional in sixteen states and that it is common practice in nineteen states.

There must be a sense of loyalty and trust when referrals take place. Jim was a 20-year-old college junior—a fine, healthy, young man, a good student and a better baseballer. He played for my semi-pro team and was a pro prospect. In April 1964, while a member of his college varsity baseball team enroute to Virginia in a station wagon driven by the coach, Jim was seriously injured in a head-on collision. His neck was broken and for three months he was confined to a hospital bed, in traction and unable to move. For the next twelve months he was a patient at the Rusk Institute in New York, a rehabilitation center. When he was released, he was permanently crippled, unable to walk without assistance.

In the interim, we filed suit against the reckless and intoxicated driver who had caused this tragedy. The insurer made little effort to settle—waiting for the young man to die. I joined a specialist in PI work from New York who got things moving in the right direction. But there were no settlement offers until the opposing attorneys met one day for lunch. Then, a substantial offer was made and a settlement was reached. The total fee was 25 percent of the gross; our agreed-on split was 50/50. The high settlement figure was due to the reputable specialist and the place of trial—New York is noted for large verdicts and settlements.

Then there was the opposite experience. An infant was seriously and permanently injured (October 6, 1975) when he stepped on a live electric wire lying on a much-used pathway. His injuries required amputation of an arm and included permanent searing of his hair and permanent damage to his hearing and bone structure. His case was referred to me by a friend and part-time investigator, known as a runner. I referred the case to a confidante, a PI specialist to whom I had in times past referred so-called "big cases." He was an expert in the field of negligence law, and the author of a book, *How to Prove Damages in Personal Injury and Wrongful Death Cases.* For the sake of the story we'll call him "The Duke."

Prior to this, The Duke and I had settled cases that brought hundreds of thousands of dollars for our clients and the fee was share and share alike. However, this case took a different turn. In a multi-thousand dollar case that meant a sizeable fee, he managed to cut me out. After two years of wrangling and threatening suit, I settled for a mere pittance. It was a costly lesson: Trust no one, even a friend.

The Need for Specialization and Certification

The move is on for specialization in law as there is in medicine, with lawyers confining their practice partially or wholly to a particular area of law, such as labor, tax, divorce, personal injury, or procedural, trial practice. Certification attests to a lawyer's competency, either generally or with respect to a specialized area, although it may simply vouch that an attorney has completed a required continuing law education couse and passed a test.

The movement springs in part from the fact that consumer groups, leading jurists, and the unrepresented middle class have begun to voice criticism of the quality and cost of legal services.[16] Specialization can assure clients that the lawyers who serve them have been trained and approved for the task. That training can lead to greater efficiency, which in turn can result in cost savings passed on to clients.

Objections have been levied against specialization by lawyers. Some fear enforced state sanctions or that general practice will be destroyed by specialists taking business away from the general practitioner. There's the fear of splinter groups forming and splitting the profession. There's fear that recognition of specialists will encourage unauthorized practice and the fear that the giant ABA is not the proper body to establish the basis for recognition and control of specialists.

Solicitation Problems

Another aspect of lawyering akin to the contingent fee is that of client solicitation or so-called "ambulance chasing," frowned on by the ABA and the state bar associations as unethical, with offenders subject to disciplinary action. Solicitation is the practice of attorneys employing laymen to procure personal injury cases for a fee or percentage. In large cities successful PI lawyers rely on highly organized methods of solicitation. These lawyers have contracts with the police, doctors, interns, nurses, cab drivers, garage mechanics, and used car dealers, who locate potentially rewarding cases. Some hospitals are even known to be controlled by certain chasers. The best organized of the chasers have automobiles patroling hospitals and using two-way radios to be informed of the admission of accident cases. At the right time and at the request of the doctor, the chaser arrives at the patient's bedside to sign him up. The personal injury case is the life blood of such specialists.

One criticism of ambulance chasing is that it stirs up litigation. And whom does that hurt? The wealthy insurance companies that are supported by bar associations and the judiciary!

Adversaries of the Sole Practitioner: The Insurance Companies

Insurance companies are typical bureaucracies—employing orderly, conventional, middle-class folk. The adjuster's job requires him to take a suspicious view of claims and of claimants, but adjusters are notoriously devious, and highly likely to interpret to their benefit the plethora of rules, regulations, and contractual provisions which govern them. As in any business, they want to maximize the amount of money in their pocket and minimize the amount of money in yours.

Take the case of Ernest Gunn, age 5, seriously injured by an insured motorist. Shortly after the accident, the insured's adjuster visited the boy's mother at home and told her there was no need to retain an attorney because the company would make a settlement as soon as the boy was out of his doctor's care. If Mrs. Gunn was not satisfied at that time, he advised, she could retain an attorney and file suit. The boy's injuries were sufficiently severe to require a doctor's care for twenty-three months. At the end of that time Mrs. Gunn made repeated efforts to reach the insurance company adjuster, but without success. She then retained a lawyer, who promptly filed suit for her. Mrs. Gunn's boy never did have his day in court, however, because the insurance company attorneys successfully pleaded a two-year statute of limitations.

One can cite many cases where adjusters have taken flagrant advantage of hapless accident victims, getting them to sign releases for a relative pittance.

And then there is the typical case in which the injured layman tries to settle his own case. The Smith car was hit from behind at an intersection, an almost absolute liability case. Smith and his wife were badly shaken but aside from a few bruises and Mrs. Smith's stiff neck, they appeared to be all right. Next evening an insurance adjuster appeared and in the Smiths' excitement and lack of thought, they accepted a small sum and executed a release. Three weeks later Mrs. Smith entered a hospital. A doctor diagnosed her condition as severe back sprain, commonly called whiplash. Mr. Smith lost time from work while his wife was in the hospital. He rode a bus and took a taxi while his car was in for repairs. Hospital bills mounted. But by signing the release, the Smiths were deprived of further financial relief.[17]

In November 1974, Earl and Leona Light, husband and wife, wearily walked into my office; both were in deep pain. Earlier that year they had lost the treasure of their life, their young adopted son and only child, Clifton, 13. He had drowned at the local YMCA swimming pool. No one was at the pool at the time and he was not discovered until hours later. After the funeral no YMCA official or its insurer bothered to talk to the parents and later the insurance company denied any liability.

Once the case reached my office, overtures of settlement began. The best offer was $5,000 for funeral expenses and a few incidentals. Investigation revealed the YMCA had been negligent. The insurer remained true to form, saying, "You'll have to sue us." It was a long, drawn out skirmish and docket entries in the case began to add up. I arranged for an associate specialist, The Duke. Under the state law, the YMCA, being a charitable institution, had to carry only a certain amount of insurance, and that was the amount for which they could be held liable. The case was settled after three years for many times the offer but it was a mere pittance in the eyes of the parents since the case had put them through much strain and anguish and caused permanent damage.[18]

Hazardous Practice: Divorce Cases

Divorce, where perjury generally flourishes, can mean hazardous practice. Law firms consider it dirty linen and shy away from it. But young Blackstones learn to crawl in the practice by taking on divorces. No smart lawyer will attempt reconciliation—give them what they want: a divorce.

Every lawyer is accustomed to tears—from husband as well as wife—when a marriage is falling apart. Probably no lawyer ever becomes so hardened to the emotional strain of divorce that he doesn't suffer along with his client. In the successful PI case, the lawyer is elated along with his client; when an innocent man is acquitted in a criminal trial, the lawyer is overjoyed. Not so in the divorce case with children standing by in tears.

Why shouldn't obtaining a divorce be as cheap as obtaining a marriage license? It's the politicians, many of whom are lawyers, who preach against streamlining divorce as though it were a viral strain of communism attacking the very health of the nation. In 1969 the State of California eliminated fault divorce and replaced it with "irreconcilable differences" as grounds, as defined by the couple and not by the lawyer. Alimony is called spousal support and is geared to economic purposes, rather than sin.

The Need for Loyalty to Clients

A central legal tenet of lawyering is the inviolability of lawyer-client confidence. That principle, like the fifth amendment privilege, guarantees the accused a fair trial. It blocks the emergence of information and like the relationship between priest and parishoner or doctor and patient, borders on sacredness. Lawyer-client privacy, the profession holds, must be inviolable. Freedom from the strict bonds of truth and the law are the chief assets of the profession. In advocacy cases, the lawyer is faced with the dilemma of either betraying the client or participating, to some degree, in deliberate deception of the court. It is believed that legal procedure must serve individual welfare at the cost of truth and, too often, of public safety as well.

Take a much discussed case that happened in New York state in July 1973. Two girls had disappeared at different times. Susan was 21, Alicia, 16. Susan's 22- year-old camping companion, Daniel, was found murdered, but there was no trace of either girl. Several months later, Susan's father, hearing that a man had been arrested and charged with murdering an 18-year-old boy in the same mountainous region, flew to New York to talk with the accused's lawyers. The lawyers gave him no information concerning his daughter. Alicia's parents, meanwhile, thinking her a runaway, continued to advertise in newspapers, begging her to come home.

Neither girl could come home. Both girls were dead, a fact that the lawyers had known when Susan's father asked their help and during the time Alicia's parents had been publicizing their pleas. In fact, the lawyers themselves had seen and photographed the mutilated bodies of the girls where they lay—one at the bottom of a well, one in the wooded brush of a cemetery. They had been directed to these locations by the girls' killer: their client.

The lawyers did not tell the victims' parents what they knew; neither did they tell the police. For six months the lawyers kept silent. Nor was it they who finally talked. Instead, their client blurted the truth from the witness stand during his trial for murdering the 18-year-old boy. Had the murderer himself not spoken, his further crimes might have remained hidden forever.[19]

What kept the lawyers silent? Nothing less than the ethics of their profession. Had the attorneys done otherwise, stated Monroe Freedman, author of *Lawyers' Ethics in an Adversary System*, "it would be a serious violation of their professional responsibility." The adversary ethic, which insists that the lawyer's first duty is to his client, required two officers of the court to conceal a killer's culpability even though that concealment might have let the killer go free.

IX

The Business of Lawyers

If a man is truly competent in his particular sphere of work, the world always anxious to obtain the best will beat a pathway to his door.

Ralph Waldo Emerson

The Practice of Law—An Ultrahazardous Occupation

When you have struggled through law school and passed the bar exam, you believe that your dues have been paid; you envision awesome paychecks and satisfied clients to come. You see yourself as entering a profession one-half trained and the other half to be obtained at the expense of your future clients, plus whatever small bits of continuing education you might undertake. You tell yourself you must get out into the field to learn the tricks of the trade, take your bumps and bite the bullet. But you will find early that the practice of law is an ultrahazardous occupation, surrounded by rules of court and procedure and professional responsibility. You're like a sailor setting out on a long voyage with inaccurate charts and compasses, and misplaced buoys and beacons.

You are an apprentice at the trade and should not expect master's fees at the outset. These will come only as you diligently seek learning, one day at a time.

If you thought law school was a jealous mistress you will find actual practice is an unsatisfied lover. There is a tremendous gap between law school and law practice and you will soon learn how much you do not know. You can toss out those illusions of kind and benevolent judges and how justice permeates the courtroom. Equal justice under the law is a myth. It has been said that justice, most of the time, is only in the courtroom walls.

Advice for the Early Years

In the first years, seek perspective and balance, not great monetary gain. That will come after you endear yourself to the business and service. The unhappy lot of every beginner is one of the fullness of confusion, doubt, inexperience and incompetence. You must develop wings before flying and that takes a minimum of five to seven years (if ever). Don't try to rush it. The certificate and license to practice law enrolls one as a professional, but not a major leaguer. Like the young baseball player who must spend time down in the minors or in the farm system, the young lawyer must do likewise. The beginner has got to hustle; dig is a better word. Hanging out a shingle is not enough.

To succeed you must achieve a command of the English language. Avoid the Latin words and phrases no one understands. Words are the tools of the law trade. When you are called to address a judge or jury, it is your words that count most and it is by them that you must persuade the court and jury of the righteousness of your cause. Words are indeed important because they are the vehicle of your thoughts; if others find it difficult to understand you, it is most often because of your own lack of clarity in thinking. Obscurity in thought leads to obscurity in language.

Solo, Associate, or Law Firm Serf?

One of the first decisions you must make—and sometimes there is no choice—is whether to go it alone, as an associate with another lawyer or a law firm, or as a law firm serf. Partnership is not plausible for the first few years. Novices make bad partners—the blind leading the blind. Who wants to join forces with a raw beginner? To the solo practitioner, business is one of independence; no bosses or alliances or dividing of fees. You may cash in on a windfall that promises to make you rich, but going solo has all the riskiness of prospecting for gold.

Becoming an associate does have some fringe benefits when one is not financially able to set up an office. But sharing the costs can also mean accepting hand-me-down cases of one's seniors. You may be forced to take the piggly-wiggly cases such as collections, bankruptcies (that the senior does not want), and, before long, that you may not want.

If you like to spend much time among the library stacks and be beholden to others, or to lean on other people, join a large law firm like the bluebloods of Yale, Columbia and Harvard do.

In any event, seek out an older and experienced helpmate who can be trusted and relied on for direction in case of fog and indecision. There is so much to learn and it comes only in bits and pieces; some of it through trial and error. Should you become involved in heavy litigation, don't hesitate to join with an experienced advocate who commands confidence and trust. Think foremost of the client's welfare and interest, no matter whether it involves negotiation or a criminal or civil trial. Do not be penny wise and dollar foolish. Seek the best. Don't go into the water without being able to swim or without a life jacket. The waters are usually rough! On my first two civil jury cases I took on an experienced associate and we won. In my first three serious criminal trials of murder, extortion and rape, I also felt inadequate to go it alone, and joined with an expert trial lawyer.

Keep Your Name Before the Public

When you appear frequently in the courtroom and gain public exposure in the media, you may find your name becoming a household word. Keep your name before the public.

Read the daily newspapers to watch for the obituaries and accidents. When a friend or kin is involved, visit the hospital or funeral home and send cards of sympathy. Remember birthdays and holidays with greeting cards; and don't forget congratulatory notes to graduates and those receiving promotions. It is difficult to place a value on a kind and timely word of praise.

Managing Your Office

Learn good office management. If going solo, the amount of capital you need depends on your life style. Mark VIIs, Corvettes and Mercedes are not necessary equipment or tools of the trade. Go with the minimum essentials. A minimum of $30,000 is needed as a beginner for solo practice.

When affordable, get yourself a part-time secretary who is qualified and of the highest calibre. Refrain from shapely Miss Americas who can strain your eyes and affect your brain and morality. Do not mix sex with business in the light of many temptations. I preferred an older head beyond the child bearing stage to the young and potentially pregnant. The latter can destroy the continuity and effectiveness of the office. My wife was a perfect choice; she served me the last twelve years of practice and managed very well to keep the ship afloat.

Maintain a high degree of accuracy, and don't overlook the fact that *you* are personally liable for the misdeeds of inefficient or dishonest secretaries. A punctuation mark misplaced in a deed, or other instrument, can invalidate it and threaten you with a possible malpractice suit. Bear in mind that insurers are always more ready to accept premiums than to pay claims.

Don't cripple yourself with excessive office expense. Bonuses to office help can be paid periodically in due time when you are successful. Do not crowd in merit pay, profit sharing and economic increases all in one year. However, recognize good work and propriety. Do not get buddy-buddy with any staff member for the possible consequence of familiarity is contempt.

Being late for office appointments annoys clients and can lose you business. Being late for court appearances annoys judges and can bring contempt of court charges against you. A judge, on the other hand, is never considered late for a hearing or a trial.

Keep an orderly desk, but not a cleared one. A client who walks into your office and sees a clean desk may think, "Hell, this lawyer doesn't have any business!" A backlog of files on your desk is a sign that someone needs you, but keep them tidy. It is the busy and dedicated lawyer who gets results.

Take on public defender criminal work, but never compromise justice so as to speed up the criminal court backlog.

When practicing criminal law and defending the corrupt of society, recognize them as such and be on your guard. As you will find someday that the civil case bankrupt client will not want to pay his fee, so the criminal client also may not pay and will use techniques to turn against you.

Charging for Your Services

Make a reasonable charge for your services. You are not in business to kill time or for health's sake but to make an honest living. Fee arrangements should be in writing; and in criminal cases and divorces, the cash must be up front. Once a criminal is behind bars, he is unable to pay; all you will get is the experience.

When your client insists the case go to trial after a settlement offer is made, protect yourself with a pre-trial awareness of settlement offer for him or her to sign. There have been cases of mine where the client refused to accept the insurance policy limits and the jury's verdict has been much less than the offer.

Some cases take years to decide and you must have the patience to wait. Insurance adjusters tend to keep putting you off. File suit and you'll see how quickly an offer of settlement is forthcoming. When possible, in the fruitful years, keep a reserve on hand for when business slackens.

Your office should be furnished simply; ornate surroundings are the mark of the fake. Clients are not interested in examining your diplomas, fraternal memberships and awards or family photos. They only want to know what you can do for them.

Choosing Your Office Location

The location of your practice, whether in a small town or a large city, is a choice of temperament. Some persons are happier surrounded by lights and busy streets, but in many instances, business can be generated more quickly in one's home town.

In the early days locate your home and office near the courthouse. As Abe Lincoln said, "A lawyer's time and advice is his stock in trade."

Use the courthouse library religiously and avoid buying law books with the exception of the state code and form books.

In law, as in other human endeavors, much depends upon the person. The workman speaks through his works. Your works will reach the ears of those in need and will be scanned by judges through whose hands each pleading must pass. Life consists of small matters and proper attention to the lesser insures success and satisfaction in the greater.

Don't Trust Your Memory

In matters of the law and statutes, never counsel off the top of your head. Drawing on one's memory can be misleading and dangerous. Strange errors seem to find their way into the mind. Guesswork near the mark cannot be as reliable as a carefully considered opinion. Statutes can be ambiguous and controversial, often passed by a series of mutual concessions, begotten by compromise out of vested interests. When they emerge as part of the law of the land, they may be quite illogical and at times incomprehensible. Go to the law books when in doubt.

Not all problems involve intricate points of law. Many depend more upon a knowledge of the world coupled with sound common sense. Do not hold yourself out as a counselor until you have paid your dues with experience. A young practitioner in our circuit, having just passed the bar and entered practice, used on his letterhead: "Attorney and Counselor at Law." Where did he get all the experience and knowledge in such a short time?

If not an experienced typist, take a short course at once. The young lawyer will be up late many nights preparing legal documents for the following day. I have typed many a legal document nights and weekends after a bedside visit to a home or hospital. If time permits, take a course in shorthand.

Communicate With Your Clients

Develop good telephone manners for yourself and all office staff. The telephone is lifeblood to new business and old. But never discuss fees over the phone or give telephone advice to new clients because they may be merely shopping. Avoid charging for telephone conversations except to confirmed clients who need your time and advice.

Keep a calendar on the desk to remind you of appointments and court appearances. Organize each day in advance and begin work early. Make yourself available at home or office seven days a week. Imitate the family doctor with his home visits to the sick and infirm. A medical practitioner owes a lot to a good beside manner and the young lawyer will do well to take that lesson to heart.

Quality stationery will serve as one of your best ads; and in signing documents, make your signature neat and clear. There is nothing more repulsive than a slipshod or abbreviated signature. Be proud of your name. One's character is often determined by the writer's signature.

Maintain a sound office accounting system with daily income and disbursements for IRS purposes and budgeting of expenses. Refer tax matters to a reputable accountant unless you majored in tax work. It is impossible to keep up with annual tax changes. From my first year (with a gross income of $3,874.55 in 1960) I relied on an experienced accountant and the IRS never knocked at my door, even when my gross annual income climbed to sizeable figures.

Communicate with your clients periodically and provide them with copies of all court pleadings and correspondence. Law practice is a battle of paper and has been characterized as "the paper chase." Cultivate unfailing courtesy in your correspondence, even to offensive letters. Let your replies be couched in language which, though firm, is nevertheless polite. Do not descend to ungentlemanly personal attacks or vulgar abuse.

In settlement of cases, the client has the last word, but he hires your ability and experience, and above all, your trust. Keep him aware of what is going on and avoid quarrels. A fair and reasonable settlement often is more satisfactory than an action fought out to the bitter end. An amicable settlement is always more conducive to happy relationships between the parties. The true lawyer is a pacifier, not a provoker. The Orientals put great stress on peaceful settlement outside a court. As a consequence, their need for lawyers is far less than ours.

Develop a love for the underdog and lost causes.

Working With Other Lawyers

Beware of referrals from other lawyers who claim they are too busy to handle a case. No lawyer passes up a good case. Bad cases are headaches to the other lawyer and worse for you. In my first year of practice I was called to the office of a prosperous attorney who wanted to impress me by being helpful in getting me started. He turned over to me an old worn-out civil case of little value that had been pending for years in court. When he gave me the file he said, "Sully, take it and keep the fee." I enthusiastically took over the case, studied the file—which included a 400-page appellant court transcript— and after a conference with the defendant's attorney a quick settlement was effected. When the settlement check arrived, my brother attorney's name was listed as one of the drawees. I took it to his office for his signature, whereupon he demanded one-half the small fee.

Hone Your Competitive Edge

If you haven't participated in any form of competition, take up something that involves winning and losing, like tennis or golf or playing cards, such as poker, blackjack or bridge. It will hone your competitive edge. Growing up I participated in football, basketball, baseball and boxing, without realizing how important it was for the experience of winning and losing. My eleven fights as an amateur—the first eight all knockouts, then win, lose, lose, win—taught me to get up from the canvas and start swinging. In boxing you are in there alone. In law, you are part of a dog eat dog profession—knock down and drag out. Queensbury rules do not apply. Life is a competition and in many situations, the laurels go to the one who outlasts the other. I am sure insurance companies teach their adjusters the spirit of competition.

Rising to the Top

Do not become discouraged at the number of competitors in the profession. Law schools are producing many more prospective lawyers than the country needs. The cream, however, always goes to the top, and it is important how that cream develops. You will run into the fixers and finaglers, the crooks and the bleeders. Successful criminal lawyers must rely at times on perjury and they are usually adept in creating evidence. They are not truth-seekers, but aim at victory and winning the fight.

A lawyer can have no attribute which contributes so much to legitimate and enduring success as the confidence of others that he can be trusted always to do the decent thing. Have an old-fashioned regard for the worth of your word in all things.

There is no substitute for courtesy and good manners. Politeness costs nothing and goes a long way. Tip your hat, be cordial to the women, and bow gracefully only to proper superiors.

Dress modestly and simply, not slovenly; nor wear rat-tailed hair. Some judges and juries are repulsed by an attorney's or client's bad grooming.

Your effectiveness as a counselor often depends on a knowledge of financial matters. Study an attorney's handbook on accounting and be primed to give sound advice on money matters, including one's own. Seek out an expert if need be. Keep the client's trust fund account separate from your own personal business. Many of the disciplinary accusations brought against lawyers, especially babes in the trade, are for mixing funds and using them as their own.

Some business depends on the popularity of the client or the attorney, but don't rely on it. A sense of humor is helpful in all walks of life. Although it is said to be worth several thousand a year, don't set a precise value on it. Have a friendly disposition; no one looks at your shoes when you wear a smile.

Don't expect to win friends and influence people easily. The great public relations expert, Dale Carnegie, was not a lawyer.

In every case there is a potential enemy. Sometimes that includes the client, if the attorney loses a close one or fails to touch all the bases in handling a case. Often, those you trust may turn against you if the prevailing situation benefits them most. Therefore, be cautious and don't provoke complaints.

Be careful, also, in selecting friends. Two of my best friends reported me to the state bar grievance committee on two separate occasions as part of a conspiracy to get me. Their efforts failed when the bar committee dismissed the complaints as nothing but smoke. However, it taught me a lesson not to get too buddy-buddy.

Avoid Prohibited Contacts

The Model Rules of Ethics or Professional Responsibility prohibit contacts for business with the police, taxi drivers, nurses and hospital workers, physicians, garage mechanics and insurance agents. This is termed "ambulance chasing" by bar grievance committees although some law firms' members use even more indirect methods of getting business. Referrals from friends and kinfolk are within the bounds of the Model Rules and will keep the disciplinary wolves away from your door.

One-third of my first year's net earnings stemmed from a relative troubled by a car accident, even though an experienced insurance company attorney got the best of me in the deal which was settled out of court.

Finding New Business

Business brings business. A deed or mortgage may lead to a will and possibly the handling of an estate. One of the better ways to obtain business is to acquire a sound reputation for speed and efficiency. A satisfied client is a valuable asset but satisfied clients who broadcast your praises among relatives and friends are worth their weight in gold.

Fraternal lodges and church associations will seek your membership, but do not rush to join. Country clubs often swarm with lawyers overworked to a frazzle, but in search of business. An attorney could be wasting time.

Bar associations will also solicit your membership. I do not know of their doing anything worthwhile for the sole practitioner, the small law firm member, or society, but they have been running the show for many years.

Make friends at the courthouse with all the clerical personnel. They can help immensely and will assist ably in preparing legal documents. They are noted business referrals on wills, deeds, and law suits; be kind to them and share the wealth.

Know Human Nature and Behavior

To be a good trial lawyer one must have a working knowledge of human nature and behavior.

Know the history of great lawyers, their experiences and their methods. Like student artists, copy the masters and read and observe them when you can. The practice of law and skill in the courtroom is a continuous education and only practice makes perfect.

My early hero was Clarence Darrow of criminal law fame. His biography should be required reading in every law school. He was the most controversial lawyer of his era and the most fearless defender of men and women charged with crime. He became the interpreter of labor and of the radical movement to lift up the common man. He used the law to promote social justice as he saw it.

One aspect of trial practice that is sensitive and dangerous for the beginner is cross-examination of witnesses. It is the phase of the trial that constitutes the severest test. Avoid asking questions merely for the sake of asking. Don't go on a fishing expedition if you do not know the probable answers.

The objectives of cross-examination are twofold: (1) To discredit damaging testimony that may have been brought out against you; and (2) to elicit further information that could be useful to your case. Do not be long and windy; and when you have touched base on one point, go to second base and thence to third and around home. Don't end up stuck on first base.

When your efforts are crowned with success, do not gloat. On the other hand, if the verdict is adverse, do not let defeat beget depression. If the client ascribes his failure to win to the attorney's ineptitude, such criticism is better ignored.

Don't take your loss home, leave it in the courtroom. A hardy old practitioner friend of mine always told clients after losing, "It was the judge's fault for ruling against us. He made a mistake." That is one way of passing the buck.

It is seldom wise to be cocksure. The best cases may be lost with a jury. I have seen many an apparent winner fall flat. It happened to me during my green years in an almost perfect case of liability. My client was a cyclist who had been seriously injured when a motorist—the defendant—crossed in front of him to make a left turn. The judge erroneously instructed the jury that "if the cyclist could have avoided the accident by turning to the right or left, then he was contributorily negligent and cannot recover if he failed to do so." Following the trial, a juror told me, "Your man had the obligation to turn left, even though it meant going into oncoming traffic."

Regardless of how trifling or insignificant the case seems, it is important to the client and can have grave consequences. An important reminder: Before going into court, always look up the laws relating to the case. Take, for example, the following:

A young lawyer gratuitously represented his neighbor accused of driving under the influence of alcohol. The attorney and defendant agreed to a plea of guilty. It appeared the easy way out and they hoped the judge would be merciful. The attorney had seen others get off with a mere slap on the wrist for manslaughter by auto. The lawyer was shaken when the judge sentenced his client to thirty days in jail, then explained to the young lawyer that because the defendant was a second offender, the law mandated a jail sentence.

The Trial Game

A fair trial is not always assured. After two centuries justice and due process are still being developed by our court system. It has taken our U.S. Supreme Court many years to acknowledge certain inalienable rights. In the early 1960s the average criminal defendant was treated like a piece of meat on its way to dressing and processing. A person was arrested, interrogated, and threatened with dire consequences if he did not cooperate and plead guilty. A judge would advise him that things would go easier if he did not contest his guilt. The system retained the unpleasant features of Nazi Germany and today's Russian courts.

Men routinely were picked up without warrants, denied food and water for hours and humiliated with insults. It was not until the 1950s, during the Warren era of the U.S. Supreme Court, that constitutional principles of due process of law were enforced. Meanwhile, hundreds of the poor and despised had gone to the gas chamber, the electric chair, or the gallows, victims of grave injustice.

Trial is an adversary or contentious procedure. It's a game with the judge as the referee. It is not an orderly search for truth, but a quest for victory. Lawyers are told they are members of a noble profession; it is only as noble as the lawyers make it. The word "profession," originally applied to religious orders, means "bound by a vow." A layman is one of the laity or, of Greek origin, one of the people. A professional professes to have some specific knowledge that others lack, which is supposed to be offered for the benefit of the whole community, or, in that mystical phrase, "the public interest." Many times cases are won, not through merit, but through cronyism and politics.

In law, there are no rewards or silver medals for coming in second-best, as in sports. In the Super Bowl of law, the awards go to the winners. Great performances by lawyers do not even go into the record book.

Learn early: Perjury runs rampant, particularly in criminal and divorce cases. Truth can't be ascertained alone by facial expressions or human behavior. Have no part of perjury, even though it means loss of a friend or a giant valuable case. The disregard for seeking truth is probably the chief reason the legal profession is held in such low esteem.

Serve the Poor and Give Community Service

Cast your bread upon the waters and it will multiply after many days. *Pro bono* or gratuitous services for the poor is a must in the early stages of practice and never depart from it after making it big. The voiceless poor, the illiterate and the helpless are ever with us and need your assistance. At my son's law school graduation exercises in June 1977 in Baltimore, the speaker of the day exhorted each graduate to take several *pro bono* cases a year. In my fourth year of practice, when the pickings were lean, I took a *pro bono* case and spent over $1,000 and hundreds of hours of time to free a life prisoner, the victim of an unfair judgment who had spent eleven long years in prison.

During all my years of practice I never charged for an interview except in those few instances when the person insisted on paying me. In my seventh year, I began a ten-year quest, spending over $4,000 and hundreds of hours of time on one case, in an attempt to make due process a reality. The long struggle is discussed fully in the chapter entitled $_{2}$it$_{3}$Justice Denied.$_{2}$bk$_{3}$

In the French cathedral at Treguier there is a memorial window to Honest St. Ives, the patron saint of lawyers. Dedicated in 1936, it was financed by contributions from American lawyers. Of him it was said in his day that "he was a lawyer but no crook, a thing which astonished the people. . . . He defends the children, the widows, and all friendless people. Not only does he accept their defense, but he seeks them as clients. . . . He gives them good counsel and he pleads for them. And for all this he receives his reward from God." St. Ives practiced seven centuries ago but it would be well to have his kind with us today.

Community service is the keystone of your success. Pitch in, even though it means a financial contribution as well as time. In my first eight years, I involved myself in teen, community, church and school activities, and I spent over $17,000 in junior and senior baseball leagues to show people I cared. Sow seeds of kindness and generosity. Don't leave it to the next fellow.

Don't join the church for business; enter where your feeling is most in conformity with its doctrine. The proper observance of the holy day has kept many an overworked person from going off the deep end. Faith in the Sovereign above can enable you to climb mountains and reach unimaginable goals. Demonstrate to the world that an honest lawyer is possible. God is justice; learn from Him. He is the divine attribute manifested in just laws or rules or ethics as they were in the Ten Commandments of the Mosaic law. The true lawyer is a pacifier in the quest for just settlements.

Dedication, Hard Work, Experience, and Professional Conduct

There is no substitute for dedication and long hours of work. If you cannot cut it in the early days, bow out and seek a new profession or vocation.

In all the world there is no experience like that which is found in one's office. Patrick Henry, the American patriot, said, "I have but one lamp by which my feet are guided and that is the lamp of experience."

Do your part to change the rules of legal professional conduct called the Code of Professional Responsibility and legal ethics. They were established and pronounced by that elite group, the ABA—called the guild or employer's union —and the bar associations in each state. Petty violations can bring disciplinary action against you and possible malpractice suits. The establishment does not like bar members to muddy the waters or cause ripples. Any technique can be used to get rid of you. In the course of twenty years, several attempts were made to oust me from practice. When, in my early days of practice, a local judge rendered an adverse verdict and I countered with a strong letter of reprobation, my first grievance hearing resulted. Seven other misconduct citations followed in the next ten years, and one involved a two-day trial, much expense and embarrassment. Fortunately, the three judges appointed to the panel to hear the case could distinguish the trees from the forest. I never received a suspension or disbarment.

Be attentive to suit filing deadlines, fees, and preparation of all documents; avoid losing files, faulty research, misinterpretation of the law, and abuse of trust funds and fiduciary duties.

Continuing education is a must for the beginner. In my first five years I attended seminars on criminal law and personal injury in Baltimore, Washington, and New York. It was there I came into contact with some of the masters of the bar. It was there, also, I learned the fine points of advocacy and the adversary system, the give and take and the hard pull of courtroom work.

There are three principal attributes any true attorney must possess: knowledge of the law, which can be found in the library; sensitivity to the needs of society, and a response to those needs that flows from within; and third, courage. As a whole, lawyers are the biggest cowards and ass-kissers of any profession.

Courage or boldness cannot be learned in any academic institution. It is molded through one's environment.

William Kunstler, in his book, *The Case for Courage*, spans more than 200 years and presents ten famous trials in which lawyers chose to involve themselves with the most explosive cases of their times and places. He describes how these men courageously accepted the unpopular cases, knowing all too well that in so doing they faced the threat of financial loss, ostracism and political extinction. These distinguished attorneys and cases included: Andrew Hamilton, who defended the impoverished journalist, John Peter Zenger, against an outraged New York governor in 1735; John Adams, destined to be the second President of the U.S., who undertook the defense of nine British soldiers indicted for murder for their part in the Boston Massacre of 1770. And there was Harold R. Medina's defense of the accused Nazi conspirator, Anthony Cramer, in 1942. And Clarence Darrow's defense in the conspiracy trial of union leader, Eugene Victor Debs, in 1895. These lawyers not only survived the experience but found it did not stand in the way of future political triumphs and rewards.

John W. Davis, renowned attorney and politician, told by a political supporter to get rid of his more controversial clients if he hoped to win the Democratic nomination for president, replied: "The only limitation upon a right-thinking lawyer's independence is the duty which he owes to his clients, once selected, to serve them without the slightest thought to the effect which such service may have upon his own personal popularity or political fortunes. Any lawyer who surrenders his independence, or shades his duty by trimming his professional course to fit the gusts of popular opinion, in my judgment not only dishonors himself, but disparages and degrades the great profession to which he should be proud to belong."

Whom to sue and whom to defend in a controversial case can be a problem. In all my dealings with clients and prospective clients I turned no one away. If the facts and law constituted a cause of action, I accepted the case. A retainer fee was never a prerequisite. Over the years I have sued churches, pastors, dentists and dental associations, banks, mayors and city councils, boards of education and school teachers, county commissioners, local unions and international unions, YMCAs, nurses and hospitals, attorneys, state attorneys—even judges. I do not recommend the latter because of the impact it may have on a client.

When the two sitting judges in my district brought contempt charges against my client—a weekly newspaper that had criticized the judges' handling of certain cases—we retaliated by bringing suit for injunctive relief in the U.S. District Court of Maryland for violation of freedom of speech. A judge from another county, appointed by the high court of Maryland appeals, ruled in our favor and applied the first amendment to the U.S. Constitution in his carefully written opinion. Freedom of speech prevailed.

My position as to who should have his day in court never wavered. When an incumbent county commissioner lost the election and filed libel charges against the same *News Weekly* for six figures damages, a petit jury in an adjoining county could not decide on a verdict; a mistrial resulted in a verdict for the defendant.

At times I have nursed slow chronic burns because of the follies and injustice of the legal system. Badgering a hostile or adverse witness in courthouse corridors has brought contempt of court citations. Searching for truth was like climbing mountains.

Building Monuments

The attorney, advocate, or solicitor, can be likened to a monument builder. From an anonymous author came these words:

> A young man desired to study law. He went to a noted jurist and asked for an opportunity to read law in his office. The lawyer replied, "My son, why do you wish to study law? Is it because you can make a great deal of money out of the profession, or because you think it will give you power and position, or because it may give you access to the political arena? What is the motive that actuates you?
>
> The young man answered that it was because he thought the law was a great profession, and one which gave opportunities.

The old lawyer said, "Young man, you should know that the chief business of a lawyer is building monuments."

"Building monuments?" asked the young man in surprise. "I do not desire to be a stonecutter."

"If you will take a walk with me," replied the lawyer, "I will show you some of the monuments I have built. Some of them are not so good, but they stand as I have built them."

As the grizzled old lawyer and the puzzled young man walked down the street, the former pointed to two elegant business buildings and said, "There are a couple of monuments. A number of years ago two men were in partnership, but they could not agree. So one came to me and asked me to institute suit against the other. I agreed to do so only after he would allow me a conference with both of them together. The conference was arranged. I said to them, 'You men are both good businessmen, both capable, you cannot get along together. Therefore, the common sense thing to do is to dissolve the partnership, and each go into business for himself.' There was no lawsuit. They dissolved the partnership by mutual agreement, and each is the head of his own great store."

As they walked along they met a well-dressed couple of middle age, accompanied by a handsome young lad. Friendly greetings were exchanged, and after the trio had passed, the lawyer said, "There is another of my monuments, of which I am very proud. A few years ago that man and woman were bride and groom. He was a young businessman doing well, but success went to his head. He began to dissipate, neglected his wife and his business, and she, broken-hearted, came to me wanting a divorce.

"I said to her, 'First, let me talk to your husband.' I brought him into my office, and told him how well he had done, what a fine businessman he was, what a wonderful wife he had, and how richly endowed he was for the great business of living. I told him also that, because of his folly and weakness, he was throwing it all away like the proverbial fool. The young man had good stuff in him. He saw where he was going, and made up his mind that he was going to right-about-face. There was no divorce, and today you see him happy with his lovely wife and young son. That is one of my monuments of which I am very proud."

Pointing to a derelict sitting on the curb, one of the shabby habitues so commonly seen at street corners, the lawyer said, "There, my son, is a monument of which I am far from being proud. But, every day as I pass along, I have to view it. That poor fellow you see sitting there was one time a bookkeeper in a store here—and doing well. He was a good bookkeeper, but succumbed to temptation and indulged in systematic peculation from his employer. Of course, in time he was found out and was brought to trial. I was a young lawyer then, and I did not have the vision of a monument-builder that I have today. My only thought was that this fellow was a thief and should go to prison. And being the prosecuting attorney, my only duty, I thought, was to convict him. With all the eloquence and fire and merciless logic that I possessed, I stood before the jury and judge, and sent him to the penitentiary. Today he is a piece of flotsam and jetsam, riding willy-nilly down the great sea of life. No friends, no ambition, no hope.

"When I look at that monument, my son, I think of what I made of a bright young man, and what I might have made of him had I talked to him and pled his case so that he might have had a chance to be the man God meant him to be."

There was quiet as the two strode along. Finally, the elder man spoke again. "Now, my son, I think you know what I mean by 'building monuments.' Everyone in life, no matter what his work or vocation, is a monument-builder, and whether you practice law, or become a digger of ditches, or a miner in the bowels of the earth, whatever you do, remember what kind of monuments you are building."

X

Advice to the Layman: Considerations When Selecting a Lawyer

Choose With Care

Using a divorce kit to save money can be disastrous to a complaining party in a lawsuit. A middle-aged lady who put together an agreement based on the kit did not include her husband's income from a pension. When the divorce decree was handed down, she discovered her husband's pension was community property, but she was left out of it.

No other profession or occupation in our society affects the finances of individuals or their status in life as does the practice of law. In many instances the selection of the right lawyer is surrounded by confusion. The selection can be a tedious task, and shouldn't be left until the need arises because when people do need legal help, they often need it in a hurry.

The best warning I've heard is: "Choose a lawyer as carefully as you choose a doctor. The doctor cures your physical ills; the lawyer cures your legal aches and pains."

Choose a Specialist for Major Problems

When you choose the right lawyer for your case, you are on second base and have won half the game. Lawyers, like doctors, are divided into two groups: the generalists and the specialists. When you need surgery, you visit the surgeon; and when you have a bone dislocation or fractures, you go to the orthopedic surgeon. It's as simple as that. When you are injured, when someone sues you, when you are arrested, financially in trouble, or when your marriage is on the rocks, or you need a will, deed or power of attorney, when you buy property, have a car accident, lend money, go into business, or speak out of turn and are sued for libel or slander—these are the times you need a lawyer, and many times, a generalist just won't do.

Many laymen have been sold down the river because their attorneys weren't sure how to handle a case. Rather than share the case with a specialist, the lawyer becomes greedy at the expense of the client. When the *big case* comes along, that is not the time to select a Blackstone Jr. He will have his day in the future; meanwhile, he must cut his teeth on the simpler cases in the lower courts.

Take, for example, a personal injury case in which the victim has spent months in the hospital and is totally disabled. This is a case for a specialist. Some are denigrated as "ambulance chasers," but you'll find they have the know-how and will touch all the bases. That's what puts you on the winning team. And isn't that what you're after? A personal injury case involves the contingent fee. That is, if you win, the lawyer gets a share of the award. But if you lose, the lawyer gets nothing. This provides a motivation factor; since the lawyer owns part of the action, he or she will work twice as hard.

Warning Signs to Avoid

There is no magic formula for guaranteeing you a successful lawyer. However, there are warning signs to watch for and some basic information you should have about the types of lawyers who handle various kinds of litigation. Some tips to follow are: Friends are not the best advisers, and neither are banks. Your employer's lawyer may do a great job for him but not be the right one for your case. Don't go to a lawyer friend out of a feeling of obligation. And be careful of doctors who refer cases to certain lawyers; they could be splitting the fee. Bar referral offices are available, but the receptionist or secretary in charge may be referring her friend, the lawyer, for a price. Newspaper and television ads extolling the virtues of Mr. Tim Grabber, Esq., can also mislead you, as can the law school professor who appears to know it all but has never tried a case.

Look for a Strong Ethical Foundation

Who should you take a chance on? Take a chance on the churchman rather than an agnostic. The latter may not have any deep-down ethics or standards to guide him. Don't let the fact a lawyer has had trouble with the bar association dissuade you. The big boys of the bar may have it in for him because he's a lone dissenter and a fighter.

Shop, and Query in Depth

When you buy a new suit or an expensive pair of shoes, you shop around. Do the same thing for a lawyer, but with greater depth. Query each prospective lawyer on his experience in your kind of case. How long has he been in practice? Is he a trial lawyer or does he prefer office work? What is his reputation as a fighter? Is he meek and timid in the courtroom or will he stand up to the judge? You want a fighter, but not one who is at odds with the judge.

Insurance companies and their adjusters are noted for evaluating a case and keeping a particularly high reserve because a certain lawyer is representing the plaintiff. The companies know whom they can force settlements on, and who will go to court. They are familiar with the fighter who doesn't let down his guard and can negotiate himself around the courtroom.

Use General Practitioners for Smaller Cases

Turn to the general practitioner for the smaller cases that don't place your life or your bankroll on the line. Some lawyers have experience but haven't been able to succeed in the more lucrative branches of the law. Many small town, country lawyers fit that description. Some considerations you will want to weigh are the extent of his legal knowledge, whether his law library is adequate and current with recent law decisions, and whether he attends seminars to keep up to date. Also, is he a nine-to-fiver who takes long lunch breaks?

"A criminal lawyer without experience is mere decoration," claim Marks and Goldfarb. "Criminal proceedings are highly specialized with hundreds of cunning maneuvers available to the knowledgeable lawyer. If your lawyer is going to plea bargain for you, he'd better be experienced in that marketplace, for plea bargaining in the courthouse is no different from bargaining [elsewhere]. You'd better know both the prices and the products or you'll wind up paying too much for too little, except this time the currency could be years of your life in the pen. [1]

How Honest a Lawyer Do You Want?

"How honest a lawyer do you want?" ask Marks and Goldfarb. "This question may sound strange, but its answer is essential to choosing the lawyer who is right for you. If you look, you can find lawyers of all shades on the honesty spectrum—from the highly ethical with profound integrity to the gross liar who cares for nothing but money and victory.[2] The latter kind may suggest you tell a white lie to get your case over the hump. But there are no shades or degrees of lies and truth; it's either one or the other. Take your pick, but suffer the consequences.

In your search you'll find many lawyers will lie about their ability and experience. They never want to pass up a case. Many of these make their rounds like a carpenter who can use a saw and hammer but cannot use a square or a circular saw. Beware of them.

Use the general practitioner for small claims and traffic cases where the eventual outcome does not threaten you with jail or loss of property. The general practitioner may have the judge as a golfing buddy or fraternal associate, and this can spell the difference between victory or defeat.

Pay little attention to attorneys who berate and denigrate their brethren. They are masking their own weaknesses. You find them in every courthouse. They are self-styled experts in every field, but in court it's a different matter. The lawyer who tells you the case is a sure win is lacking in honesty, but more important, he is lacking in experience. There are no sure wins.

Avoid Settlements Between the Lawyer and Judge

Anne Strick warns against settlements reached between your attorney and the judge. "Never allow your lawyer to settle your case in the judge's chambers where it may be the scene of a civil sellout," she wrote. "What goes on in chambers is off-the-record secrecy, the lawyer may well make an agreement that scuttles his client's case. That agreement will appear in court as the Bench's order, against which, the lawman assures his client, appeal is impracticable."[3]

Choosing a Lawyer in Personal Injury Cases

Personal injury practice—the PI game—is incomparably the richest area of law practice in the United States. Even Wall Street lawyers, the highest-paid corporate lawyers in the country, don't do as well as PI lawyers. Why? Because PI lawyers aren't paid by the hour; they get a piece of the action, a contingency fee which can be as much as 50 percent of the total amount recovered for a client.

Lawyers who represent plaintiffs in PI cases are, like criminal and divorce lawyers, often looked down on by blue chip law firms. In turn, PI lawyers look on their moneybag opponents, the insurance companies, as the scum of the earth. "The contingent fee is like a cancer!" exclaimed one frustrated insurance executive.

So, if you find yourself thrust into the personal injury system, how do you find the right lawyer to lead you through it? The answer depends on one key question: How honest will you be? Answer that and your path is clear cut.

If you look, you can find a personal injury attorney of impeccable integrity who will, if you insist, present your case quite truthfully. You can, if you choose, be relatively honest, but will you be?

An example has been provided by Marks and Goldfarb. "Assume, for instance, that you've been in an accident and your neck hurts. You decide, quite properly, that you want to be compensated for you pain and suffering. You seek out a lawyer. He sees his duty. . . in 'maximizing your recovery.' In other words, he wants to get you all the money he can. And if this is going to happen, you must receive medical treatment—and the more the better: The more doctor bills you have, the worse your injury is presumed to be, and a bad injury is obviously 'worth' more than a minor one. The lawyer may insist you visit certain doctors for diagnosis and treatment. This he calls the 'medical management' of your case.

"The insurance companies play the PI game too, and in similar ways. They, too, hire consulting physicians, as they have a legal right to do, to examine claimants and report on their health. And these physicians, as well, tend to do the bidding of their employers."[4]

Rosenthal has cited the expert insurance adjuster who admits: "Frankly, we are in the business to wear out plaintiffs. In the process we take our percentage of interest for as long as we can. Companies are smart to do this. This is big business. It's dirty business. We're not a charity out to protect the plaintiff's welfare."[5]

Rosenthal goes on to say, "And then there is the element of delay, instigated and promoted by the insurance company defeating the claims of accident victims; for him, the costs of delay are great. Not only does this work against the injured's rehabilitation by denying him money at the time rehabilitation expenses are incurred, it increases pressures to take an unfairly low settlement, and plays on his psychological uncertainties—but it hampers the plaintiff's problems of proving it if the case is ever tried. Witnesses die and move away. Details are forgotten. Injuries cease to be visually dramatic."[6]

It bears repeating: "Choose a lawyer as carefully as you choose a doctor. The doctor cures your physical ills; the lawyer cures your legal aches and pains."

Part III

RECOMMENDATIONS

XI

Recommendations for Reformation

Institutions are created for the purpose of resisting change; that's their main function. And they preserve all kinds of things that one doesn't want.

Prof. A. J. Taylor, 1982

While law schools have stressed conceptual trial skills, they have placed insufficient emphasis on the practical training in litigation techniques and ethical sensitivity necessary to turn out competent trial lawyers.

Irving R. Kaufman[1]

The Need: Scrape Off the Barnacles of Tradition

All the conservatism and exclusiveness of old institutions are to be found in the legal profession. It is a closed and self-regulating community with all its strengths and weaknesses. Lawyers have resisted reforms more stubbornly than anyone. They enjoy the most restrictive monopoly of all, protected by a company guild, the American Bar Association.

To quote John Frank: "Just as the ship that is in the water too long becomes encrusted with barnacles, so legal education and proceedings may become encrusted with traditions and some of them from time to time need to be scraped off."[2]

How to improve lawyer training has been on the agenda of the American Bar Association and the American Association of Law Schools for many years. Some strides have been taken to correct the inadequacies but hardly enough. Martine B. Reed, in a special article to the *Maryland Daily Record*, a law newspaper, wrote: "A system is only as good as the humans who make it work. The soundest way to improve the legal system is to improve the training of lawyers."

"It would be unthinkable," says Reed, "for a physician to graduate from medical school without ever having seen a real patient. Yet, lawyers start their careers in ignorance of what lawyering really entails. A period of mandatory and substantial clinical experience should be part of every law school curriculum."

In Reed's opinion "The clinical experience must be mandatory out of simple respect for the public upon whom graduates will be unleashed. . . . Who would agree to be operated upon by a solo surgeon holding a scalpel for the first time?" she asks. "Yet new admittees to the bar are legally allowed to handle claims with no idea of the anatomy of a case and no prior experience with legal tools."[3]

Former Chief Justice Burger has said, "The legal profession never really dedicated itself to making our legal system work. Not a single law school in this country gives a course on court administration or goes out of its way to alert students of the need to help courts dispose of calendars in the interest of the general public."

As for our jury system, Burger asked, rhetorically, "Can a jury of one's peers grasp today's sophisticated problems, especially when business executives, lawyers and teachers are freely excused from jury duty?" In his view we should expand our use of the "English rule" which stipulates that when a case is too complex for a jury of lay people to understand, it is to be decided by a judge alone.

A jury trial is not necessarily the better way of deciding cases. It is said juries are vested with the import of democracy and the safeguard of liberty, but the truth is, their occupational status and education is low par. England at one time called the jury the most sacred of institutions and the glory of English law, but time and experience led to the abolition of juries there in all civil matters except libel and false imprisonment.

Burger, who has long advocated creation of special courts and the use of arbiters to ease the workload of the nation's judges, also said, "Our distant forebears moved slowly from trial by battle and other 'barbaric' means of resolving conflicts and disputes, and we must move away from total reliance on the adversary contest for resolving all disputes.

"For some disputes," he acknowledged, "trials will always be the only means, but for many claims we do not need trials by the adversary contest."

As practiced, he said, the system is "too costly, too painful, too destructive and too inefficient."

Saying he believed a lawyer's "highest obligation" is to keep clients out of the courtroom if possible, Burger nonetheless noted that within the federal appeals court system, lawsuit filings have increased 600 percent in twenty-five years.[4]

Whitney N. Seymour Jr., in his book, *Why Justice Fails,* wrote: "Our method of picking judges is catch as catch can. Whether appointive or elective, too much emphasis is on regarding the party faithful and not enough on finding men who have professional qualifications, temperament, and personality to make top flight judges. An obvious direction for reform is developing a career service for the judiciary and an education system of professional graduate training and promotion from the lower ranks to the higher courts, based on merit and performance."[5]

As for the grand jury, called the guardian of justice and the watchdog of our rights, it too must go, as it has in England where it was found to be out of place in 20th Century jurisprudence.

And then there is the problem of the media which is allowed too much leeway in reporting criminal trials. Prejudicial newspaper influence may be brought to bear at every stage, beginning with the initial investigation of a crime to the finale of the suspect's trial. Yet the press rarely concerns itself with whether the accused was advised of his rights or appointed an adequate lawyer.

These and other matters that affect our judicial system we must examine and must change whatever is needed to meet the demands of our times, as well as those in the future. Anyone who has better alternatives should propose them. In short, those who disagree have an obligation to advance other solutions.

Improve the Training of Lawyers

Before reviewing the legal educational system, let us examine the educational requirements of the medical profession. The medical schools do not teach surgery merely from books. What would we say of the doctor who was taught only from the printed page? More than 80 percent of medical teaching is done by practicing physicians and surgeons in the laboratory and in clinics.

Undergraduate course requirements for admission to medical schools include a sound and strong foundation in the natural sciences, biology, chemistry, mathematics and physics, with a solid background in social sciences and the humanities. In medical school, there is a major emphasis on contact with clinical problems early in the curriculum. Students are usually assigned to a hospital service, responsible for working up cases to present to the faculty. They associate with post-graduate trainees (residents) and teaching physicians in the care of patients. Then, following graduation, med students are exposed to the various branches and aspects of medicine. By the beginning of their second graduate year, most students have decided on the area of medicine in which they will specialize.

In addition, all states require written examinations for licensure and approximately 84 percent of state boards require graduate training to obtain a license to practice.

But admission to law schools generally requires no particular pre-law preparedness. A physical education major, a music major, an English or a psychology major, or any other major may qualify if he or she has a respectable Grade Point Average (GPA) and passes the LSAT (Law School Admission Test). What we need is mandatory pre-law requirements in the humanities, political science, English, history, economics, social studies, psychology, philosophy, accounting, and English composition. All pre-law studies should have some bearing on the law field. Foreign languages, for example, serve no useful purpose.

Not more than one year is needed in case or analytical study of the law. The second year should be shared with law specialty and clinical work so as to prepare for the third year out in the field. A third-year law student should be exposed to actual practice as an apprentice, to become familiar with what practice is all about and determine if he wants additional study to prepare for specialization.

Law students need intimate contact with clients, their needs, and with the courts, to learn what a lawyer actually does. Each case study should take the student through the entire process—from the initial filing of court papers to appellate opinions.

We need more than one kind of bar examination. The bar exam should not be of one dimension but have some relativity to future work, such as actual practice, government work, or teaching.

"One of the myths of contemporary legal education," Joel Seligman wrote, "is the goal to teach students to think as lawyers. Legal reasoning is nothing more than purposive problem solving about legal materials or judicial opinions. It is no different than just plain simple reasoning. No one has ever adequately defined what is thinking like a lawyer."[6]

The practice of law involves problem solving. The fundamental skills necessary for competence include factual investigating, interviewing, counseling and negotiation. The complete law school must train, as well as educate, not simply lead to practicing at the expense of the client.

Seligman wrote: "The current model of legal education is comparable to a system of medical education that prepares only general practitioners, leaving surgeons, psychiatrists and medical researchers to gain the most important aspects of their training during their first jobs or by reading on the side."[7]

One of the most overrated aspects of law education is the law review system. How does one rise to the occasion of law reviews? It is through academic honors, letters of recommendation and optional personal statements. They should be open to all who want to contribute. The ones who need it do not get it. It is limited to the intellectual aristocracy, the academic giants, who do not necessarily make the best lawyers.

Justice Burger, commenting on the wasted third year of law school said, "I am satisfied that at least one-half and perhaps all of the third year could be spent to better use than is now the case."[8]

We put too great stress on test scores on the LSAT and the GPA. This can leave the hard working, highly motivated nontester out in the cold unless he can get special consideration as a member of a minority group, by being disadvantaged or disabled, or as a pre-law school high achiever. Great men like Lincoln might not have made it into law school.

What does being a good first-year student and examination tester have to do with becoming a good trial lawyer? Are college grades and performances, including making law review, the best criteria for choosing humane and compassionate practitioners of justice? The brightest student may become the most ineffective lawyer. Often, the more successful a student undergraduate has been the more difficult is his adjustment to the rigors of law study.

How can tests measure integrity, industry, reliability, patience, honesty, moral values, compassion, sensitivity to others' needs, trial advocacy, counseling, persistence, conscientiousness and above all, courage? No value is more recognizable and admirable in human experience than courage.

Philip M. Stern, in *Lawyers on Trial*, said:

> Unhappily, law schools exhibit at best a secondary interest in such traits, contenting themselves with a single comparative narrow aptitude, the ability to do well on examinations, both in college and special multiple choice bar admission tests. Most law schools reduce their screening process to pure mechanics and numbers with a centralized computer which serves all ABA-approved law schools. That procedure flattens the applicant's many qualities into a single numerical index, LSAT and GPA,

> which becomes the most important single factor in the yea-nay decision, with the LSAT often making the decisive difference. The designers and administrators of the LSAT (Educational Testing Services), acknowledge the test has a 60-point error factor. That is, the applicant's "true score" may be 30 points higher or lower than the test result.[9]

The continued widespread use of grades in prediction statistics is due largely to the fact they are conveniently available. It is very simple to examine LSAT and GPA scores, yet it is recognized, psychologically and statistically, that grades do not represent a universal and unvarying value which their numerical or literal definitions often implies.

Errors in the prediction of law school performance are still fairly high, so it is apparent that no prediction technique has as yet even approached infallibility.

The LSAT was never intended to produce better lawyers, but to prevent glutting the market. What kind of lawyer you'll make is not a consideration, the focus is on doing well on law school and bar examinations.

Wigmore, the great jurisprudence writer and lecturer of law studies, held: "The only way to find out whether a boy has the making of a competent lawyer is to see what he can do in a first year of law school."

Robert R. Ramsay wrote in *Journal of Law Education*: "The most serious gap in our knowledge of legal planning continues to be the assessment of those non-intellectual influences. The need for more research to develop and evaluate different law school selection procedures has never been greater."[10]

These are some of my suggestions for improving law education:

1. *Make law review available for everyone, not just the academic giants.*
2. *Add term papers to law school curriculum to bolster the poor tester's grades.*
3. *Increase law student enrollment so that every prospective student gets a first year chance. Get rid of the LSAT and GPA.*
4. *Compel all law school faculty members to pass the bar examination in at least one state and to have a minimum five years of law practice.*
5. *Add clinical study to the second year of law school and do away with internships in judges' offices, clerks of courts offices, and legislative halls.*

6. *Include the study of the masters or experts of law practice for those students who plan trial work.*
7. *Provide government subsidies to students who cannot pay their way, as England does. (We spend billions for weapons for defense that become obsolete within a few years.)*
8. *Allow students to major in specialized fields, such as taxation, personal injury, corporate practice, estate planning, etc.*
9. *Model the licensing of law grads after the current system of licensing engineers. (Electrical engineers are thoroughly tested on practicality, such as the ability to design an electric generator.)*
10. *Give more minorities the opportunity for admission. Open wide the gates.*

Revise and Update Rules for Practicing Attorneys

The American Bar Association and its state affiliates are overly concerned with rules for the practicing attorney. Each year committees on rule-making ordain more rules to make practicing law more difficult. The old worn out ethical standards are kept intact and new ones are added without rhyme or reason.

Strictures against soliciting clients are out of place. Lawyers have a duty to advise people who may be ignorant of their rights, to seek justice in the courts. Bar association disciplinary committees have used anti-solicitation rules to harass public-interest lawyers and solo practitioners—even those working gratis—who represent unpopular clients or causes.

Nader and Green wrote, "A number of leading critics consider anti-solicitation rules unrelated to professional ethics but rather the rules of the guild. That is, they are directed against competition rather than for the maintenance of moral standards in the public interest. Other authors have also emphasized the effect of these rules in protecting established lawyers and large firms from undesired competition from young lawyers and small firms."[11]

Provisions of the codes of professional representation pertaining to division of fees should be abolished. When a lawyer must be retained by a client miles away, common sense dictates that the referring lawyer should not lose a fee or part of a fee because he has to take in another lawyer. Yet the model Code De 2-107 states, "A lawyer shall not divide a fee for legal services with another lawyer who is not a partner in or associate of his law firm" unless the referring lawyer participates in some fashion and there is a written contract disclosing how the fees will be shared. No rule is more unconscionable and no rule is broken more often among attorneys.

The time for certification and specialization within the legal system has arrived if competency is to increase. The medical field has twenty-seven specialities; the dental field, eight. Specialization allows lawyers to confine their practice partially or entirely to a particular area of law. There should be mandatory continuing legal education for the seasoned lawyer to keep up with current laws. Every member of the bar should be required to attend advanced courses or lectures.

Addressing this, Nader and Green wrote, "Certification, specialization and continuing education can assure the public of more noteworthy representation in and out of the courts and of getting their dollar's worth of service.

"There is no place for the jack of all trades in lawyering in the weighty cases of capital criminal offenses and the civil cases that could involve millions of dollars in recovery," the authors contend.[12]

We must take our hats off to the English who stress expert advocacy in court with their system of solicitors and barristers. It is the solicitor who handles the office work of wills, deeds, corporate work, and the preparation of the case for trial. The barrister confines his work to the courtroom, whether representing the state or a defendant in criminal cases and the plaintiff or defendant in civil cases.

The American legal system does not conform to the textbook appearance of due process and equal justice for all. Legal services must be available equally to rich and poor, young and old. There must be a right to the counsel of their choice for civil and criminal litigants who are unable to pay. Meaningful representation, not simply a pro forma compliance with the law, requires more than a warm body with a law degree; and counsel should confer with the client well in advance of trial to properly prepare the case.

Public criticism of the legal system shares a common thrust: There is too much law and too little justice, and the attorneys are to blame.

We need a nationwide law foundation to replace the ABA in representing lawyers, judges and laymen. People, that is, who are interested in promoting equality and justice for the rich and the poor, people who are dissatisfied with the status quo and are willing to crusade for changes in the practice of law. Further, we need an organization, such as organized labor has, to stand up for the individual lawyer faced with a grievance. Today's lawyer has no one but another lawyer retained to represent him, in a conflict with the strong and mighty bar association grievance committee.

An honest effort must be made to kick out the dishonest; the profession can be honorable only with honest men who place the dollar second to service to his fellow men.

The adversary system with its dog-eat-dog attitude must give way to peaceful settlement of disputes within society. Arbitration should replace the expensive and time-consuming lawsuit. This is successfully practiced in the far east, in countries such as China and Japan.

We need lawyers motivated by good will. Law and lawyers have failed to function well. Reform and honest appraisal demands radicals.

Improve the Procedures for Selecting Judges

The public knows little about judges. There is little public discussion or awareness of the quality of less competent judges. The media remains quiet despite obvious wrongdoings and unfair decisions. Analyses of published opinions or public appraisal of a judge's performance are almost nonexistent. Spend awhile inside courtrooms and you'll see judges with unmistakable biases, unstable temperaments; judges who are insulting and sarcastic, who open the chambers at 9:00 and go home at 4:00. The 40-hour work week is unheard of among many of the judiciary. There are judges who favor the clients of clubhouse cronies. Such conduct leads to substantial injustice. Judges, except for a few, form a close-knit group which closes ranks for self protection.

Lawyers know all about the judges but they cannot speak out without jeopardizing their clients' cases.

How long must we tolerate judges who have never tried a case in court, written a brief, or argued an appeal? Why is legal education important for the aspiring lawyer but nonexistent for the new judge? The most important prerequisite for a judgeship is to be a member of the local and state bar associations which are made up of the elitists or members of the influential law firms. A serious defect of the bar associations has been their restricted memberships and class bias. Most are white males associated with large firms. Few have specialized in criminal law or domestic relations.

Many American lawyers and judges pay homage to the English system which may indeed produce the best qualified judges anywhere. In England, judges are appointed by the Crown from a limited cadre of barristers having at least ten years' experience in the courtroom. It is a thing of beauty to watch the barrister and judge at work. Only after years of trial experience is the barrister ready to take on a judgeship. In France and some other European countries, judges are civil servants who, through specialized education, work themselves up the judicial ladder.

As to the selection process in our country, only ten states do not elect trial judges. Political considerations play a large part in the selection and election. Judicial aspirations under all systems of selection must, except in extraordinary situations, have political backing. Political support entails contributions to a political party. A judicial candidate must either pay it himself or raise it from friends and supporters. There are three groups of people interested in a judicial candidate: friends and family, businessmen who have dealings with the courts, and members of the bar. This system puts the judges under direct obligation to the lawyers and litigants who appear before them. There are many ways in which a judge can show favoritism in the course of a trial, such as in the admissibility of evidence, granting or refusing to grant certain instructions to the jury, during *voir dire* when the attorneys are trying to prune the jury, motions for change of venue, continuances, and the deciding of close cases.

Despite the problems inherent in the election process there is some merit in election rather than appointment: It gives the nonestablishment lawyers, women, and minorities, a chance at judgeships, and arrogant, unfair and corrupt judges can be voted out of office.

And there is the cult of the robe. Judges clad in the solemn black or red silk automatically believe themselves endowed as sacred and touched by divinity. We must face the fact that judges are human public officers with human weaknesses and foibles. They are born with predispositions and through education—formal and informal—and experiences, adopt the attitudes which affect them in judging situations. Some attitudes precede reasoning in particular instances, and are therefore by definition, prejudices.

Appellate judges have the same biases and interests and at times these are more pronounced. State appellate decisions have the binding force of state statutes. So that the public may know judges' rights, obligations and limitations, their opinions should be clear and concise, and widely published. Appellate judges spend too much time writing windy opinions; they are too willing to follow precedent rather than establish new law to effect change in current conditions. One of their pet maxims is: Let the legislature change established common law rather than changing it through judicial fiat. Plainly, this is passing the buck.

Judges who must decide many and varied questions affecting great numbers of individuals and society as a whole, are handicapped not merely by lack of information, but by the narrowness of their training and backgrounds.

Most appellate courts refuse to examine the facts of a case on appeal regardless of the relevancy to justice—the civilizing and humanizing element in any society. In most of our state appellate courts, the court can reverse a lower court only for errors of law. They are bound by the lower judge's and jury's finding, however wrong they may consider the conclusion. The appellate courts of Britain review both the law and the facts because they are interested, above all, in justice.

Some considerations worthy of change:

1. *Get rid of the cult of the robe.* It's awesome both to the client and young lawyer, placing them in a state of fear. In the service of the government no one other than judges wears a uniform, except the police and elevator operators. The judge's robe is an antique garment, impractical and of no aesthetic value. Robes and courthouse verbiage symbolize the notion that courts must preserve the ancient ways, that the past is sacred and that the public may not change inherited customs and institutions. It was democratically-inspired Thomas Jefferson who opposed any distinctive judicial raimant. Some lawyers call the judges priestly tribes with superhuman force. Such belief is delusional. Unfrock the judge and let him appear as an ordinary person. Plain dress may encourage plain speaking.
2. *Develop pre-judge education toward a career in judging.* Promotion should be from the lower to the higher courts and be based on merit and performance.
3. Judges' orders or opinions should never be decided in chambers and suit parties should accompany their attorney in approaching the bench.
4. *A judge should interfere in the proceedings when an incompetent attorney is fumbling* the ball, so as to prevent injustice.
5. *We need court administrators.* Postponement of cases beyond scheduled trial dates is a major factor in delaying the administration of justice—civil as well as criminal. Court and court-supporting services spend substantial time spinning their wheels. Court time is lost, witnesses disappear, and all are inconvenienced and frustrated at repeatedly being called needlessly into court. Judges and lawyers cannot blame the system, they are the people who run the system.

6. *Trial judges should be well versed in constitutional law.* Why need the criminal defendant go all the way to the U.S. Supreme Court to establish his rights in a simple matter of due process?
7. *Get rid of those cases that do not belong in the courts,* such as traffic, divorce, custody, prostitution, vagrancy, drunkenness, gambling, and drug use—cases that involve no infringement upon property rights and that so preoccupy the courts they are prevented from dealing effectually with more weighty matters.
8. *Let trial judges come from the ranks of trial lawyers and appellate judges from trial judges.*
9. *Judges should be rotated within the state* so that no judge becomes too friendly or familiar with lawyers appearing before him. Let's get rid of the buddy-buddy system in the judiciary.

Eliminate or Greatly Reduce Jury Trials

The jury is not without its critics. Many thoughtful persons urge that it be abolished either in whole or in part. There are numerous jury verdicts that are difficult to explain. It is not unlikely that juries are often arbitrary, and subject to sentiment.

"One of the features of our legal system that distinguishes us from the rest of the world," a *New York Times* article stated, "is our continued reliance upon the jury. By one estimate, we conduct eight times as many criminal jury trials as does the rest of the world.

". . .Today, almost 90 percent of British criminal prosecutions are decided by a judge or magistrate without a jury. Even serious criminal cases can be tried without juries in Northern Ireland, under anti-terrorist laws authorizing special tribunals composed solely of judges."[13]

There have always been Americans who distrusted the ability of ordinary citizens to pass judgment in complicated legal matters. Roscoe Pound, Jerome Frank and Erwin Griswold are among the eminent legal scholars to express the view that a jury system, as Griswold, a former solicitor general, put it, "is the apotheosis or glorification of the amateur."

Chief Justice Burger is among a growing number of bench and bar leaders who question whether modern juries can understand, much less fairly decide, complex, protracted cases. "In a trial that lasted 96 days, the jury heard 87 witnesses and examined 3,000 exhibits," *Time* reported. "After deliberating 115 days, the jury could not reach a unanimous verdict and the judge had to declare a mistrial. Following this the judge queried the jury and their answers became confused.

"The jury is rarely a cross section of those best fitted to serve 12 of one's peers," the magazine article concluded. "In the 14-month trial of *Scott v. Xerox*, a $1.5 million trust suit, the average education revealed of the jury was the tenth grade."[14]

Lloyd E. Moore claimed that "Many jurors are intimidated by the trial judge and give negative responses even to a judge's most penetrating questions."[15]

Howard James cited critics' reasons for scrapping the jury system:

1. The jury system creates delays and causes court congestion.
2. Jury trials are too costly.
3. Because testimony is so often technical, many jurors do not comprehend what is going on. Or they may not understand the law. Or follow the thread of logic in a case.
4. It is hard to round up a jury that really represents a fair cross section of the community. Many citizens are "too busy to serve." Or feel compensation is too low for the time spent. So they ask to be excused by the hundreds.
5. Juries are unpredictable.[16]

"Most lawsuits present a plurality of complicated issues which single track minds are utterly unable to grasp," James wrote.

"To discriminate between conflicting items of evidence, to determine whether a skillful prevaricator is twisting facts to his own profit, to see when they are being grossly exaggerated or manufactured out of whole cloth, requires the highest degree of judgment, education, experience, and mental alertness."

Granville Williams, an English scholar, said during a series of lectures in 1955:

> . . .There seems to be a formidable weight of argument against the jury system. To begin with, the 12 men and women are chosen haphazardly. Exemption is given to some professional people who would seem to be among the best qualified to serve—clergymen, ministers of religion,

> lawyers, doctors, dentists, chemists, justices of the peace, as well as all rank of the armed forces.
>
> The subtraction of relatively intelligent classes means that it is an understatement to describe a jury, with Herbert Spencer, as a "group of 12 people of average ignorance."
>
> There is no guarantee that members of a particular jury may not be quite unusually ignorant, credulous, slow-witted, narrow-minded, biased, or temperamental. The danger of this happening is not one that can be removed by some slight procedural change or adjustment.

In his 1962-63 report to the Harvard Law School, Dean Erwin Griswold, said: "Why should anyone think that 12 persons brought in from the street, selected in various ways, for their lack of general ability, should have any special capacity for deciding controversies between persons?"

Lawyer Walter J. Bilder says: "The minds of jurors are notoriously susceptible to influences which are extraneous to the merits of the controversy and. . .the jury's verdict is likely to be determined by considerations which are irrelevant to a just determination of the case."[17]

Bilder contends:

> Aside from automobile collision cases, a lawsuit is almost certain to involve a set of facts. . .which relates to. . .[an] experience which is wholly alien to. . .most, if not all, persons who become members of a jury.
>
> Confronted with such a set of facts, the members of a jury will. . .[have] an attitude of incomprehension and inattentiveness and even boredom, aggravated undoubtedly by a feeling of resentment at having been compelled to leave their ordinary pursuits in order to settle a controversy which even fails to arouse [in] them [even] an academic interest.[18]

"In many instances," says James, "lawyers, when selecting a jury, will refuse to accept business executives or others holding responsible positions. And they reject jurors for other reasons that are not always explained in a way that makes citizens feel that the system must be wrong."[19]

Warren Burnett of Odessa, Texas, an experienced trial lawyer, contends that "one of the majesties of the jury system is the uncertainty of it. The only thing a trial lawyer is sure of is a darned good seat at the trial."[20]

In *Law and the Modern Mind* Jerome Frank wrote:

> It is unlikely that 12 persons summoned from all kinds of occupations, unaccustomed to the machinery of the law, unacquainted with their own mental workings and not known to one another, can, in the scant time allowed them for deliberation, do as good a job in weighing conflicting testimony as an experienced judge. Can they see as well through the glib liar, or of the unconsciously biased but conscientious witness, or as ably allow for the stage fright which often makes the honest but cautious man speak falteringly on the witness stand? A judge who has sat for 10 to 15 years on the criminal bench is usually keener to detect a liar or see through a faked defense than any 12 men drawn indiscriminately from different walks of business activity.[21]

Juries are "notoriously gullible and impressionable," Frank charged.[22] In *Courts on Trial* he pointed out that ". . .juries often do not find the facts in accordance with the evidence, but distort or fudge the facts and find them in such a manner that (by applying the legal rules laid down by the judge to the fact, deliberately misfound) the jury is able to produce the result which it desires in favor of one party or the other. The facts are found in order to reach the result."[23]

Juries have been known to arrive at verdicts in civil cases by one of two methods, Frank submits. "(1) Each juror. . .writes down the amount he wants to award; the total is added and the average taken as the verdict. (2) The jurors, by agreement, decide for one side or the other by the flip of a coin."[24]

"Many juries in reaching their verdicts," Frank wrote, "rely on their emotional responses to the lawyers and witnesses; they like or dislike, not any legal rule, but they do like an artful lawyer for the plaintiff, the poor widow, the brunette, the soulful eyes; and they do dislike the big corporation, the foreigner with a thick accent.

"The jury system almost completely wipes out the principle of equality before the law which supremacy of law and the reign of law symbolize and does too, at the expense of justice, which requires fairness and competence in finding facts in specific cases."[25]

It is the personal injury cases that hog tie the court system and keep many claimants waiting years for recovery in a case. Accidents that cause loss of employment, loss for damaged automobiles and medical expenses, take years to be compensated. Those matters should be deferred to experienced panels of arbitration rather than clogging the court system. The right to trial should exist when the parties cannot agree to the arbitrator's decision, as in workman compensation cases.

In all cases in which a jury trial is applicable, let us resort to the majority rule rather than a unanimous verdict. Since majority rule governs the elective process and many other matters, why is the jury system so unique as to warrant unanimity?

And there are those who would prefer a professional jury that travels about, hearing and deciding cases based on the facts and current laws. Aren't we seeking justice rather than lopsidedness?

Removing Abuses in the Criminal Law Jungle

The challenge in the last decades of the 20th century is to make equal protection of the laws not merely a nominal right, but an actual, feasible, and available means of redress and defense for every person. To do this, the system must be modified to conform to due process. There is no quick fix or panacea. This chapter is not a blueprint for redoing the legal system but is meant to present ideas for change—for the promotion of justice.

In a land flowing with an abundance of lawyers there should be enough for anyone with a particular need. People charged with a crime are constitutionally entitled to adequate defense counsel. The litigant should be entitled to select his attorney. A young lawyer foisted upon the client is not the answer. Our whole system of criminal law must be examined, beginning with the grand jury.

"The Grand Jury has served too often to harass the poor and unpopular," Frankel and Naftalis wrote. "Its large and secret powers have proved too frequently to be terrifying weapons in the hands of righteous or cynical prosecutors. Many witnesses have been badgered, trapped, defamed by leaks and scarred by the high-handed perverse employment of the Grand Jury's great authority. The most sweeping design for change remains the still-powerful body of opinion that favors its abolition."[26]

The alternative in England and in European judicial systems is to have the preliminary inquisitorial proceedings conducted by a magistrate.

The role of the prosecutor has been delineated by John Lofton. "Prosecutors are most addicted to publicity seeking," he observed. "As Roscoe Pound once wrote: 'When a sensational crime has been committed, coroner, police, and district attorney may each go out for glory or publicity. Politics require taking advantage of possibilities of publicity.'"

Explained Lofton:

> A prosecutor's election or re-election depends largely on the reputation he has with the public. And the press

> is one means of building a reputation. If he is running for the first time, a district attorney candidate may be able to cite his experience as a special prosecutor. If he is running to succeed himself in office, a frequent tactic is to appeal for votes on the basis of his record of convictions.
>
> It has been observed that at prosecutors' conventions there is often talk that successful prosecutions of a sensational nature can send a district attorney to new heights, as shown by the career of Thomas Dewey. Yet there is grave danger to justice in such an attitude. The late Judge Jerome Frank made it clear when he said: "The menace to the guiltless becomes singularly great when a politically ambitious prosecutor seeks to advance himself through newspaper renown for the large number of convictions he obtains."[27]

"A prosecutor, eager to prove a suspect guilty," wrote Lofton, "will carelessly, or even sometimes deliberately, neglect painstaking investigation, before indictment or trial, of leads that might well show the suspect's innocence. Such a prosecutor will all too easily develop what Sam Hobbs (a lawyer with much experience in prosecution) calls an 'occupational disease,' a 'habit of drifting into a chronic spirit of hostility toward each new suspect.'

"Prosecuting attorneys, like other law enforcement officials, are attuned to what the public wants and tend to reflect popular demands. In the South this may mean the excusing of lynching or failure to prosecute. Or in any region it may mean harsh treatment of defendants in cases in which public passion is excited. Sometimes the zeal to convict becomes so intense that the prosecutor casts aside caution and even honesty."[28]

Reduce Plea Bargaining

Plea bargaining distorts the ideas of right and wrong, justice and injustice. Those guilty of a crime may assume that the acts they commit are only worth the crime they ultimately admit. Conversely, those who have committed no crime may plead guilty to a lesser offense to avoid being found guilty of the crime with which they were originally charged. Such a possibility is perhaps the most serious objection to plea bargaining. Our entire criminal law system has its being in the plea bargain institution.

Harry Douglas Siegler was tried in Richmond, Virginia, for the murder of an insurance agent. Siegler maintained his innocence throughout the trial. After the jury retired, fear of a death sentence overcame him and he pled guilty to first degree murder and robbery. The jury returned three minutes later. They had found him not guilty. The judge then sentenced him to sixty years on his plea bargain.

Many defendants plea bargain for a lesser charge and assume the judge will be more lenient. Some judges will even state that under certain circumstances a defendant should be penalized for wasting the court's resources by trying an unmeritorious case. It appears to be highly unjust for a defendant to be given a greater sentence for stubbornly maintaining his innocence.[29]

Eliminate the Insanity Defense

The insanity plea should no longer be used as a defense. No aspect of the insanity defense enrages the public more than seeing a defendant acquitted as insane and then released to commit yet more crimes. Jurors are asked to determine the sanity of a person and grasp for guidelines from forensic psychiatrists who only add to the confusion by presenting varying and opposing opinions. The insanity defense may be an intriguing intellectual exercise for psychiatrists, psychologists and lawyers, but the welfare of society should be the most important issue at stake. People who commit heinous crimes may or may not know what they are doing at the time of the crime. They are in need of control and need to be confined to an institution, no matter how upsetting the confinement. They need society's protection and society needs protection from them.

Why not create new verdicts of guilty but mentally ill, with sentences to be served at a state hospital. If cured, the guilty could then be remanded to a state prison for the remainder of sentence. They must be segregated from a society in which they cannot live peaceably.

Abolish Capital Punishment

More than seventy nations have acted to reduce human violence by abolishing the death penalty. Among advanced nations the United States remains the chief advocate of death as a punishment for crime. We are characterized in the eyes of millions as much by our executions as by the general violence of our environment.

History shows that the death penalty has been unjustly imposed, innocents have been killed by the state, effective rehabilitation has been impaired, judicial administration has suffered and crime has not been deterred.

The major argument for capital punishment today is the belief that fear of death will keep people from committing serious crimes. But most studies of the death penalty have concluded that it has failed as a deterrent. A comprehensive United Nations report found that abolition of the death penalty has no effect on murder rates. With or without capital punishment, murder rates are the same.

Capital crimes are more often committed on impulse in a moment of passion without thought of gain or loss. Only extreme fear of punishment, so emotionally severe that basic instincts are cowed, can deter unpremeditated crime. It is, after all, meditation before the act that may cause a person, aware of the risks and consequences of being caught, to refrain from prohibited conduct.

The hardened criminal, devoid of human compassion, will not be deterred by the fear of death or severe punishment. He lives among the springs of American violence, where sudden death is no stranger. Society must protect itself by rehabilitating him or isolating him. To seek some satisfaction from his execution will only brutalize others.[30]

There is no justification for the death penalty. It demeans life. Its inhumanity raises basic questions about our institutions and our purpose as a people. Why must we kill? What do we fear? What do we accomplish besides our own embitterment? We must revere life and in so doing create in the hearts of our people a love for mankind that will finally still violence.[31]

The Administration of Equal Justice

The purpose of our legal system should be the administration of justice equally.

"Justice is not possible in a society that denies social justice," Gregg Barak wrote. "Social conditions have been squarely recognized as the primary cause of crime. Most of our corrective efforts have been directed toward rehabilitating the criminal rather than revamping the socio-economic system. The convicted criminal is only given attention after he commits the crime. When released and returned to society he must be able to adjust to inequities that were at the root of his crime. His ability to tolerate his position in society dictates his success as a reformed citizen. It has been more advantageous to condemn the common criminal and ignore the crimes committed by the more elite members of society."[32]

We will never have criminal justice as long as we have political influence involved in our legal systems. We will never have criminal justice as long as the bar associations refuse to accept their responsibility and role in defending the poor and unwanted. When money becomes the purpose and end of law practice, justice goes out the window.

The poor, the needy, the unwanted, the despised, we will always have with us. They need help from the professionals.

White collar crime converts billions of dollars annually in tax evasion, price fixing, embezzlement, swindles and consumer fraud. The mother of a 19-year-old boy serving a four-year term for stealing a $116 welfare check from a hallway mailbox, reads in the morning paper that a corporate executive has been convicted of evading $60,000 in income taxes and received a suspended sentence.

The U.S. criminal justice system maintains a double standard. When E. F. Hutton pleaded guilty to 2,000 counts of mail fraud involving kited checks, its top officers denied any knowledge of the wrongdoing, despite an FBI investigation which disclosed that several managerial level executives had conspired to bilk millions of dollars from more than 400 banks; the net effect of this all too common practice is to steal interest by using someone else's money. The Justice Department, under Attorney General Ed Meese, allowed plea bargaining. All guilty individuals were let off the hook. Corporate E. F. Hutton was fined $1,000 for each of the 2,000 criminal charges—a total of $2 million—and required to make restitution. No one went to jail. Neither real justice nor the appearance of justice was satisfied by the E. F. Hutton plea bargaining arrangements. Hutton's president, Scott Pierce, is the brother-in-law of Vice President George Bush.

No industry has drawn more fire than the defense business. General Electric, the sixth largest U.S. military contractor, pleaded guilty to defrauding the Air Force of $800,000 on a Minuteman missile project in 1980. The company agreed to pay fines of more than $2 million.

Law enforcement officials claim that the growing corporate wrongdoing and the consequences of its acts create a double standard and is destructive to society.

Organized crime reaps hundreds of millions in gambling, loan sharking, drug trafficking, extortion, prostitution, corruption of government officials and resorting to force, including murder when necessary, to accomplish its purpose. A General Accounting Office survey released May 2, 1985, revealed that 75 percent of 1,044 Cosa Nostra crime figures and big drug dealers drew shorter time behind bars, and 68 percent were fined less than the law allowed. Life sentences were handed to only one.[33]

"If we are to deal meaningfully with crime we must examine its nature and causes,'' Ramsey Clark said. ''We must see the dehumanizing effect on the individual of slums, racism, ignorance and violence, of corruption in high places, of poverty and unemployment. We must see and realize the effect of prenatal neglect, sickness and disease, pollution, alcoholism and narcotic addiction. These are the fountainheads of crime we must deal with. Respect for all people of all races. We must have a humane and generous concern for each individual, for his safety and health. When society seeks vengeance, it cheapens and demeans one's life. Violence will only nourish violence as long as we do not revere human life."[34]

Said Clark, "We must recognize the effect of organized crime with its involvement in the drug trade and its involvement in street crime. Narcotics furnished by the professionals nourish thefts, burglaries, muggings and killings."[35]

In a century characterized by growth and advancement in scientific technology and economics, the legal fraternity is still living in the past. The mainstream of progress passes us by when justice is denied any citizen because of faulty administration. The failure to act becomes inexcusable.

In classrooms and meeting halls, we pledge allegiance "to the United States of America and to the republic for which it stands, one nation, under God, indivisible, with liberty and justice for all." For many it has little or no significance. Many refuse to participate in the ceremony because it has little meaning in real life.

Endnotes

I. The ABA: Overlords of Lawyering

1. Carson, Gerald. *A Good Day at Saratoga*. American Bar Association, 1978.

2. Lieberman, Jethro K. *Crisis at the Bar*. New York: W.W. Norton & Co., 1978, p. 57.

3. Gerson, Allen, Ed. *Lawyer's Ethics*. Transatlantic Books, 1980, p. 41.

4. Stern, Philip M. *Lawyers on Trial*. New York Times Book Co., Inc., 1980, p. xviii.

5. *Ibid*. p. 90.

6. *Ibid*. p. 88.

7. Gerson. pp. 42-43.

8. Dayton, David McKean. *Intergrated Bar*. Houghton-Mifflin Co., 1963, pp. 84-111.

9. Stern. pp. 77-78.

10. Nader, Ralph and Green, Mark, Eds. *Verdict on Lawyers*. Thomas Y. Crowell Co., 1976, p. 98.

11. Lieberman. pp. 79-87, 562 Pac 2nd 1326, 1977.

12. Lieberman. pp. 87-90, 97 Sup Ct., 2691, 1977.

13. Lieberman. pp. 71-75, 389 U.S. 217, 1967.

14. Lieberman. pp. 77-78, 401 U.S. 576, 1971.

15. Lieberman. pp. 110-113, 421 U.S. 773, 783, 1975.

16. Strock, Barbara R. *It's Easy to Avoid Probate*. Orlando, Florida: Linch Publishing, 1983.

17. Dacey, Norman F. *How to Avoid Probate*. New York: Crown Publishers, Inc., 1983.

II. The Judiciary: High Priests Of The Legal System

1. Frankfurter, Justice Felix. *In Re Sawyer.* 360 U.S. 622, 669, 1959.

2. Wright, John A. *How to Get Good Judges.* 1892.

3. Goldberg, Louis and Levenson, Elanaore. *Lawless Judges.* New York: Negro Press Inc., 1969, p. 7.

4. *Ibid.* p. 11.

5. *Ibid.* p. 9.

6. *St Petersburg Times.* Feb. 5, 1984.

7. Forer, Judge Lois F., *Money and Justice, Who Owns the Courts.* New York: W.W. Norton & Co., 1984, pp. 75-76, 79, 81, 83.

8. Jackson, Donald Dale. *Judges.* New York: Atheneum, 1974, p. 9.

9. Botein, Judge Bernard. *Trial Judge.* Simon & Schuster Inc., 1952, and Da Capa Press, 1974, p. 308.

10. Frank, Jerome. *Courts On Trial: Myths and Reality in American Justice.* Princeton Univ. Press, 1949 & 1973, pp. 151-152.

11. Jackson. pp. vii-viii.

12. *Ibid.* pp. 7, 8.

13. *Ibid.* p. 155.

14. *Ibid.* p. 239.

15. *Ibid.* pp. 378-379.

16. Nader, Ralph and Green, Mark, Eds. *Verdicts On Lawyers.* New York: Thomas Y. Crowell Company, 1976, pp. 269-270.

17. Strick, Anne. *Injustice For All.* Penguin Books, 1977, p. 142.

18. Frank, Jerome. *Law and the Modern Mind.* Anchor Books, 1963, Peter Smith, 1970, p. 108.

19. *Ibid.* p. 112.

20. James, Howard. *Crisis in the Courts.* David McKay Co. Inc., 1967, pp. 6-10.

21. Rosenblatt, Stanley. *Justice Denied.* Los Angeles, CA: Nash Publishing Co., 1971, pp. 257-258.

22. Murphy, William H., former Circuit Judge of Baltimore City, Md. *The Baltimore Sun.* Baltimore, Maryland: 1984.

23. Rosenblatt. p. 258.

24. O'Connell, Jeffery. *Law Suit Lottery.* Free Press, A Div. of Macmillan Pub. Co., Inc., 1979, pp. 108-10.

25. Strick. p. 165.

26. *Model Rules of Professional Conduct and Code of Judicial Conduct.* American Bar Assoc., August, 1983.

27. Traynor, Judge Rodger J., California.

28. *Model Rules of Professional Conduct and Code of Judicial Conduct*. ABA, 1983, p. 135.

29. *United States* vs. *Manton*. 107 Fed 2nd 834, 1938, 309 U.S. 664.

30. *Judicial Ethics*. Canon II, 1983, p. 135.

31. *St. Petersburg Times*. Dec. 8, 1983.

32. *Ibid*. August 9, 1984.

33. *Judicial Ethics*. Canon III, 1983, p. 136.

34. *St. Petersburg Times*. March 15, 1983; March 18, 1983; March 19, 1983; May 11, 1983; Dec. 11, 1983; Dec 15, 1983.

35. No. 13950 Circuit Court of Allegany County, Md. *Appeal No. 614*. Maryland: Special Court of Appeals, Sept. Term 1980.

36. *Judicial Ethics*. Canon 7, Model Rules, 1983, p. 145.

37. *Lawless Judges*. p. 232.

38. Strick. pp. 147-166.

39. O'Connell. p. 112.

40. Frank *Courts on Trial, Myths and Reality in American Justice*. p. 152.

41. *Lawless Judges*. pp. v-viii.

42. Justice Douglas in *Craig* vs. *Harvey*. 331 U.S. 367, 1947.

43. Justice Medina. *Some Reflections on the Judiciary Function, A Personal Viewpoint*, p. 38 ABA Journal, 1952, pp. 107-108.

44. Justice Frankfurter in *Bridges* vs. *Calif.* 314 U.S. 252, 289, 1941.

45. Mellinkoff, David. *Lawyers and the System of Justice*. West Publishing Co., 1976, pp. 559-564.

46. Supreme Court of Kansas. *State* vs. *Nelson*. 210 Kans. 637, 204 Pac 2nd 211, 1972.

47. Strick. p. 155.

48. *Garrison* vs. *U.S.* 379 U.S. 64, 1964.

Additional Sources:

Kunstler, William M., Esq. *The Case for Courage*. Wm. Morrow Co., 1962.

No. 10,601 Law. Circuit Court for Allegany County, Md., Ruppert vs. Cumberland Brewery Co.

III. Appellate Courts: The Red Barons

1. Ingersoll, Robert J. Speech at Civil Rights Meeting. Lincoln Hall, Washington, D.C. Oct. 22, 1883.

2. Parker, John J., Former Chief Judge of U.S. Court of Appeals Fourth Circuit.

3. Davis, John W. *ABA Journal*. 1941, p. 221.

4. Marks, Burton and Goldfarb, Gerald. *Winning with your Lawyer.* New York: McGraw Hill, Book Co., 1980, p. 68.

5. No. 12376 Circuit Court, Allegany County, Maryland: Case by Jury, Washington County, 1975.

6. Neely, Judge Richard, of the W. Va. Supreme Court. *How Courts Govern America*. Yale U. Press, 1980, expanded by 1983 interview, Charleston, W. Va., Court Chambers.

7. Traynor, Roger J. *Riddle of Harmless Error.* Columbus, Ohio State University Press,1970, p. 16.

8. Sunderland, Edson R. *Proper Function of the Appellate Court*. 5 Indiana Law Journal, 1930, pp. 483, 504, and 505.

9. Llewellyn, Karl. *The Common Law Tradition Deciding Appeals*. Little Brown & Co., Inc., 1960, p. 240.

10. Watson, Richard W. and Downing, Rondal. *Politics of the Bench and Bar.* 1969 Judicial Selection Under the Missouri non-Partisan Court Plan, New York: John Wiley & Sons, Inc., p. 181 and others.

11. Forer, Judge Lois F. *Money & Justice, Who Owns the Courts*. New York: W.W. Norton & Co., 1984, p. 168.

12. *Ibid*. p. 170.

13. LeFlar, Robert Allen, Ed. *Appellate Judicial Decisions*. St Paul Minnesota: West Publishing Co.; and Institute of Judicial Administration, 1974, pp. 272-291.

14. Neely. pp. 103-104.

15. Gregory, Herbert H., Former Justice of the Virginia Supreme Court. *Virginia Law Review.* 1948, pp. 363-364.

16. Vanderbilt, Arthur T. *Improving the Administration of Justice*. 1957, pp. 106-116.

17. Denning, Lord. *Due Process of Law.* London: Butterworth, 1980, p. 3.

18. LeFlar. p. 116.

19. Jerome Frank. *Courts on Trial, Myth and Reality in American Justice*. Princeton U. Press, 1949 & 1973, p. 270.

20. Forer. p. 163.

21. *Baltimore Sun*. March 20, 1983.

22. *Murphy* vs. *Baltimore Gas and Electric Co.* No. 59 Sept. Term 1980, 290 Md. 186.

23. *Butterfield* vs. *Forester.* 11 East 60, English Reports 926, 1809, and *Harrison* vs. *Montgomery County School Board, et al*. 295 Md. 442, March, 1982.

IV. The Veniremen: Juries And Justice

1. Moore, Lloyd E. *Jury, The Tool of Kings*. Paladium of Liberty, W. H. Anderson Co., 1973, pp. 86-89.

2. Joiner, Charles W. *Civil Justice of the Jury*. Prentice Hall, 1962, p. 162. Bloomstein, Morris J.*The Jury System*. New York: Bobbs-Merrill and Co., 1968. Forsyth, William. *History of Trial by Jury*. Lenox Hill Publishing and Distributing Co., 1971, p. 199.

3. McCart, Samual W. *Trial by Jury*. Chilton Book Co., 1964, pp. 3-4.

4. *Ibid*. p. 4.

5. *Ibid*. pp. 5-6.

6. *Ibid*. pp. 6-7.

7. *Ibid*. pp. 6-7.

8. Moore. pp. 97-99.

9. Bloomstein. p. 22.

10. McCart.

11. Moore. pp. 107-109.

12. Bloomstein. pp. 23-24.

13. Moore. p. 110-111.

14. Moore. p. 101.

15. Moore. p. 102.

16. McCart. p. 11.

17. Joiner. p. 180.

18. McCart. p. 16.

19. McCart. p. 17.

20. Hastie. pp. 1-2.

21. Hastie. p. 3, and *Burch* vs. *LA*. 1979.

22. Jerome Frank. *Law and the Modern Mind*. Coward-McCann Inc., 1970, pp. 327-28.

23. *St. Petersburg Times Newspaper*. Florida: March 18, 1984.

24. Frank. *Law and the Modern Mind*. p.186.

25. Frank. *Law and the Modern Mind*. p 187.

26. Frank,*Law and the Modern Mind,* p. 191.

27. O'Connell, Jeffrey. *Lawsuit Lottery*. New York: Free Press Div. of MacMillan Co., Inc., 1977, pp. 90-91.

28. O'Connell. p. 94.

29. O'Connell. p. 101.

30. *Kiddy* vs. *Memorial Hospital & Dorsey*. No. 9920 Circuit Court, Allegany County, Maryland: jury case in Garrett County, Maryland.

31. *Liberty Magazine*. March/April, 1983, p. 7.

32. *Ibid*. p. 8.

33. *Ibid*. p. 10.
34. Kelly, John. *Baltimore Sun*. April 3, 1984.
35. *St. Petersburg Times*. Florida: April 30, 1984.
36. McCart. p. 35.
37. Criminal case, Oakland, Md: Garrett County Circuit Court., Nos. 921, 922, 923.
38. *St Petersburg Times*. January 1, 1983.
39. King, Larry L. *Book of Outlaws, Con Men, Whores, Politicians, and other Artists*. Penquin Books, 1973, pp. 165-201.
40. *St. Petersburg Times*. October 27, 1984.
41. *St. Petersburg Times*. October 24, 1984.
42. *Tampa Tribune*. Florida: February 4, 1984.
43. *St. Petersburg Times*. March 31, 1983.
44. *St. Petersburg Times*. May 18. 1983.

V. The Criminal Law Jungle

1. Freedman, Monroe H. *Lawyer's Ethics in an Adversary System*, Bobbs Merrill, Inc., 1975, p. 84.
2. James, Howard. *Crisis in the Courts*. David McKay & Co., Inc., 1967.
3. James. pp. 126-142.
4. Barak, Gregg. *In Defense of Whom: A Critique of Criminal Justice Reform*. Anderson Publishing Co., 1980.
5. *Ibid*. p. 21.
6. *Ibid*. p. 28.
7. Winters, Glenn R. and Schoenbaum, Richard J., Eds. *American Judicature Series of Articles*. 1976, p. 86.
8. Barak. p. 40.
9. Barak. p. 41.
10. *St. Petersburg Times*. April 26, 1984.
11. Rosenblatt, Stanley. *Justice Denied*. Los Angeles: Nash Publishing Co., 1971, p. 93.
12. *University of Pennsylvania Law Review*. No. 103, p. 1057.
13. James. p. 92.
14. Rosenblatt. pp. 95-96.
15. Nader, Ralph, and Green, Mark, Eds. *Verdicts on Lawyers*. New York: Thomas Y. Crowell Co., 1976, pp. 231-232.
16. Dorsen, Norman, and Friedman, Leonard. *Disorder in the Court*. Pantheon Books, 1973.
17. Freedman. p. 88.

18. Freedman. p. 89.
19. Freedman. p. 89.
20. Barak.
21. Freedman. p. 89.
22. Freedman. p. 96.
23. *St. Petersburg Times*. March 3, 1984.
24. *New York Times*. July 3, 1984.
25. Rosenblatt. p. 106.
26. Rosenblatt. pp. 92-132.
27. Abourez, James G. "The Inquisition Revisited," *Barrister*. Winter 1980, pp. 19-20.
28. Mellinkoff, David. *Lawyers and the System of Justice*. West Publishing Co., 1976, p. 733.
29. *Smith* vs. *Texas*. 311 U.S. 128, 132, 1940.
30. *Taylor* vs. *Louisiana*. 419 U.S. 530, 1975.
31. *In re Groban*. 352 U.S. 330, 1957.
32. *83 Harvard Law Review*. 1970, pp. 1388-1390.
33. Gorecki, Jan. *Capital Punishment, Criminal Law and Social Revolution*. Columbia University Press, 1983, p. 12.
34. Gorecki. p. 103.
35. Burger, Chief Justice Warren. *Santobello* vs. *NY*. 404 U.S. 257, 1971.
36. Neumann, Milton. *Plea Bargaining*. University of Chicago Press, 1978, p. 163.
37. *Daily Record*, February 11, 1985, p. 4.
38. *Baltimore Sun*. June 22, 1984.
39. *St. Petersburg Independant*. January 3, 1982.
40. *St. Petersburg Times*. February 16, 1984.
41. James. p. 144.
42. James. p. 147.
43. James. pp. 148-149.
44. Anaya, Toney, Former Governor of New Mexico. With a Death Penalty Law and 15 Inmates on Death Row.
45. *St. Petersburg Times*. November 27, 1984.
46. Anaya, Toney.
47. McCafferty, James A. *Capital Punishment*. Lieber Atherton, 1974, p. 219.
48. Black, Jr., Charles L. *Capital Punishment, the Inevitability of Caprice and Mistake*. W.W. Norton, 1981; Adam Bedau, Tufts University; and Chester M. Pierce, Harvard. AMS Press, 1975, p. 481.
49. Black. p. 158.
50. McCafferty. pp. 141-143.

51. Williams, Edward B. *One Man's Freedom*. New York: Atheneum, 1965, pp. 238-239.
52. McCafferty. p. 198.
53. McCafferty. p. 199.
54. McCafferty. p. 145.
55. *University of Baltimore Law Review.* 1971.
56. Bedau and Pierce. p. 420.
57. McCafferty. p. 177.
58. Bedau and Pierce. p. 432.
59. McCafferty.
60. *St. Petersburg Times*. December 7, 1983.
61. *St. Petersburg Times*. November 10, 1984.
62. McCafferty. p.146.
63. *Furman* vs. *Georgia*. 408 U.S. 238, 33 L Ed2nd 346, 1972.
64. *St. Petersburg Times*. November 10, 1984.
65. Gorecki. p. 23.

Additional Sources:

Frankel, Marvin E. and Naftalis, Gary P. *Grand Jury.* Hill & Wang, 1977.

Auerbach, Jerold S. *Unequal Justice*. New York: Oxford University Press, 1976.

Felsher, Howard and Rosen, Michael. *Press in the Jury Box*, Macmillan Co., 1966.

Winslade, William J., PhD. and Ross, Judith W. *Insanity Plea*. New York: Charles Scribner's Sons, 1983.

Kennedy, Ludovic H. C. *Airman and the Carpenter.* New York: Viking Press, 1985.

VI. Justice Denied

1. *St. Petersburg Times*. March 20, 1980, Sec. A, p. 22.
2. Friedman, Leon, Ed. *Southern Justice*. Pantheon Books, 1965, p. 156.
3. Forer, Lois G. *Money and Justice, Who Owns the Courts*. W.W. Norton and Co., 1984, p. 9.
4. Downie, Leonard Jr. *Justice Denied, the Case for Reform of the Courts*. New York: Praeger Publications, 1971.
5. *Ibid*. pp. 15-16.
6. *Ibid*. p. 113.

7. Carlin, Jerome E. *Lawyers on Their Own*. New Brunswick: Rutgers University Press, 1962, p.8.

8. *Bill Of Rights*.

9. Denning, Rt. Hon. Lord. *Due Process of Law.* London: Butterworth, 1980.

10. *The Case of Kermit Twigg* vs. *The Cumberland Brewing Co.* Cumberland, MD: 1502, No. 27728 Equity 7/19/65, Allegany County Circuit Court, 7/9/65.

11. Frankel, Marvin E. *Partisan Justice*. Hill & Wang, 1978, p. 3.

12. Borchard, Edwin M. *Convicting the Innocent*. Archon Books, 1961, pp. vii-viii.

13. *Ibid*. pp. xiii and xiv.

14. *Ibid*. pp. xv and xvi.

15. *Ibid*. p. xviii.

16. *Ibid*. pp. xx-xxi.

17. *Ibid*. pp. 33-39.

18. *Ibid*. pp. 245-256.

19. *Newsweek*. May 20, 1985, pp. 69-73.

20. *State of Maryland* vs. *Gary Lee Miller.* Criminal Trials No. 911, Circuit Court of Allegany County, MD: 21502, October 1967 25, 26, 27, 30, and 31st.

21. *State of Maryland* vs. *Gary Lee Miller.* Court of Appeals of Maryland, No. 385 1967 Term reported in 251 Md. 362 1968, decided 11/12/68. Lower Court affirmed.

Writ of Certiorari to the U.S. Supreme Court. Filed 3/6/69, No. 685008, Opinion 6-29-72 408 US 934; 92 S. Ct. 2857.

Writ of Habeas Corpus U.S. District Court. September 1973, No. Civil 73456Y. Denied and sent back for process through Maryland Courts.

Post Conviction. Filed 7/24/75; Denied September 30, 1975, Judge Irvine Rutledge, Washington County Circuit Court Judge.

Application to Court of Special Appeals of Maryland from Post Conviction Denial. Filed October 29, 1975, in 92 September Term 1975, unreported, denied 11/14/75.

Writ of Habeas Corpus U.S. District Court of Maryland. Filed January 1976, No. 67727, denied by Judge Young.

Appeal to the U.S. Circuit Court of Appeals. Richmond Virginia: denied 2 to 1 decision, 6/22/78, 577 Fed 2nd 1158.

22. *Miranda* vs. *Arizona*. 384 US 436, 1966.

23. *Furman* vs. *Georgia*. 408 US 238, 92 S Ct 2726, 33 L ED 2nd 346, 1972.

24. *Bartholomew* vs. *State of Maryland*. 267 Md 175 1973.

25. *State* vs. *Gary Lee Miller*. No. 911 Criminal Trials, Allegany County, MD: Sentencing 1/11/73.

26. *Gallegos* vs. *Colorado*. 370 US 49, 1962.

VII. Legal Education In America

1. Reed, A. Z. *Training for the Public Profession of Law*.

2. Whitehead, A. N. *Organization of Law*. London.

3. Stevens, Robert. *Law School, Legal Education from 1850's to 1980's*. Chapel Hill: University of North Carolina Press, 1983.

4. Brown, Esther Lucille. *Lawyers and the Promotion of Justice*. Brattleboro, E.L. Hildreth and Co., 1938, p. 74.

5. Llewellyn, Karl. *Current Crisis in Legal Education*. p. 215.

6. Frank, Jerome. "Why Not a Clinical Law School," *81 University of Pennsylvania Law Review*. 909, 1933.

7. *Ibid*.

Additional Sources:

Friedman, Lawrence M. *History of American Law*. Simon and Schuster, 1973.

McKirdy. "Lawyer as Apprentice, Legal Education in the 18th Century," *Massachusetts Journal of Legal Education*. 1976, 125, 228.

Blaustein, Albert P. and Porter, Charles A. *American Lawyer, a Summary of the Survey of the Legal Profession*. University of Chicago Press, 1954, p. 161.

Goldfarb, Sally F. *Profiles Inside the Law Schools*. New York: E.P. Dutton, Inc., 1980.

Barrons Educational Series. 4th Ed. Woodbury, New York: 1980.

Glotzer, Arline: *Monarch's Complete Guide to Law School*. New York: Monarch Press, 1981.

PreLaw Handbook, 1984-85. American Bar Association & American Association of Law Schools.

Richardson. *W.R. History of the Inns of Court*. 1975.

VIII. The Ethical Challenges Of Lawyering

1. *Comme* vs. *US*. 350 US 399, 1956.

2. Gerson, Allen, Ed. *Lawyer's Ethics*. New Brunswick: Transaction Books, 1980, p. 59.

3. *Ibid*. p. 60.

4. *Ibid*. p. 102.

5. *Ibid*. p. 115.
6. *Ibid*. p. 121.
7. *Ibid*. p. 126.
8. *Ibid*. p. 127.
9. *Model Rules of Professional Conduct*. August 1983, pp. 23-26.
10. Shaffer, Thomas and Elkins, James R. *Legal Interviewing and Counseling in a Nutshell*. West Publishing Co., 1976, p. 111.
11. Freedman, Monroe H. *Lawyer's Ethics in an Adversary System*. New York: Bobbs-Merrill, Inc., p. 62.
12. *Ibid*. p. 68.
13. *Ibid*. p. 75.
14. Miller, Henry H. Chapter 4, 4.00 to 4.2.
15. *Ibid*. 16.20 and 16.30.
16. Nader, Ralph and Green, Mark, Eds. *Verdicts on Lawyers*. Thomas Y. Crowell Co., 1976, pp. 118, 119.
17. *Ibid*. pp. 269-270.
18. *Light* vs. *YMCA*. No. 12079 Law Circuit Court of Allegany County, Maryland.
19. Strick, Anne. *Injustice for All*. New York: Penguin Books, 1977, pp. 14-15.

Additional Sources:

Gugle vs. *Ohio State*. 362, 55 NE 2nd 580, 1944.
Carson vs. *McMahan*. 215 Ore 38, 332 Pac 2nd 84, 1958.
37 Va. Law Rev...399. p. 415, 1951.
W. Burger at Fordham, Law School, November 17, 1963.

IX. The Business Of Lawyers

Darrow, Clarence S. *Crime, Its Causes & Treatment*. New York: Thomas Y. Crowell, 1922.

Denning, Rt. Hon. Lord. *Due Process of Law*. London: Butterworth, 1980.

Foonberg, Jay G. *How to Start and Build a Law Practice*. Chicago: American Bar Association, 1984.

Harris, Arthur M. *Letter to a Young Lawyer*. St. Paul: West, 1953.

Kunstler, William M. *Case for Courage*. New York: Wm. Morrow & Co., 1962.

Lock, H. O. *Advice to the Young Solicitor...*London: Stevens Sons Ltd., 1974.

Neely, Judge Richard. *How Courts Govern America*. Yale University Press, 1980.

Neely, Judge Richard. *Why Courts Don't Work*. New York: McGraw Hill Book Co., 1982.

Nader, Ralph and Green, Mark, Eds. *Verdict on Lawyers*. New York: Thomas Y. Crowell, 1976.

Also interview with the Hon. Judge Richard Neely in his court chambers, June 1983, and an interview with the Rt. Hon. Lord Denning in his Lincoln Inn office, London, England: April 1984.

X. Advice To The Layman; Considerations When Selecting A Lawyer

1. Marks, Burton and Goldfarb, Gerald. *Winning with your Lawyer*. McGraw Hill, 1980, p. 18.

2. *Ibid*. p. 30.

3. Strick, Anne. *Injustice For All*. Penguin Books, 1977, p. 139.

4. Marks and Goldfarb. pp. 80-81.

5. Rosenthal, Douglas G. *Lawyer and Client, Who's in Charge?* Russell Sage Foundation, 1974, p. 82.

6. *Ibid*. pp. 89-90.

XI. Recommendations For Reformation

1. Kaufman, Irving R. "Attorney Incompetence, a Plea for Reform," *69 ABA Journal*. 308, 1983.

2. Frank, John Paul. *American Law, the Case for Radical Opinion*. Macmillan Co., 1969.

3. Martine Reed. "Improve Lawyer Training." *Daily Record*.

4. Reske, Henry J. "Trial by Trial Wasteful, Burger Says," *United Press International*.

5. Seymour, Whitney N., Jr. *Why Justice Fails*. William Morrow and Co., 1973, p. 226.

6. Seligman, Joel. *The High Citadel*. p. 203.

7. Seligman. p.203.

8. Burger, Warren. *Wisconsin Law Bulletin*. 1969, p. 16.

9. Stern, Philip M. *Lawyers on Trial*. Times Books, 1980, p. 175.

10. Ramsay, Robert R. *Journal of Law Education*. No. 20, 514, 519.

11. Nader, Ralph, and Green, Mark, Eds. *Verdicts on Lawyers*. Thomas Y. Crowell, 1976.

12. *Ibid*. p. 121.

13. *New York Times*. "The Verdict on Juries." April 1, 1984.

14. *Time*. September 3, 1979, p. 61.

15. Moore, Lloyd E. *Jury, Tolls of Kings, Palladium of Liberty*. W. H. Anderson Co., 1973, p. 158.

16. James, Howard. *Crisis in the Courts*. David McKay & Co., Inc., 1967, p. 193.

17. *Ibid*. p. 196.

18. *Ibid*. p. 198.

19. *Ibid*. p. 199.

20. *Ibid*. p. 203.

21. Frank, Jerome. *Law and the Modern Mind*. Gloucester, Mass.: Peter Smith, 1963, p. 193.

22. *Ibid*. p. 192.

23. Frank, Jerome. *Courts on Trial, Myth and Reality in American Justice*. Princeton University Press, 1949 & 1973, p. 111.

24. *Ibid*. pp. 114.

25. *Ibid*. pp. 130 and 132.

26. Frankel, Marvin C. and Naftalis, Gary P. *Grand Jury*. New York: Hill & Wang, 1977, p. 117.

27. Lofton, John. *Justice and the Press*. Boston: Beacon Press, 1966, p. 220.

28. *Ibid*. p. 221.

29. "Plea Bargaining." *ABA Journal*. January 1983.

30. Clark, Ramsey. *Crime in America*. New York: Simon and Schuster, 1970, pp. 308-309.

31. *Ibid*. pp. 314-315.

32. Barak, Gregg. *In Defense of Whom, a Critique of Criminal Justice Reform*. University of California, 1980.

33. *Daily Record*. May 23, 1985.

34. Clark. pp. 5-6.

35. Clark. p. 22.

Index

B

C

D

K

L

M

N